A-Level Year 1 & AS
Mathematics

Exam Board: AQA

Right. This book is 100% focused on helping you revise for AQA's new AS Maths exams in summer 2018 and beyond. Except this bit, which won't help you much at all.

But once you've turned the page, you'll be thrown head-first into a high-octane frenzy of brilliantly clear revision notes and worked examples covering the whole year — plus plenty of practice questions to test you on what you've learned.

And if you don't like turning pages, you can read the whole book online instead...

How to get your free Online Edition

Just go to **cgpbooks.co.uk/extras** and enter this code:

3630 7441 5477 8815

This code only works for one person. If somebody else has used this book before you, they might have already claimed the Online Edition.

A-Level revision? It has to be CGP!

Contents

Pure Mathematics

Statistics

Mechanics

Published by CGP

Based on the classic CGP style created by Richard Parsons.

Editors:
Chris Corrall, Sammy El-Bahrawy, Will Garrison, Paul Jordin, Caley Simpson, Dawn Wright.

Contributors:
Andrew Ballard, Claire Jackson, Mark Moody, Garry Rowlands, Chris Worth.

ISBN: 978 1 78294 805 6

With thanks to Ruth Wilbourne for the proofreading.

Clipart from Corel®
Printed by Elanders Ltd, Newcastle upon Tyne.

Proof

Like an annoying child who keeps asking 'But whyyyyyyyy?', sometimes the examiners expect you to prove something is true. The next two pages feature two classic maths ways of proving things, plus a bonus way to disprove stuff.

Some Notation

There are certain bits of **notation** that'll be **useful** not only for **proofs**, but for the **rest** of this course too.

A **set** is just a **collection** of objects or numbers (called **elements**), shown using **curly brackets**.
A set is often represented by a capital letter — e.g. A = {0, 1, 2}. There are different ways of writing sets:
- A list of elements — e.g. {1, 3, 5, 7, 9}
- A rule — e.g. {odd numbers between 0 and 10}
- Mathematical notation — e.g. {$x: x < 0$} (this means "the set of values of x such that x is less than 0")

The symbols $\Rightarrow$ and $\Leftrightarrow$ are **logic symbols** — they show when one thing **implies** another.
- '$p \Rightarrow q$' means 'p implies q' or 'if p then q'. E.g. $x = 2 \Rightarrow x^2 = 4$.
- '$p \Leftrightarrow q$' means 'p implies q and q implies p' or 'p if and only if q'. E.g. $x^2 = 4 \Leftrightarrow x = \pm 2$

'If and only if' is sometimes written as 'iff'.

There are a few variations on the **equals sign** that you need to know:
- $\neq$ means **not equal to** — e.g. $\sin 90° \neq \cos 90°$
- $\approx$ means **approximately equal to** — e.g. $1 \div 3 \approx 0.33$
- $\equiv$ is the **identity symbol**. It means that two things are **identically equal** to each other.
  So $(a + b)(a - b) \equiv a^2 - b^2$ is true for all values of a and b
  (unlike an equation like $a^2 = 9$, which is only true for certain values of a).

Proof by Exhaustion

In **proof by exhaustion** you break things down into two or more **cases**. You have to make sure that your cases cover **all possible situations**, then prove **separately** that the statement is true for **each case**.

Example: Prove the following statement: "For any integer x, the value of $f(x) = x^3 + x + 1$ is an odd integer."

To prove the statement, split the situation into **two cases**:
    (i) x is an **even number**,   and   (ii) x is an **odd number**

(i)   If x is an **even integer**, then it can be written as $x = 2n$, for some integer n — *this is the definition of an even number.*
     Substitute $x = 2n$ into the function: $f(2n) = (2n)^3 + 2n + 1 = 8n^3 + 2n + 1$
$$= 2(4n^3 + n) + 1$$

     n is an integer $\Rightarrow (4n^3 + n)$ is an integer — *the sum or product of any integers are also integers.*
$$\Rightarrow 2(4n^3 + n) \text{ is an even integer} - 2 \times \text{an integer is the definition of an even number.}$$
$$\Rightarrow 2(4n^3 + n) + 1 \text{ is an odd integer} - \text{since even + odd = odd.}$$

     So $f(x)$ is **odd** when x is **even**.

(ii)   If x is an **odd integer**, then it can be written as $x = 2m + 1$, for some integer m — *this is the definition of an odd number.*
     Substitute $x = 2m + 1$ into the function:
$$f(2m + 1) = (2m + 1)^3 + (2m + 1) + 1 = (8m^3 + 12m^2 + 6m + 1) + 2m + 1 + 1$$
$$= 8m^3 + 12m^2 + 8m + 3 = 2(4m^3 + 6m^2 + 4m + 1) + 1$$

You can use the binomial expansion formula on p.29 to help you find these coefficients.

     m is an integer $\Rightarrow (4m^3 + 6m^2 + 4m + 1)$ is an integer
$$\Rightarrow 2(4m^3 + 6m^2 + 4m + 1) \text{ is an even integer}$$
$$\Rightarrow 2(4m^3 + 6m^2 + 4m + 1) + 1 \text{ is an odd integer}$$

     So $f(x)$ is **odd** when x is **odd**.

We have shown that $f(x)$ is **odd** when x is even **and** when x is odd. As any integer x **must** be either odd or even, we have therefore shown that $f(x)$ is **odd** for **any** integer x.

Proof

Proof by *Deduction*

A **proof by deduction** (or **direct proof** or '**proof by direct argument**') is when you use **known facts** to **build up** your argument and show a statement **must** be true.

> **Example:** A definition of a rational number is: 'a number that can be written as a quotient of two integers, where the denominator is non-zero'.
> Use this definition to prove that the following statement is true:
> "The product of two rational numbers is always a rational number."

Take **any two** rational numbers, call them a and b.

By the **definition** of rational numbers you can write them in the form $a = \frac{p}{q}$ and $b = \frac{r}{s}$, where p, q, r and s are all integers, and q and s are non-zero.

The **product** of a and b is $ab = \frac{p}{q} \times \frac{r}{s} = \frac{pr}{qs}$

pr and qs are the products of integers, so they must also be integers, and because q and s are non-zero, qs must also be non-zero.

We've shown that ab is a quotient of two integers and has a non-zero denominator, so by definition, ab **is rational**.

Hence the original statement is **true**.

Disproof by *Counter-Example*

Disproof by **counter-example** is the easiest way to show a mathematical statement is **false**. All you have to do is find **one case** where the statement doesn't hold.

> **Example:** Disprove the following statement:
> "For any pair of real numbers x and y, if $x > y$, then $x^2 + x > y^2 + y$."
>
> To **disprove** the statement, it's enough to find just **one example** of x and y where $x > y$, but $x^2 + x \leq y^2 + y$.
> Let $x = 2$ and $y = -4$.
> Then $2 > -4$, so $x > y$
> but $x^2 + x = 2^2 + 2 = 6$ and $y^2 + y = (-4)^2 + (-4) = 12$, so $x^2 + x < y^2 + y$
> So when $x = 2$ and $y = -4$, the first part of the statement holds, but the second part of the statement doesn't.
> So the statement is not true.

Practice Questions

Q1 Write out the following sets as lists of elements:
   a) {even prime numbers}   b) {factors of 28}   c) $\{x: x^2 = 1\}$

Q2 Disprove the following statements by giving a counter-example:
   a) If $\frac{x}{y} < 1$, then $x < y$ for all values of x and y b) If $x^2 + y = y^2 + x$, then $x = y$

Exam Questions

Q1 Prove that, for any integer n, $(n + 6)^2 - (n + 1)^2$ is always divisible by 5. [3 marks]

Q2 Prove that the difference between an integer and its square is always even. [3 marks]

Q3 Is the following statement true or false? $(x + 2)(x - 1) > 2x - 2$ for all values of x.
   Give either a proof or a counter-example. [3 marks]

If you've exhausted all options, just stick it in a proving drawer for an hour...

When you're trying to disprove something, don't be put off if you can't find a counter-example straight away. Sometimes you have to just try a few different cases until you find one that doesn't work.

Laws of Indices and Surds

You use the laws of indices all the time in maths — when you're integrating, differentiating and ...er... well loads of other places. So take the time to get them sorted now.

Three mega-important **Laws of Indices**

You **must** know these three rules. I can't make it any clearer than that.

$$a^m \times a^n = a^{m+n}$$

If you **multiply** two numbers — you **add** their powers.

$a^2 a^3 = a^5$
$x^{-2} x^5 = x^3$
$p^{\frac{1}{2}} \cdot p^{\frac{1}{4}} = p^{\frac{3}{4}}$

The dot just means 'multiplied by'.

$(a+b)^2 (a+b)^5 = (a+b)^7$
$y \cdot y^3 = y^4$ ← *Since $y = y^1$.*
$ab^3 \cdot a^2 b = a^3 b^4$

Add the powers of a and b separately.

$$\frac{a^m}{a^n} = a^{m-n}$$

If you **divide** two numbers — you **subtract** their powers.

$\dfrac{x^5}{x^2} = x^3$

$\dfrac{x^{\frac{3}{4}}}{x} = x^{-\frac{1}{4}}$

$\dfrac{x^3 y^2}{xy^3} = x^2 y^{-1}$

Subtract the powers of x and y separately.

$$(a^m)^n = a^{mn}$$

If you have a **power** to the **power of something else** — **multiply** the powers together.

$(x^2)^3 = x^6$
$\{(a+b)^3\}^4 = (a+b)^{12}$
$(p^3)^{-2} = p^{-6}$
$(ab^2)^4 = a^4 (b^2)^4 = a^4 b^8$

This power applies to both bits inside the brackets.

Other important stuff about **Indices**

You can't get very far without knowing this sort of stuff. Learn it — you'll definitely be able to use it.

$$a^{\frac{1}{m}} = \sqrt[m]{a}$$

You can write **roots** as powers...

$x^{\frac{1}{5}} = \sqrt[5]{x}$
$4^{\frac{1}{2}} = \sqrt{4} = 2$
$125^{\frac{1}{3}} = \sqrt[3]{125} = 5$

$$a^{\frac{m}{n}} = \sqrt[n]{a^m} = \left(\sqrt[n]{a}\right)^m$$

A power that's a **fraction** like this is the **root of a power** — or the **power of a root**.

It's often easier to work out the root first, then raise it to the power.

$9^{\frac{3}{2}} = (9^{\frac{1}{2}})^3 = (\sqrt{9})^3 = 3^3 = 27$
$81^{\frac{3}{4}} = (81^{\frac{1}{4}})^3 = (\sqrt[4]{81})^3 = 3^3 = 27$

$$a^{-m} = \frac{1}{a^m}$$

A **negative** power means it's on the bottom line of a fraction.

$2^{-3} = \dfrac{1}{2^3} = \dfrac{1}{8}$

$(x+1)^{-1} = \dfrac{1}{x+1}$

$$a^0 = 1$$

This is true for **any** number or letter.

$x^0 = 1$
$2^0 = 1$
$(a+b)^0 = 1$

Surds are sometimes the only way to give an **Exact Answer**

If you put $\sqrt{2}$ into a calculator, you'll get something like 1.414213562...
But if you square 1.414213562, then you get 1.999999999.
And no matter how many decimal places you use, you'll never get **exactly** 2.

To write the exact, spot on value you can **use surds**.
There are three **rules** you'll need to know to be able to use surds properly.

Rules of Surds

$\sqrt{ab} = \sqrt{a}\sqrt{b}$

$\sqrt{\dfrac{a}{b}} = \dfrac{\sqrt{a}}{\sqrt{b}}$

$a = (\sqrt{a})^2 = \sqrt{a}\sqrt{a}$

Laws of Indices and Surds

Use the Three Rules to deal with Surds

Examples: a) Simplify (i) $\sqrt{12}$ (ii) $\sqrt{\frac{3}{16}}$ b) Find $\left(2\sqrt{5}+3\sqrt{6}\right)^2$

a) To **simplify** a surd, make the number in the $\sqrt{}$ sign **smaller**, or get rid of a **fraction** in the $\sqrt{}$ sign.

(i) $\sqrt{12}=\sqrt{4\times3}=\sqrt{4}\times\sqrt{3}=2\sqrt{3}$

Using $\sqrt{ab}=\sqrt{a}\sqrt{b}$.

(ii) $\sqrt{\frac{3}{16}}=\frac{\sqrt{3}}{\sqrt{16}}=\frac{\sqrt{3}}{4}$

Using $\sqrt{\frac{a}{b}}=\frac{\sqrt{a}}{\sqrt{b}}$.

b) Multiply surds very **carefully** — it's easy to make a silly mistake.
$$\left(2\sqrt{5}+3\sqrt{6}\right)^2=\left(2\sqrt{5}+3\sqrt{6}\right)\left(2\sqrt{5}+3\sqrt{6}\right)$$
$$=\left(2\sqrt{5}\right)^2+\left(2\times2\sqrt{5}\times3\sqrt{6}\right)+\left(3\sqrt{6}\right)^2$$
$$=\left(2^2\times\sqrt{5}^2\right)+\left(2\times2\times3\times\sqrt{5}\times\sqrt{6}\right)+\left(3^2\times\sqrt{6}^2\right)$$
$$=20+12\sqrt{30}+54$$
$$=\mathbf{74+12\sqrt{30}}$$

$=4\times5=20$ $=12\sqrt{5}\sqrt{6}=12\sqrt{30}$ $=9\times6=54$

You might need to Rationalise the Denominator

Rationalising the denominator means getting rid of the surds from the bottom of a fraction.

Example: Show that $\frac{9}{\sqrt{3}}=3\sqrt{3}$

Multiply the top and bottom by the denominator.

$$\frac{9}{\sqrt{3}}\times\frac{\sqrt{3}}{\sqrt{3}}=\frac{9\sqrt{3}}{\sqrt{3}\times\sqrt{3}}$$
$$=\frac{9\sqrt{3}}{3}$$
$$=3\sqrt{3}$$

Example: Rationalise the denominator of $\frac{1}{1+\sqrt{2}}$

Multiply the top and bottom by the denominator (but change the sign in front of the surd).

$$\frac{1}{1+\sqrt{2}}\times\frac{1-\sqrt{2}}{1-\sqrt{2}}$$
$$=\frac{1-\sqrt{2}}{(1+\sqrt{2})(1-\sqrt{2})}=\frac{1-\sqrt{2}}{1^2-\sqrt{2}+\sqrt{2}-\sqrt{2}^2}$$
$$=\frac{1-\sqrt{2}}{1-2}=\frac{1-\sqrt{2}}{-1}=-1+\sqrt{2}$$

This works because:
$(a+b)(a-b)=a^2-b^2$

Practice Questions

Q1 Simplify these:

a) $x^3\cdot x^5$ b) $a^7\cdot a^8$ c) $\frac{x^8}{x^2}$ d) $(a^2)^4$ e) $(xy^2)\cdot(x^3yz)$ f) $\frac{a^2b^4c^6}{a^3b^2c}$

Q2 Work out the following: a) $16^{\frac{1}{2}}$ b) $8^{\frac{1}{3}}$ c) $16^{\frac{3}{4}}$ d) x^0 e) $49^{-\frac{1}{2}}$

Q3 Simplify: a) $\sqrt{28}$ b) $\sqrt{\frac{5}{36}}$ c) $\sqrt{18}$ d) $\sqrt{\frac{9}{16}}$

Q4 Find $\left(6\sqrt{3}+2\sqrt{7}\right)^2$

Q5 Rationalise the denominator of: $\frac{2}{3+\sqrt{7}}$

Bruce lived by the sword and died by the surd.

Exam Questions

Q1 Simplify a) $\left(5\sqrt{3}\right)^2$ [1 mark]

b) $\left(5+\sqrt{6}\right)\left(2-\sqrt{6}\right)$ [2 marks]

Q2 Given that $10000\sqrt{10}=10^k$, find the value of k.   [2 marks]

Q3 Express $\frac{5+\sqrt{5}}{3-\sqrt{5}}$ in the form $a+b\sqrt{5}$, where a and b are integers.   [4 marks]

Where does Poseidon keep his powers — indices...

For lots of these questions you can check your answers on your calculator. If you ever forget the rules of surds you can even write $\sqrt{}$ as $^{\frac{1}{2}}$ and manipulate the indices instead — e.g. $\sqrt{ab}=(ab)^{\frac{1}{2}}=a^{\frac{1}{2}}b^{\frac{1}{2}}=\sqrt{a}\sqrt{b}$. Very sneaky.

Polynomials

A polynomial is just an expression of algebraic terms. In AS Maths you need to manipulate them all the time.

Expand brackets by Multiplying them out

Here are the basic types you have to deal with — you'll have seen them all before.

Single Brackets

$a(b + c + d) = ab + ac + ad$

Double Brackets

$(a + b)(c + d) = ac + ad + bc + bd$

Squared Brackets

$(a + b)^2 = (a + b)(a + b) = a^2 + 2ab + b^2$

Use the middle stage until you're comfortable with it.
Just **never** make this **mistake**: $(a + b)^2 = a^2 + b^2$

Difference of Two Squares

$(a + b)(a - b) = a^2 - ab + ab - b^2 = a^2 - b^2$

The difference of two squares can be applied to surds:
$(\sqrt{x} + \sqrt{y})(\sqrt{x} - \sqrt{y}) = x - y$

Long Brackets

Write it out again with **each term** from one bracket separately multiplied by the **other bracket**.

$(x + y + z)(a + b + c + d)$
$= x(a + b + c + d) + y(a + b + c + d) + z(a + b + c + d)$

Then **multiply out each** of these **brackets**, one at a time.

Example: Expand and simplify $(2x^2 + 3x + 6)(4x^3 + 6x^2 + 3)$

Multiply each term in the first bracket by the second bracket:

$2x^2(4x^3 + 6x^2 + 3) + 3x(4x^3 + 6x^2 + 3) + 6(4x^3 + 6x^2 + 3)$

Multiply out each bracket individually:

$= (8x^5 + 12x^4 + 6x^2) + (12x^4 + 18x^3 + 9x) + (24x^3 + 36x^2 + 18)$

Simplify it all:

$= \mathbf{8x^5 + 24x^4 + 42x^3 + 42x^2 + 9x + 18}$

Look for Common Factors when Simplifying Expressions

Something that is in each term of an expression is a **common factor** — this can be **numbers**, **variables** or even **brackets**. If you spot a common factor you can '**take it outside**' a bracket.

Example: Simplify $(x + 1)(x - 2) + (x + 1)^2 - x(x + 1)$

There's an $(x + 1)$ factor in each term, so we can take this out as a common factor (hurrah):

$(x + 1)\{(x - 2) + (x + 1) - x\}$

The terms inside the curly bracket are the old terms with an $(x + 1)$ removed.

At this point you should check that this multiplies out to give the original expression. (You can just do this in your head, if you trust it.)
Then simplify the big bracket's innards:

$(x + 1)\{x - 2 + x + 1 - x\}$
$= (x + 1)(x - 1) = x^2 - 1$

Use the "difference of two squares" (or multiply out) to get this answer

Factorise a Quadratic by putting it into Two Brackets

Factorising a quadratic in the form $ax^2 + bx + c$ is pretty easy when $a = 1$:

Factorising Quadratics

1) Write down the two brackets:
$(x \quad)(x \quad)$

2) Find two numbers that **multiply** to give 'c' and **add/subtract** to give 'b' (ignoring signs).

3) Put the numbers in the brackets and choose the correct **signs**.

Example: Factorise $x^2 + 4x - 21$

1) $x^2 + 4x - 21 = (x \quad)(x \quad)$

2) 1 and 21 multiply to give 21 — and add/subtract to give 22 and 20.
3 and 7 multiply to give 21 — and add/subtract to give 10 and **4**.

3) $x^2 + 4x - 21 = (x \quad 7)(x \quad 3)$
$= (x + 7)(x - 3)$

This is the value of 'b' you're after — 3 and 7 are the right numbers.

These get much easier with practice — you might even be able to do them in your head.
Make sure you always check your answer by multiplying the brackets out.

Section 1 — Algebra and Functions

Polynomials

Use a *Similar Method* for *Factorising* a quadratic when *a ≠ 1*

Example: Factorise $3x^2 + 4x - 15$

As before, write down two brackets — but instead of having
x in each, you need two things that will multiply to give $3x^2$: $3x^2 + 4x - 15 = (3x \quad)(x \quad)$

It's got to be 3x and x here.

This is where it gets a bit fiddly. You need to find two numbers that multiply together to make 15
— but which will give you 4x when you multiply them by x and 3x, and then add/subtract them:

$(3x \quad 1)(x \quad 15) \Rightarrow x$ and $45x$ — which then add or subtract to give $46x$ and $44x$.

$(3x \quad 15)(x \quad 1) \Rightarrow 15x$ and $3x$ — which then add or subtract to give $18x$ and $12x$.

$(3x \quad 3)(x \quad 5) \Rightarrow 3x$ and $15x$ — which then add or subtract to give $18x$ and $12x$.

$(3x \quad 5)(x \quad 3) \Rightarrow 5x$ and $9x$ — which then add or subtract to give $14x$ and $\mathbf{4x}$.

This is the value you're after — so this is the right combination.

You know the brackets must be like these... $(3x \quad 5)(x \quad 3) = 3x^2 + 4x - 15$
so all you have to do is put in the plus or minus signs:

$(3x + 5)(x - 3) = 3x^2 - 4x - 15$

or...

$(3x - 5)(x + 3) = 3x^2 + 4x - 15$ ⟵ So it's this one.

You've only got two choices — if you're unsure, just multiply them out to see which one's right.

'c' is negative — that means the signs in the brackets are different.

Simplify algebraic fractions by *Factorising* and *Cancelling Factors*

Algebraic fractions are a lot like normal fractions — and you can treat them in the **same way**, whether you're
multiplying, dividing, adding or subtracting them. All fractions are much **easier** to deal with when they're in their
simplest form, so the first thing to do with algebraic fractions is to **simplify** them as much as possible.

1) Look for **common factors** in the numerator and denominator — **factorise** top and bottom
   and see if there's anything you can **cancel**.

Examples: Simplify the following: a) $\dfrac{ax + ay}{az}$ b) $\dfrac{3x + 6}{x^2 - 4}$

Watch out for the difference of two squares.

a) $\dfrac{ax + ay}{az} = \dfrac{\cancel{a}(x + y)}{\cancel{a}z} = \dfrac{x + y}{z}$

b) $\dfrac{3x + 6}{x^2 - 4} = \dfrac{3\cancel{(x+2)}}{\cancel{(x+2)}(x-2)} = \dfrac{3}{x - 2}$

2) If there's a **fraction** in the numerator or denominator (e.g. $\frac{1}{x}$), **multiply** the **whole thing** (i.e. top and bottom)
   by the same factor to get rid of it (e.g. for $\frac{1}{x}$, you'd multiply through by x).

Example: Simplify $\dfrac{2 + \frac{1}{2x}}{4x^2 + x}$

$\dfrac{2 + \frac{1}{2x}}{4x^2 + x} = \dfrac{\left(2 + \frac{1}{2x}\right) \times 2x}{x(4x + 1) \times 2x} = \dfrac{4x + \cancel{1}}{2x^2 \cancel{(4x + 1)}} = \dfrac{1}{2x^2}$

3) You **multiply** algebraic fractions in exactly the same way as normal fractions — multiply the **numerators**
   together, then multiply the **denominators**. It's a good idea to **cancel** any **common factors** before you multiply.

4) To **divide** by an algebraic fraction, you just **multiply** by its **reciprocal** (the reciprocal is 1 ÷ the original thing
   — for fractions you just turn the fraction **upside down**).

Examples: Simplify the following: a) $\dfrac{x^2 - 2x - 15}{2x + 8} \times \dfrac{x^2 - 16}{x^2 + 3x}$ b) $\dfrac{3x}{5} \div \dfrac{3x^2 - 9x}{20}$

Turn the second fraction upside down.

a) $\dfrac{x^2 - 2x - 15}{2x + 8} \times \dfrac{x^2 - 16}{x^2 + 3x} = \dfrac{(x+3)(x-5)}{2\cancel{(x+4)}} \times \dfrac{\cancel{(x+4)}(x-4)}{x\cancel{(x+3)}}$

Factorise both fractions.

$= \dfrac{(x - 5)(x - 4)}{2x} \quad \left(= \dfrac{x^2 - 9x + 20}{2x}\right)$

b) $\dfrac{3x}{5} \div \dfrac{3x^2 - 9x}{20} = \dfrac{\cancel{3x}}{5} \times \dfrac{20}{\cancel{3x}(x - 3)}$

$= \dfrac{4}{x - 3}$

Polynomials

Add and Subtract fractions by finding a Common Denominator

You'll have come across **adding** and **subtracting fractions** before, so here's a little reminder of how to do it:

Example: Simplify $\dfrac{2y}{x(x+3)} + \dfrac{1}{y^2(x+3)} - \dfrac{x}{y}$

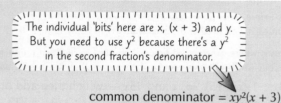

The individual 'bits' here are x, (x + 3) and y.
But you need to use y^2 because there's a y^2
in the second fraction's denominator.

1) Find the common denominator

Take all the individual 'bits' from the bottom lines and multiply them together. Only use each bit once unless something on the bottom line is raised to a power:

common denominator = $xy^2(x + 3)$

2) Put each fraction over the common denominator

Make the denominator of each fraction into the common denominator. Multiply the top and bottom lines of each fraction by whatever makes the bottom line the same as the common denominator:

$$\frac{y^2 \times 2y}{y^2 x(x+3)} + \frac{x \times 1}{xy^2(x+3)} - \frac{xy(x+3) \times x}{xy(x+3)y}$$

3) Combine into one fraction

Once everything's over the common denominator you can just add the top lines together and simplify the numerator:

$$= \frac{2y^3 + x - x^2 y(x+3)}{xy^2(x+3)} = \frac{2y^3 + x - x^3 y - 3x^2 y}{xy^2(x+3)}$$

All the bottom lines are the same
— so you can just add the top lines.

Practice Questions

Q1 Expand the brackets and simplify the following expressions:
 a) $(x + y)(x - y)$
 b) $(x + y)(x + y)$
 c) $35xy + 25y(5y + 7x) - 100y^2$
 d) $(x + 3y + 2)(3x + y + 7)$

Q2 Show that $(\sqrt{x} + \sqrt{2})(\sqrt{x} - \sqrt{2}) = x - 2$.

Q3 Take out the common factors from the following expressions:
 a) $2x^2y + axy + 2xy^2$
 b) $a^2x + a^2b^2x^2$
 c) $16y + 8yx + 56x$
 d) $x(x - 2) + 3(2 - x)$

Q4 Factorise the following quadratics:
 a) $x^2 + 6x - 7$
 b) $x^2 - 4x - 12$
 c) $9x^2 - 64$
 d) $4x^2 - 11x - 20$

Q5 Simplify the following:
 a) $\dfrac{4x^2 - 25}{6x - 15}$
 b) $\dfrac{2x + 3}{x - 2} \times \dfrac{4x - 8}{2x^2 - 3x - 9}$
 c) $\dfrac{x^2 - 3x}{x + 1} \div \dfrac{x}{2}$

Exam Questions

Q1 Write $\dfrac{2x^2 - 9x - 35}{x^2 - 49}$ as a fraction in its simplest form. [3 marks]

Q2 Factorise $2x^4 - 32x^2$ completely. [2 marks]

Q3 Write each of the following polynomials as a single fraction in its simplest form.
 a) $\dfrac{x}{2x + 1} + \dfrac{3}{x^2} + \dfrac{1}{x}$ [3 marks]

 b) $\dfrac{2}{x^2 - 1} - \dfrac{3x}{x - 1} + \dfrac{x}{x + 1}$ [3 marks]

What do you call a hungry parrot? Polynomials...

Nothing on these pages should be a big shock to you — you've been using normal fractions for years, and algebraic fractions work in just the same way. They look a bit scary, but they're all warm and fuzzy inside.

Algebraic Division

I'm going to spoil you with three methods for algebraic division — these can be a bit tricky so take your time with them. I know you can't wait to get stuck into them, but first you'll need to learn the Remainder Theorem.

There are some **Terms** you need to **Know**

These words will keep popping up over the next few pages, so make sure you know what they all mean.

1) **DEGREE** — the highest power of x in the polynomial (e.g. the degree of $4x^5 + 6x^2 - 3x - 1$ is 5).
2) **DIVISOR** — this is the thing you're dividing by (e.g. if you divide $x^2 + 4x - 3$ by $x + 2$, the divisor is $x + 2$).
3) **QUOTIENT** — the stuff that you get when you divide by the divisor (not including the remainder).
4) **REMAINDER** — the bit that's left over at the end (for AS Maths this will be a constant).

The **Remainder Theorem** is an easy way to work out **Remainders**

If f(x) is a **polynomial** then the **Remainder Theorem** states that:

> When you divide f(x) by ($x - a$), the remainder is f(a).
>
> When you divide f(x) by ($ax - b$), the remainder is $f\left(\frac{b}{a}\right)$.

Example: Find the remainder when you divide $2x^3 - 3x^2 - 3x + 7$ by $2x - 1$.

f(x) = $2x^3 - 3x^2 - 3x + 7$. The **divisor** is $2x - 1$, so $a = 2$ and $b = 1$.

Using the Remainder Theorem, the **remainder** must be $f\left(\frac{1}{2}\right) = 2\left(\frac{1}{8}\right) - 3\left(\frac{1}{4}\right) - 3\left(\frac{1}{2}\right) + 7 = 5$

The **Factor Theorem** is just the Remainder Theorem with a **Zero Remainder**

If you get a **remainder of zero** when you divide f(x) by ($x - a$), then ($x - a$) must be a **factor**. That's the **Factor Theorem**:

> If f(x) is a polynomial, and f(a) = 0, then ($x - a$) is a factor of f(x).
>
> If $f\left(\frac{b}{a}\right) = 0$, then ($ax - b$) is a factor of f($x$).

In other words: If you know the roots, you also know the factors — and vice versa.

Example: Show that ($2x + 1$) is a factor of f(x) = $2x^3 - 3x^2 + 4x + 3$.

Use the second version of the Factor Theorem — in this case, $a = 2$ and $b = -1$.

This means that if you show that $f\left(-\frac{1}{2}\right) = 0$, then, by the Factor Theorem, ($2x + 1$) is a factor.

$$f(x) = 2x^3 - 3x^2 + 4x + 3 \text{ and so } f\left(-\frac{1}{2}\right) = 2\left(-\frac{1}{8}\right) - 3\left(\frac{1}{4}\right) + 4\left(-\frac{1}{2}\right) + 3 = 0$$

So, by the **Factor Theorem**, ($2x + 1$) is a factor of f(x).

Method 1 — Divide by Subtracting Multiples of the Divisor

This is the first of **three methods** I'm going to show you for dividing a polynomial by a **linear expression**.
To do **algebraic division** you can keep **subtracting** chunks of the **divisor**, ($x - k$), until you get the **remainder**.

Algebraic Division

① Subtract a multiple of ($x - k$) to get rid of the highest power of x.

② Repeat step 1 until you've got rid of all the powers of x.

③ Work out how many lumps of ($x - k$), you've subtracted, and read off the remainder.

For this course you'll only have to divide by a linear expression — i.e. $ax + b$, where a and b are constants. This means that the remainder will always be a constant because the degree of the remainder has to be less than the degree of the divisor.

Algebraic Division

Always get **Rid** of the **Highest Power** of x

Example: Divide $(2x^3 - 3x^2 - 3x + 7)$ by $(x - 2)$

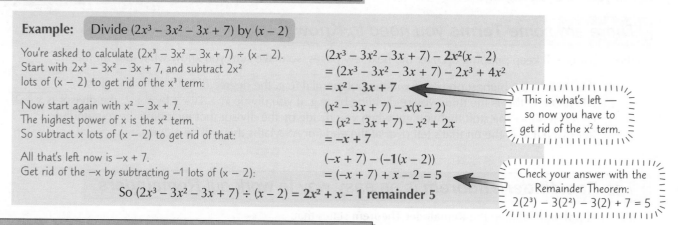

You're asked to calculate $(2x^3 - 3x^2 - 3x + 7) \div (x - 2)$.
Start with $2x^3 - 3x^2 - 3x + 7$, and subtract $2x^2$
lots of $(x - 2)$ to get rid of the x^3 term:

$(2x^3 - 3x^2 - 3x + 7) - \mathbf{2x^2}(x - 2)$
$= (2x^3 - 3x^2 - 3x + 7) - 2x^3 + 4x^2$
$= x^2 - 3x + 7$ ◄

This is what's left —
so now you have to
get rid of the x^2 term.

Now start again with $x^2 - 3x + 7$.
The highest power of x is the x^2 term.
So subtract x lots of $(x - 2)$ to get rid of that:

$(x^2 - 3x + 7) - x(x - 2)$
$= (x^2 - 3x + 7) - x^2 + 2x$
$= -x + 7$

All that's left now is $-x + 7$.
Get rid of the $-x$ by subtracting -1 lots of $(x - 2)$:

$(-x + 7) - (-\mathbf{1}(x - 2))$
$= (-x + 7) + x - 2 = 5$ ◄

So $(2x^3 - 3x^2 - 3x + 7) \div (x - 2) = \mathbf{2x^2 + x - 1}$ **remainder 5**

Check your answer with the
Remainder Theorem:
$2(2^3) - 3(2^2) - 3(2) + 7 = 5$

Method 2 — use **Algebraic Long Division**

To divide two **algebraic** expressions, you can use **long division** (using the same method you'd use for numbers).

Example: Divide $2x^3 - 7x^2 - 16x + 11$ by $x - 5$.

If the original polynomial doesn't have an x term, for
example, just put Ox where the x term should be.

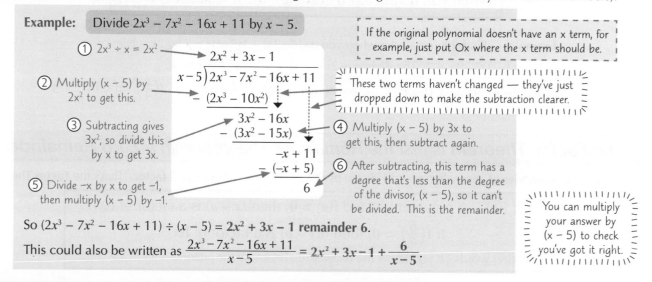

① $2x^3 \div x = 2x^2$

② Multiply $(x - 5)$ by
$2x^2$ to get this.

③ Subtracting gives
$3x^2$, so divide this
by x to get 3x.

⑤ Divide $-x$ by x to get -1,
then multiply $(x - 5)$ by -1.

$$\begin{array}{r} 2x^2 + 3x - 1 \\ x-5\overline{\smash{)}2x^3 - 7x^2 - 16x + 11} \\ -\ \underline{(2x^3 - 10x^2)} \\ 3x^2 - 16x \\ -\ \underline{(3x^2 - 15x)} \\ -x + 11 \\ -\ \underline{(-x + 5)} \\ 6 \end{array}$$

These two terms haven't changed — they've just
dropped down to make the subtraction clearer.

④ Multiply $(x - 5)$ by 3x to
get this, then subtract again.

⑥ After subtracting, this term has a
degree that's less than the degree
of the divisor, $(x - 5)$, so it can't
be divided. This is the remainder.

So $(2x^3 - 7x^2 - 16x + 11) \div (x - 5) = \mathbf{2x^2 + 3x - 1}$ **remainder 6.**

This could also be written as $\dfrac{2x^3 - 7x^2 - 16x + 11}{x - 5} = 2x^2 + 3x - 1 + \dfrac{6}{x - 5}$.

You can multiply
your answer by
$(x - 5)$ to check
you've got it right.

Method 3 — use the **Formula f(x) = q(x)d(x) + r(x)**

There's a **formula** you can use to do **algebraic division**. It comes from the Remainder Theorem and looks like this:

> A polynomial f(x) can be written in the form $\mathbf{f}(x) \equiv \mathbf{q}(x)\mathbf{d}(x) + \mathbf{r}(x)$,
> where q(x) is the quotient, d(x) is the divisor and r(x) is the remainder.

You'll be given f(x) and d(x) in the **question**, and it's down to you to **work out** q(x) and r(x). Here's how you do it:

Using the Formula

① First, you have to work out the **degrees** of the **quotient** and **remainder**, which depend on the
degrees of the polynomial and the divisor. The degree of the quotient is **deg f(x) – deg d(x)**,
and the degree of the remainder, **deg r(x)**, has to be less than the degree of the divisor.

For this course, you'll
only get questions
where deg d(x) = 1
and deg r(x) = 0.

② Write out the division using the **formula** above, but replace q(x) and r(x) with
general polynomials (i.e. a general polynomial of degree 2 is $Ax^2 + Bx + C$, and a
general polynomial of degree 1 is $Ax + B$, where A, B, C, etc. are constants to be found).

③ The next step is to work out the values of the **constants** — you do this by
substituting in values for x to make bits disappear, and by **equating coefficients**.
It's best to start with the constant term and work backwards from there.

Equating coefficients means
comparing the coefficients
of each power of x on the
LHS and the RHS.

④ Finally, **write out** the division again, replacing A, B, C, etc.
with the values you've found.

The method looks a bit **intense**, but follow through the **example** on the next page to see how it works.

Algebraic Division

Start with the **Remainder** and **Work Backwards**

When you're using this method, you might have to use **simultaneous equations** to work out some of the coefficients.

Example: Divide $x^4 - 3x^3 - 3x^2 + 10x + 5$ by $x - 2$.

① The polynomial f(x) has degree 4 and the divisor d(x) has degree 1, which means that the quotient q(x) has degree $4 - 1 = 3$ (i.e. a **cubic**). The remainder r(x) has degree 0.

Remember, it's easiest to start by finding the constant term.

② Write out the division in the form **f(x) ≡ q(x)d(x) + r(x)**:
$$x^4 - 3x^3 - 3x^2 + 10x + 5 \equiv (Ax^3 + Bx^2 + Cx + D)(x - 2) + E$$

③ **Substitute** $x = 2$ into the identity to make the q(x)d(x) bit disappear. This gives the remainder as **E = 5**.
Now, using this value of E and putting $x = 0$ into the identity gives the equation $5 = -2D + 5$, so **D = 0**.

Using the values of D and E you now have:
$$x^4 - 3x^3 - 3x^2 + 10x + 5 \equiv (Ax^3 + Bx^2 + Cx)(x - 2) + 5$$
$$\equiv Ax^4 + (B - 2A)x^3 + (C - 2B)x^2 - 2Cx + 5$$
Equating coefficients of x^4, x^3 and x gives A = 1, B − 2A = −3 (so **B = −1**) and −2C = 10 (so **C = −5**).

④ Putting these values into the original identity gives: $x^4 - 3x^3 - 3x^2 + 10x + 5 \equiv (x^3 - x^2 - 5x)(x - 2) + 5$.
So the answer is $(x^3 - x^2 - 5x)$ **remainder 5**.

Practice Questions

Q1 Find the remainder when f(x) = $x^4 - 3x^3 + 7x^2 - 12x + 14$ is divided by:
   a) $x + 2$ b) $2x + 4$ c) $x - 3$ d) $2x - 6$

Q2 Which of the following are factors of f(x) = $x^5 - 4x^4 + 3x^3 + 2x^2 - 2$?
   a) $x - 1$ b) $x + 1$ c) $x - 2$ d) $2x - 2$

Q3 Use algebraic long division to divide $x^3 + 2x^2 - x + 19$ by $x + 4$.

Q4 Write the following functions f(x) in the form f(x) = ($x + 2$)q(x) + r(x), where q(x) is a quadratic:
   a) f(x) = $3x^3 - 4x^2 - 5x - 6$,   b) f(x) = $x^3 + 2x^2 - 3x + 4$,   c) f(x) = $2x^3 + 6x - 3$

Q5 Write $2x^3 + 8x^2 + 7x + 8$ in the form $(Ax^2 + Bx + C)(x + 3) + D$.
   Using your answer, state the result when $2x^3 + 8x^2 + 7x + 8$ is divided by ($x + 3$).

Exam Questions

Q1   f(x) = $2x^3 - 5x^2 - 4x + 3$
   a) Find the remainder when f(x) is divided by:
      (i)   ($x - 1$)   [1 mark]
      (ii) ($2x + 1$)   [1 mark]
   b) Show using the Factor Theorem that ($x + 1$) is a factor of f(x).   [2 marks]
   c) Factorise f(x) completely.   [3 marks]

Q2   f(x) = $(4x^2 + 3x + 1)(x - p) + 5$, where p is a constant.
   a) State the value of f(p).   [1 mark]
   b) Find the value of p, given that when f(x) is divided by ($x + 1$), the remainder is −1.   [2 marks]
   c) Find the remainder when f(x) is divided by ($x - 1$).   [1 mark]

Q3   Write $x^3 + 15x^2 + 43x - 30$ in the form $(Ax^2 + Bx + C)(x + 6) + D$,
   where A, B, C and D are constants to be found.   [3 marks]

Just keep repeating — divide and conquer, divide and conquer...

There's a lot to take in about algebraic division so feel free to go over it again. It's up to you which method you prefer but I'd recommend either long division or the formula — these are a bit quicker than the first method. Using the Remainder Theorem to find remainders (rather than actually dividing) can also save you time in the exam.

Solving Quadratic Equations

You've probably been solving equations since before you could walk, so lots of this should be familiar. Here, you'll be finding x for lovely quadratic equations of the form ax² + bx + c = 0.

Solve quadratic equations by *Factorising*

Factorising is probably the quickest way to solve a quadratic equation — if it looks fairly **simple**, try to factorise it. The examples below use the methods described on pages 6-7.

Example: Solve $x^2 - 8 = 2x$ by factorising.

Put into $ax^2 + bx + c = 0$ form: $\qquad x^2 - 8 = 2x \Rightarrow x^2 - 2x - 8 = 0$

Solve the equation by factorising: $\qquad (x + 2)(x - 4) = 0$
$$\Rightarrow x + 2 = 0 \text{ or } x - 4 = 0$$
$$\Rightarrow x = -2 \text{ or } x = 4$$

Watch out for **'disguised quadratics'**, where there's some **function of x** instead of x. To solve quadratics of the form $a(f(x))^2 + b(f(x)) + c$ use the **substitution** $y = f(x)$, solve to find values of y, then use these to find values of x.

Example: Solve $x^{\frac{2}{3}} + 3x^{\frac{1}{3}} - 40 = 0$.

$f(x) = x^{\frac{1}{3}}$, so use the substitution: $\qquad y = x^{\frac{1}{3}}$ $\qquad$ Using $x^{\frac{2}{3}} = \left(x^{\frac{1}{3}}\right)^2 = y^2$
$$y^2 + 3y - 40 = 0$$

Solve the quadratic in y by factorising: $\qquad (y + 8)(y - 5) = 0$
$$\Rightarrow y + 8 = 0 \text{ or } y - 5 = 0$$
$$\Rightarrow y = -8 \text{ or } y = 5$$

Use the values of y to find the values of x: $\quad y = -8 \Rightarrow -8 = x^{\frac{1}{3}} \Rightarrow x = (-8)^3 = \mathbf{-512}$
$$y = 5 \Rightarrow 5 = x^{\frac{1}{3}} \Rightarrow x = 5^3 = \mathbf{125}$$

'Disguised quadratics' might involve trig functions (see Section 3) or exponentials and logs (see Section 4).

The quadratics were becoming more cunning with their disguises.

Completing the Square *puts any old quadratic in a* Special Form

Completing the square sounds really confusing. For starters, what does "Completing the Square" **mean**? **What** is the square? **Why** does it need completing? Well, there is **some** logic to it:

1) The **square** looks like this: $\qquad (x + \text{something})^2$

   It's basically the factorised equation (with two identical factors), but there's something missing...

2) ...so you need to **'complete'** it by adding a number to the square to make it equal to the original equation.

$$(x + \text{something})^2 + ?$$

You start with something like this... $\qquad$ ...sort the x-coefficients... $\qquad$ ...and end up with something like this.

$$\boxed{2x^2 + 8x - 5} \implies \boxed{2(x + 2)^2 + ?} \implies \boxed{2(x + 2)^2 - 13}$$

The method below can be used to complete the square of a quadratic expression:

Completing the Square of $ax^2 + bx + c$

① Take a **factor of a** out of the x^2 and x terms: $a\left(x^2 + \frac{b}{a}x\right) + c$.

② Rewrite the bit in the bracket as **one bracket squared**.
The number in the brackets is always $\frac{b}{2a}$, so the bracket is $a\left(x + \frac{b}{2a}\right)^2$.

③ Add d to the bracket to complete the square and **find d** by setting the new and original expressions **equal** to each other:

$$a\left(x + \frac{b}{2a}\right)^2 + d = ax^2 + bx + c$$

Expanding the LHS gives:
$$\cancel{ax^2} + \cancel{bx} + \frac{b^2}{4a} + d = \cancel{ax^2} + \cancel{bx} + c.$$
Then cancel and rearrange to get d.

④ **Solving** this equation always gives $d = \left(c - \frac{b^2}{4a}\right)$, so:

$$a\left(x + \frac{b}{2a}\right)^2 + \left(c - \frac{b^2}{4a}\right) = ax^2 + bx + c$$

Solving Quadratic Equations

Complete the square to find Exact Solutions

Completing the square probably isn't the easiest way to solve an equation but it is useful
if you are asked to **sketch a graph** or find an **exact solution** — usually this means **surds** will be involved.

Example: a)   Rewrite $2x^2 - 8x + 3$ by completing the square.

You can also use the quadratic formula to find exact solutions (see p.16).

Take out a factor of 2 out of the x^2 and x terms: $2(x^2 - 4x) + 3$

Rewrite the bracket as one bracket squared: $b = -8$, so $\dfrac{b}{2a} = \dfrac{-8}{2 \times 2} = -2$, so the bracket is $2(x - 2)^2$

Add d to the bracket. Then find d by setting the new and original equation equal to each other:

$$2(x - 2)^2 + d$$
$$2(x - 2)^2 + d = 2x^2 - 8x + 3$$
$$2x^2 - 8x + 8 + d = 2x^2 - 8x + 3$$
$$8 + d = 3 \implies d = -5, \text{ so the completed square is } \boxed{2(x - 2)^2 - 5}$$

b)   Hence find exact solutions to $2x^2 - 8x + 3 = 0$.

Set your answer from part a) equal to O and solve to find x:

$$2(x - 2)^2 - 5 = 0$$
$$\implies (x - 2)^2 = \frac{5}{2}$$

Using $d = c - \dfrac{b^2}{4a}$ also gives
$d = 3 - \dfrac{8^2}{4 \times 2} = 3 - 8 = -5$.

There's a positive and negative square root:

$$\implies x - 2 = \pm\sqrt{\frac{5}{2}} = \pm\frac{\sqrt{10}}{2}$$

Rationalise the denominator
$\sqrt{\dfrac{5}{2}} = \dfrac{\sqrt{5}}{\sqrt{2}} = \dfrac{\sqrt{5}\sqrt{2}}{\sqrt{2}\sqrt{2}} = \dfrac{\sqrt{10}}{2}$

You're asked for the exact solutions so leave your answer in surd form:

$$x = 2 + \frac{\sqrt{10}}{2} \text{ and } x = 2 - \frac{\sqrt{10}}{2}$$

Sometimes it's best just to use the Formula

Factorising or completing the square can be really messy for some equations — in which case your best bet is to use the **quadratic formula** (see page 16). But be careful, the question probably won't tell you which method is best.

For example, if you are asked to solve $6x^2 + 87x - 144 = 0$ things can get **tricky**.

This will actually **factorise**, but there are 2 possible bracket forms to try:
$(6x \quad)(x \quad)$ or $(3x \quad)(2x \quad)$ For each of these, there are 8 possible ways of making 144 to try.

And completing the square would be much **slower** than using the formula.

Practice Questions

Q1 Solve the following equations. While you're doing this, sing a jolly song to show how much you enjoy it.
  a) $x^2 + x - 12 = 0$ b) $2 + x - x^2 = 0$ c) $4x^2 - 1 = 0$ d) $3x^2 - 15x - 14 = 4x$

Q2 Solve $3(x + 2)^2 - 17(x + 2) - 6 = 0$ by substitution.

Q3 Solve these quadratic equations by completing the square, leaving your answers in surd form where necessary.
  a) $x^2 - 6x + 5 = 0$ b) $3x^2 - 7x + 3 = 0$ c) $2x^2 - 6x - 2 = 0$ d) $x^2 + 4x + 6 = 12$

Q4 Solve the equation $5x^2 + 4x - 36 = x^2 - 3x$.

Exam Questions

Q1 a) Write $3x^2 + 2x - 2$ in completed square form.   [3 marks]

    b) Hence, or otherwise, solve the equation $3x^2 + 2x - 2 = 0$. Give your answers to 2 decimal places.   [1 mark]

Q2 Find the exact solutions of the equation $6x^2 = 1 - 3x$, by completing the square.   [4 marks]

I'm popular with squares — they always tell me how I complete them...

Completing the square is useful when you're sketching graphs (see page 15). It's worth making sure that you're comfortable with all the methods discussed here, they'll all come in handy at some point. If you've got a fancy calculator it might even solve quadratic equations for you — but don't forget to write some working out in the exam.

Quadratic Functions and Graphs

If a question doesn't seem to make sense, or you can't see how to go about solving a problem, try drawing a graph. It sometimes helps if you can actually see what the problem is, rather than just reading about it.

Quadratic graphs are **Always** u-shaped or n-shaped

The **coefficient of x^2** tells you whether a quadratic curve (called a **parabola**) is u-shaped or n-shaped. When sketching a graph you might have to consider the following things:

Sketching Quadratic Graphs

① **Up or down:** Decide on the shape of the curve
   — if the coefficient of x^2 is positive, then the graph is u-shaped.
   — if the coefficient of x^2 is negative, then the graph is n-shaped.

② **Axes:** Find where the curve crosses the y-axis (set $x = 0$) and x-axis (set $y = 0$).

③ **Maximum or minimum:** Find the maximum or minimum point by using the fact that it's halfway between the roots or by completing the square (see next page).

④ **Sketch the graph:** Make sure that you label all the bits that you need to.

> A u-shaped graph has a minimum and a n-shaped graph has a maximum.

Examples: Sketch $y = 8 - 2x - x^2$.

① **Up or Down**
$$y = 8 - 2x - x^2$$
The coefficient of x^2 is negative so the graph is n-shaped.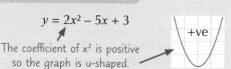

② **Axes**
When $x = 0$, $y = 8 - 2(0) - 0^2 = \mathbf{8}$
When $y = 0$, $8 - 2x - x^2 = 0$
$(2 - x)(x + 4) = 0$
$x = \mathbf{2}$ or $x = \mathbf{-4}$

This means that the curve crosses the y-axis at (O, 8) and the x-axis at (2, O) and (−4, O).

③ **Max or Min**
The maximum value is halfway between the roots because the curve is symmetrical:
$(2 + -4) \div 2 = -1$

So the maximum value is at $x = -1$.
The maximum is $y = 8 - 2(-1) - (-1)^2 = 9$

i.e. the graph has a maximum at the point **(−1, 9)**.

④ **Sketch**

> You can also find the maximum/minimum by completing the square (see the next page).

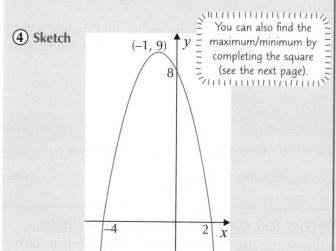

Sketch $y = 2x^2 - 5x + 3$.

$$y = 2x^2 - 5x + 3$$
The coefficient of x^2 is positive so the graph is u-shaped.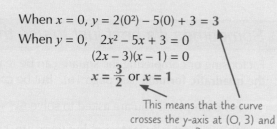

When $x = 0$, $y = 2(0^2) - 5(0) + 3 = 3$
When $y = 0$, $2x^2 - 5x + 3 = 0$
$(2x - 3)(x - 1) = 0$
$x = \dfrac{3}{2}$ or $x = 1$

This means that the curve crosses the y-axis at (O, 3) and the x-axis at $\left(\dfrac{3}{2}, \text{O}\right)$ and (1, O).

The minimum value is halfway between the roots:
$$\left(\dfrac{3}{2} + 1\right) \div 2 = \dfrac{5}{4}$$

The minimum value is at $x = \dfrac{5}{4}$.

The minimum is $y = 2\left(\dfrac{5}{4}\right)^2 - 5\left(\dfrac{5}{4}\right) + 3 = -\dfrac{1}{8}$

i.e. the graph has a minimum at the point $\left(\dfrac{5}{4}, -\dfrac{1}{8}\right)$.

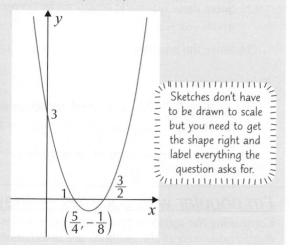

> Sketches don't have to be drawn to scale but you need to get the shape right and label everything the question asks for.

Quadratic Functions and Graphs

Completing the square can be **Useful**

Once you've completed the square, you can very quickly say **loads** about a quadratic function.
And it all relies on the fact that a squared number can **never** be less than zero... **ever**.

> **Example:** Sketch the curve of $f(x) = 3x^2 - 6x - 7$.
>
> Complete the square of f(x) (see page 12): $\qquad f(x) = 3x^2 - 6x - 7 = 3(x - 1)^2 - 10$
>
> Find where y = f(x) crosses the axes:
>
> When $x = 0$, $y = -7$, the curve crosses the y-axis at -7.
>
> When $y = 0$, $3(x - 1)^2 - 10 = 0$
>
> $$(x - 1)^2 = \frac{10}{3}$$
>
> *Rationalise the denominator (p.5).*
>
> $$x - 1 = \pm\sqrt{\frac{10}{3}}$$
>
> $$x = 1 \pm \frac{\sqrt{30}}{3}$$
>
> So the curve crosses the x-axis at $x = 1 + \dfrac{\sqrt{30}}{3}$ and $x = 1 - \dfrac{\sqrt{30}}{3}$
>
> $(x - 1)^2 \geq 0$ so the smallest value occurs when $(x - 1) = 0$, i.e. when $x = 1$.
> Find the minimum by substituting x = 1 into f(x):
>
> $f(x) = 3(x - 1)^2 - 10$, $\Rightarrow f(1) = 3(1 - 1)^2 - 10 = -10$ $\quad$ *Now you can sketch the graph.*
> So the minimum is at **(1, –10)**.

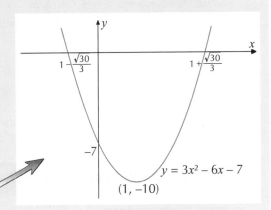

Some functions don't have **Real Roots**

By completing the square, you can also quickly tell if the graph of a quadratic function ever crosses the x-axis.
It'll only cross the x-axis if the function changes sign (i.e. goes from positive to negative or vice versa).

> **Example:** $f(x) = x^2 + 4x + 7$. Does $f(x) = 0$ have any real roots?
>
> The smallest this bit can be is zero (at x = −2). $\qquad f(x) = (x + 2)^2 + 3$
>
> $(x + 2)^2$ is never less than zero, so the minimum of $f(x)$ is 3.
>
> This means that: $\quad$ a) $f(x)$ can never be negative.
> $\qquad\qquad\qquad$ b) The graph of $f(x)$ never crosses the x-axis.
>
> So the function has **no real roots**.

To sketch a graph like this you'd need to show the correct shape, y-intercept, and coordinates of the minimum or maximum.

> If the coefficient of x² is negative, you can do the same sort of thing to check whether f(x) ever becomes positive.

Practice Questions

Q1 Sketch the following curves, labelling the maximum/minimum and the points where it crosses the axes.
$\quad$ a) $y = x^2 + 4x - 5$ $\qquad$ b) $y = 2x^2 - 7x + 6$ $\qquad$ c) $y = 11x - 10 - 3x^2$ $\qquad$ d) $y = 25 - 4x^2$

Q2 Show that the equation $f(x) = 0$, where $f(x) = 2x^2 - 12x + 23$, has no real roots.

Exam Questions

Q1 a) $f(x) = x^2 - 14x + k$, where k is a constant. Given that one of the roots of $f(x) = 0$ is $x = 7 + 2\sqrt{6}$,
$\qquad$ find the value of k, and hence verify that the other root is $x = 7 - 2\sqrt{6}$. $\qquad$ [4 marks]
$\quad$ b) Sketch the curve of $y = f(x)$. Label the minimum and the points of intersection with the axes. $\qquad$ [3 marks]

Q2 a) Rewrite $x^2 - 12x + 15$ in the form $(x - a)^2 + b$, for integers a and b. $\qquad$ [2 marks]
$\quad$ b) Find the minimum value of $x^2 - 12x + 15$ and state the value of x at which this minimum occurs. $\qquad$ [2 marks]

Sketches really help you get to the root of the problem...

Completing the square is really useful here — you can use it to find where the curve crosses the x-axis and also to find the minimum. Sketching graphs is probably the most fun you'll have in this section, so draw away to your heart's content. And once you've had your fill of quadratics there's a load of other graphs to sketch later in the section.

The Quadratic Formula

Unlike factorising, the quadratic formula always works... no ifs, no buts, no butts, no nothing...

I shall teach you the ways of the Formula

If you want to solve a quadratic equation $ax^2 + bx + c = 0$, then the answers are given by the **quadratic formula**:

$$x = \frac{-b \pm \sqrt{b^2 - 4ac}}{2a}$$

Example: Solve the quadratic equation $3x^2 - 4x = 8$, leaving your answer in surd form.

Get the equation into the standard $ax^2 + bx + c = 0$ form: $\quad 3x^2 - 4x - 8 = 0$

Plug the values $a = 3$, $b = -4$, $c = -8$ into the formula (be very careful with all the minus signs):

$$x = \frac{-(-4) \pm \sqrt{(-4)^2 - 4 \times 3 \times -8}}{2 \times 3}$$

$$= \frac{4 \pm \sqrt{112}}{6} = \frac{2 \pm 2\sqrt{7}}{3}$$

Use the rules of surds (see p.4).

There are two answers (one using + and one using −): $\quad x = \dfrac{2 + 2\sqrt{7}}{3}$ or $x = \dfrac{2 - 2\sqrt{7}}{3}$

Some **calculators** have a quadratic equation solver — you just enter the values of a, b and c and hey presto. This can be quite useful for **checking** your answers but make sure you show your working in the exam.

How Many Roots? Check the b² − 4ac bit...

$$x = \frac{-b \pm \sqrt{b^2 - 4ac}}{2a}$$

When you try to find the roots of a quadratic equation, this bit in the square root sign ($b^2 - 4ac$) can be positive, zero, or negative. It's this that tells you if a quadratic equation has **two real roots**, **one real root**, or **no real roots**.

The $b^2 - 4ac$ bit is called the **discriminant** (sometimes written D, or Δ).

It's good to be able to picture what the graphs will look like in these different cases:

$b^2 - 4ac > 0$ Two real roots	$b^2 - 4ac = 0$ One real root	$b^2 - 4ac < 0$ No real roots

The graph crosses the x-axis twice and these values are the roots:

$$y = x^2 - 6x + 8$$
$$= (x - 3)^2 - 1$$
$$= (x - 2)(x - 4)$$

The graph just touches the x-axis from above (or from below if the x^2 coefficient is negative).

$$y = x^2 - 6x + 9$$
$$= (x - 3)^2$$

The graph doesn't touch the x-axis at all.

$$y = x^2 - 6x + 10$$
$$= (x - 3)^2 + 1$$

You might also see the term 'equal roots' — this means the same as 'one real root'.

In some areas of maths, you can take the square root of negative numbers and get 'imaginary' numbers — that's why we say no 'real' roots when the discriminant is negative.

Identify a, b and c to find the Discriminant

Make sure you get them the **right way round** — it's easy to get mixed up if the quadratic's in a **different order**.

Example: Find the discriminant of $15 - x - 2x^2$. How many real roots does $15 - x - 2x^2 = 0$ have?

First identify a, b and c: $\quad a = -2$, $b = -1$ and $c = 15$ (NOT $a = 15$, $b = -1$ and $c = -2$)

Work out the discriminant: $\quad b^2 - 4ac = (-1)^2 - (4 \times -2 \times 15) = 1 + 120 = \textbf{121}$.

The discriminant is > 0: $\quad$ so $15 - x - 2x^2 = 0$ has **two distinct real roots**.

The Quadratic Formula

a, *b* and *c* might be *Unknown*

In exam questions, you might be given a **quadratic** where one or more of *a*, *b* and *c* are given in terms of an **unknown** (such as *k*, *p* or *q*). This means that you'll end up with an **equation** or **inequality** for the discriminant **in terms of the unknown** — you might have to **solve** it to find the **value** or **range of values** of the unknown.

Example: If $f(x) = 3x^2 + 2x + k$, find the range of values of *k* for which:
   a) $f(x) = 0$ has 2 distinct roots,   b) $f(x) = 0$ has 1 root,   c) $f(x) = 0$ has no real roots.

Using $a = 3$, $b = 2$ and $c = k$, work out what the discriminant is:

$b^2 - 4ac = 2^2 - 4 \times 3 \times k = 4 - 12k$

The only difference is the (in)equality symbol.

a) Two distinct roots means:

$b^2 - 4ac > 0 \Rightarrow 4 - 12k > 0$
$\Rightarrow 4 > 12k$
$\Rightarrow k < \frac{1}{3}$

b) One root means:

$b^2 - 4ac = 0 \Rightarrow 4 - 12k = 0$
$\Rightarrow 4 = 12k$
$\Rightarrow k = \frac{1}{3}$

c) No real roots means:

$b^2 - 4ac < 0 \Rightarrow 4 - 12k < 0$
$\Rightarrow 4 < 12k$
$\Rightarrow k > \frac{1}{3}$

You might have to *Solve* a *Quadratic Inequality* to find *k*

When you put your values of *a*, *b* and *c* into the formula for the **discriminant**, you might end up with a **quadratic inequality** in terms of *k*. You'll have to solve this to find the range of values of *k* — there's more on this on p.20.

Example: The equation $kx^2 + (k + 3)x + 4 = 0$ has two distinct real solutions.
Show that $k^2 - 10k + 9 > 0$, and find the set of values of *k* which satisfy this inequality.

Using $a = k$, $b = (k + 3)$ and $c = 4$, work out what the discriminant is:

$b^2 - 4ac = (k + 3)^2 - (4 \times k \times 4) = k^2 + 6k + 9 - 16k = k^2 - 10k + 9$

The equation has two distinct real solutions, so the discriminant must be > 0:

$k^2 - 10k + 9 > 0$

Now, to find the set of values for k, you have to factorise the quadratic:

$k^2 - 10k + 9 = (k - 1)(k - 9)$

This expression is zero when $k = 1$ and $k = 9$.
From the graph, you can see that this is a u-shaped quadratic which is > 0 when:

$k < 1$ or when $k > 9$

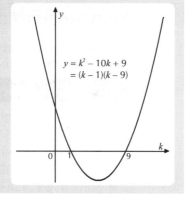

$y = k^2 - 10k + 9$
$= (k - 1)(k - 9)$

Practice Questions

Q1 For each of the following: (i)   Find the discriminant and state the number of real roots of the quadratic.
                                        (ii) Find the exact values of its real roots, if it has any.
   a) $4x^2 + 28x + 49 = 0$ b) $3x^2 + 3x + 1 = 0$ c) $9x^2 - 6\sqrt{2}x + 2 = 0$ d) $2x^2 + 9x - 5 = 0$

Q2 If the quadratic equation $x^2 + kx + 4 = 0$ has two distinct real roots, find the possible values of *k*.

Exam Questions

Q1   The equation $x^2 + 2kx + 4k = 0$, where *k* is a non-zero integer, has equal roots. Find the value of *k*.   [3 marks]

Q2   The equation $(p + 1)x^2 + (p + 1)x + 1 = 0$ has 2 distinct real solutions for *x* (*p* is a constant).
   a) Show that $p^2 - 2p - 3 > 0$ [3 marks]
   b) Hence find the range of possible values for *p*.   [3 marks]

All the best mathematicians are raised on quadratic formula...

Don't panic if you're not sure how to solve quadratic inequalities — they're covered in more detail on page 20. Although it might be tempting to hide under your exam desk and hope a discriminant question doesn't find you, there's no escaping these questions — so get practising until you can recite the quadratic formula in your sleep.

Simultaneous Equations

Solving simultaneous equations is one of those things that you'll have to do again and again
— so it's definitely worth practising them until you feel really confident.

Solving **Simultaneous Equations** by **Elimination**

Solving **simultaneous equations** means finding the answers to two equations **at the same time**
— i.e. finding values for x and y for which both equations are true.

Example: Solve the following equations: $3x + 5y = -4$
$-2x + 3y = 9$

Label the equations 1 and 2.

Go for the lowest common multiple (LCM). e.g. LCM of 2 and 3 is 6

1) Match the coefficients

Multiply the equations by numbers that will make either
the x's or the y's match in the two equations
(ignoring minus signs):

$$①\quad 3x + 5y = -4$$
$$②\quad -2x + 3y = 9$$

$$\Rightarrow \quad ① \times 2 \quad 6x + 10y = -8 \quad ③$$
$$② \times 3 \quad -6x + 9y = 27 \quad ④$$

Label these 3 and 4.

2) Eliminate to find one variable

The coefficients of x have different signs, so you need to
add the equations (if the coefficients have the same sign,
you'll need to subtract one equation from the other):

$$③+④ \quad 6x + 10y + (-6x) + 9y = -8 + 27$$
$$\Rightarrow 19y = 19$$
$$\Rightarrow y = 1$$

3) Find the variable you eliminated

Put y = 1 into one of the equations to find x:

$$y = 1 \text{ in } ① \quad 3x + 5 = -4 \Rightarrow 3x = -9$$
$$\Rightarrow x = -3$$

4) Check your answer

Put x = –3 and y = 1 into the other equation:

$$x = -3, y = 1 \text{ in } ② \quad -2(-3) + 3(1) = 9 \checkmark$$

Use **Substitution** if one equation is **Quadratic**

Sadly elimination won't always work. Sometimes one of the equations has not just x's and y's in it — but bits with
x^2 and y^2 as well. When this happens, you can **only** use the **substitution** method:

One Quadratic and One Linear Equation

1) Isolate one variable in the linear equation by
   rearranging to get either x or y on its **own**.

2) **Substitute** the variable into the quadratic equation
   (to get an equation in just one variable).

3) Solve to get values for **one variable** — either by
   factorising or using the quadratic formula.

4) Stick these values in the linear equation to find
   the **corresponding values** for the other variables.

Substitute this for your own
hilarious caption.

Example: Solve $-x + 2y = 5$ and $x^2 + y^2 = 25$.

Call the linear equation L and the quadratic equation Q.

Rearrange the linear equation so that either x or y is
on its own on one side of the equals sign:

$$Ⓛ \; -x + 2y = 5 \Rightarrow x = 2y - 5$$

Substitute this expression into the quadratic equation:

$$Ⓠ \; x^2 + y^2 = 25 \Rightarrow (2y - 5)^2 + y^2 = 25$$

Rearrange this into the form ax² + bx + c and then solve it:

$$\Rightarrow (4y^2 - 20y + 25) + y^2 = 25$$
$$\Rightarrow 5y^2 - 20y = 0$$
$$\Rightarrow 5y(y - 4) = 0$$
$$\Rightarrow y = 0 \text{ or } y = 4$$

$x^2 + y^2 = 25$ is actually a circle about the origin with radius 5 (see p.32).

Finally put both these values back into the linear equation
to find corresponding values of x:

When $y = 0$: $Ⓛ \; -x + 2(0) = 5 \Rightarrow x = -5$
When $y = 4$: $Ⓛ \; -x + 2(4) = 5 \Rightarrow x = 3$
So the solutions are $x = -5, y = 0$ and $x = 3, y = 4$.

Check your answers by putting them back into $Ⓛ$ and $Ⓠ$:

$$x = -5, y = 0 \Rightarrow -(-5) + 2 \times 0 = 5 \text{ and } (-5)^2 + 0^2 = 25 \checkmark$$
$$x = 3, y = 4 \Rightarrow -3 + 2 \times 4 = 5 \text{ and } 3^2 + 4^2 = 25 \checkmark$$

Simultaneous Equations

Number of **Solutions** = number of **Intersections**

When you have to interpret something **geometrically**, you have to sketch the graphs of the two functions and 'say what you see'. The number of **solutions** affects what your picture will look like:

Two Solutions	One Solution	No Solutions
The graphs meet in **two places**.	The graphs meet in **one place** — the straight line is a **tangent** to the curve.	The graphs **never meet**.

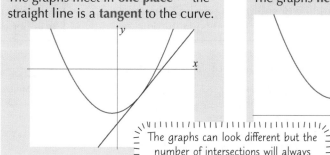

The graphs can look different but the number of intersections will always equal the number of solutions.

Example: Interpret geometrically: $y = x^2 - 4x + 5$
$$y = 2x - 4$$

Substitute the expression for y from ② into ①:
$$2x - 4 = x^2 - 4x + 5$$

Rearrange and solve:
$$x^2 - 6x + 9 = 0$$
$$(x - 3)^2 = 0$$
$$\Rightarrow x = 3$$

Putting x = 3 in ② gives: $x = 3 \Rightarrow y = 2 \times 3 - 4 = 2$

There's only 1 solution: $x = 3, y = 2$

Geometric Interpretation

Since the equations have only one solution, the two graphs only meet at one point — (3, 2):

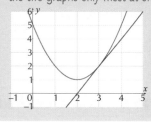

The straight line is a tangent to the curve at (3, 2).

Practice Questions

Q1 Solve these sets of simultaneous equations:

a) $3x - 4y = 7$ and $-2x + 7y = -22$ b) $2x - 3y = \frac{11}{12}$ and $x + y = -\frac{7}{12}$

Q2 Find where the following lines meet:

a) $y = 3x - 4$ and $y = 7x - 5$ b) $y = 13 - 2x$ and $7x - y - 23 = 0$ c) $2x - 3y + 4 = 0$ and $x - 2y + 1 = 0$

Q3 Find the possible solutions to these sets of simultaneous equations. Interpret your answers geometrically.

a) $y = x^2 - 7x + 4$ b) $y = 30 - 6x + 2x^2$ c) $x^2 + 2y^2 - 3 = 0$
$\quad 2x - y - 10 = 0$ $\quad y = 2(x + 11)$ $\quad y = 2x + 4$

Exam Questions

Q1 Find the coordinates of the points of intersection of $x^2 + 2y^2 = 36$ and $x + y = 6$.   [6 marks]

Q2 The line l has equation $y = 2x - 3$ and the curve C has equation $y = (x + 2)(x - 4)$.

a) Sketch the line l and the curve C on the same axes, showing the coordinates of the x- and y- intercepts.   [4 marks]

b) Show that the x-coordinates of the points of intersection of l and C satisfy the equation $x^2 - 4x - 5 = 0$.   [2 marks]

c) Hence, or otherwise, find the points of intersection of l and C.   [2 marks]

The Eliminator — a robot sent back through time to destroy one variable...

For a linear and quadratic equation you have to use substitution, but for a pair of linear equations elimination is usually the easiest method. Knowing how to sketch a graph is handy here, but there's no need to be a Van Gogh about it. Simultaneous equations pop up all over AS Maths so it's worth spending some time now to get them sorted.

Inequalities

Solving inequalities is very similar to solving equations. You've just got to be really careful that you keep the inequality sign pointing the right way.

When **Multiplying** or **Dividing** by something **Negative** flip the inequality sign

Like I said, these are pretty similar to solving equations — because whatever you do to one side, you have to do to the other. But multiplying or dividing by **negative** numbers **changes** the direction of the inequality sign.

> **Adding** or **subtracting** doesn't change the direction of the inequality sign.

> **Multiplying** or **dividing** by a **positive** number doesn't affect the inequality sign.

Examples: Find the range of values of x that satisfies: a) $x - 3 < -1 + 2x$ b) $8x + 2 \geq 2x + 17$

a) Adding 1 to both sides leaves the inequality sign pointing in the same direction.
$$x - 3 < -1 + 2x$$
$$\Rightarrow x - 2 < 2x$$
Subtracting x from both sides doesn't affect the inequality.
$$\Rightarrow -2 < x$$
so $x > -2$

b) Subtract 2, and then 2x, from both sides.
$$8x + 2 \geq 2x + 17$$
$$\Rightarrow 8x \geq 2x + 15$$
$$\Rightarrow 6x \geq 15$$
Divide both sides by 6 and simplify.
$$\Rightarrow x \geq \frac{5}{2}$$

> **Multiplying** or **dividing** an inequality by a **negative** number changes the direction of the inequality sign.

Example: Find the range of values of x that satisfies $4 - 3x \leq 16$

Subtract 4 from both sides.
$$4 - 3x \leq 16$$
Then divide both sides by -3
$$\Rightarrow -3x \leq 12$$
— but change the direction of the inequality.
$$\Rightarrow x \geq -4$$

The reason for the sign changing direction is because it's just the same as swapping everything from one side to the other:
$$-3x \leq 12 \Rightarrow -12 \leq 3x \Rightarrow x \geq -4$$

Sketch a **Graph** to solve a **Quadratic** inequality

With quadratic inequalities, you're best off sketching the **graph** and taking it from there.
You've got to be really careful when you divide by variables that might be **negative** — basically, don't do it.

Example Find the range of values of x that satisfies $36x \leq 6x^2$

Rearrange into the form $f(x) \geq 0$.
Start by dividing by 6:
Take 6x from both sides and rearrange:
$$36x \leq 6x^2$$
$$\Rightarrow 6x \leq x^2$$
$$\Rightarrow 0 \leq x^2 - 6x$$
So $x^2 - 6x \geq 0$

You shouldn't divide by x here because it could be negative (or zero).

The coefficient of x^2 is positive, so the graph of y is u-shaped.

Write the inequality as an equation: Let $y = x^2 - 6x$

Find where the curve crosses the x-axis by setting $y = 0$ and factorising:
$$x^2 - 6x = 0 \Rightarrow x(x - 6) = 0$$
So $x = 0$ and $x = 6$.

Use a sketch to find where $x^2 - 6x \geq 0$: The graph is positive to the left of $x = 0$ and to the right of $x = 6$ (inclusive).
So $x \leq 0$ or $x \geq 6$.

You might be asked to give your answer in **set notation**:

In set notation, the answer to the example above is $\{x: x \leq 0\} \cup \{x: x \geq 6\}$.

Set Notation

- Set notation uses **curly brackets**: $\{x: x < a\}$ means 'the set of values of x such that x is less than a'.
- The **empty set**, written $\varnothing$, contains **nothing**. For example, $\{x: x^2 < 0\} = \varnothing$ (as x^2 is never < 0).
- The **union** ($\cup$) of two sets is **everything** contained in **either set**: $x < a$ or $x > b$ is written as $\{x: x < a\} \cup \{x: x > b\}$.

- The **intersection** ($\cap$) of two sets is **only the things** present in **both sets**: $x > c$ and $x < d$ is written as $\{x: x > c\} \cap \{x: x < d\}$.
- You can also use **brackets** to show an interval — **round** means the value **isn't** included, and **square** means it **is**. So $(3, 5]$ means $3 < x \leq 5$.

Inequalities

Test **Both Sides** of a curve to find a **Region**

You might be given two (or more) inequalities and asked to find the **region** that satisfies them. All you need to do is **sketch** the curves or lines and **test** the coordinates of a point (usually the origin) in each of the inequalities. The region you're after will include the **areas** where each inequality holds **true** for any tested point.

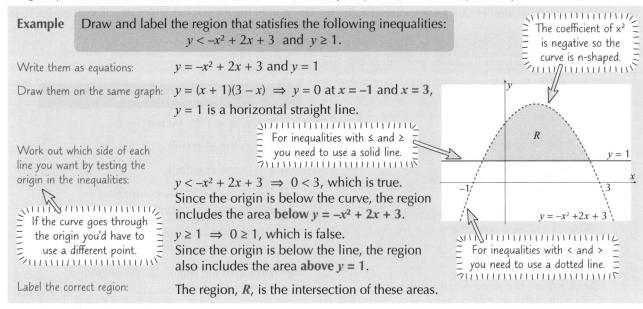

Example Draw and label the region that satisfies the following inequalities:
$y < -x^2 + 2x + 3$ and $y \geq 1$.

The coefficient of x^2 is negative so the curve is n-shaped.

Write them as equations: $y = -x^2 + 2x + 3$ and $y = 1$

Draw them on the same graph: $y = (x + 1)(3 - x) \Rightarrow y = 0$ at $x = -1$ and $x = 3$,
$y = 1$ is a horizontal straight line.

For inequalities with $\leq$ and $\geq$ you need to use a solid line.

Work out which side of each line you want by testing the origin in the inequalities:

If the curve goes through the origin you'd have to use a different point.

$y < -x^2 + 2x + 3 \Rightarrow 0 < 3$, which is true.
Since the origin is below the curve, the region includes the area **below** $y = -x^2 + 2x + 3$.

$y \geq 1 \Rightarrow 0 \geq 1$, which is false.
Since the origin is below the line, the region also includes the area **above** $y = 1$.

For inequalities with < and > you need to use a dotted line.

Label the correct region: The region, R, is the intersection of these areas.

Practice Questions

Q1 Find the ranges of x that satisfy these inequalities:
a) $x + 6 < 5x - 4$ b) $4x - 2 > x - 14$ c) $7 - x \leq 4 - 2x$

Q2 Solve: a) $7x - 4 > 2x - 42$ b) $12y - 3 \leq 4y + 4$ c) $9y - 4 \geq 17y + 2$

Q3 Find the ranges of x that satisfy the following inequalities:
a) $3x^2 - 5x - 2 \leq 0$ b) $6 - x - 2x^2 < 0$ c) $3x^2 + 7x + 4 \geq 2(x^2 + x - 1)$

Q4 Find the ranges of x that satisfy these jokers. Give your answers in set notation.
a) $x^2 + 3x - 1 \geq x + 2$ b) $2x^2 > x + 1$ c) $3x^2 - 12 < x^2 - 2x$

Q5 Draw and label the region that satisfies the following inequalities:
$y \leq 3$, $y > x - 1$ and $y > 4 - 2x$.

Exam Questions

Q1 Find the set of values for x that satisfy the inequalities below.
a) $3x + 2 \leq x + 6$ [1 mark]
b) $20 - x - x^2 > 0$ [2 marks]
c) both $3x + 2 \leq x + 6$ and $20 - x - x^2 > 0$ [1 mark]

Q2 Solve the inequalities:
a) $3 \leq 2p + 5 \leq 15$ [2 marks]
b) $q^2 - 9 > 0$ [2 marks]

Q3 Draw and label the region that satisfies the following: $y > 2x^2 - x - 3$ and $y \geq 1 - \frac{1}{2}x$ [4 marks]

Inequalities ≥ vectors > biology...

For inequality questions you could be given any linear and/or quadratic inequalities to sketch (or find intersection points). Don't forget to use a solid line for inequalities with ≤ or ≥ and a dotted line for < or > — this could cost you marks in the exam. There are plenty of inequality questions to get stuck into here, so get cracking.

Cubics

Remember how much you enjoyed factorising quadratics? Well factorising cubics is a little bit similar — only harder, better, faster, stronger. Okay maybe just harder, but at least you still get to do a bit of sketching.

Factorising a cubic given One Factor

A **cubic** function has an x^3 term as the highest power. When you factorising a cubic, you put it into (up to) three **brackets**. If the examiners are feeling nice they'll give you **one** of the factors, which makes it a bit **easier** to factorise.

Example: Given that $(x+2)$ is a factor of $f(x) = 2x^3 + x^2 - 8x - 4$, express $f(x)$ as the product of three linear factors.

The first step is to find a quadratic factor. So write down the factor you know, along with another set of brackets:

$(x + 2)($ $) = 2x^3 + x^2 - 8x - 4$

Put the x^2 bit in this new set of brackets. These have to multiply together to give you this:

$(x + 2)(2x^2$ $) = 2x^3 + x^2 - 8x - 4$

Find the number for the second set of brackets. These have to multiply together to give you this:

$(x + 2)(2x^2$ $- 2) = 2x^3 + x^2 - 8x - 4$

These multiply to give you $-2x$, but there's $-8x$ in f(x) — so you need an 'extra' $-6x$. And that's what this $-3x$ is for:

$(x + 2)(2x^2 - 3x - 2) = 2x^3 + x^2 - 8x - 4$

Before you go any further, check that there are the same number of x^2's on both sides:

$4x^2$ from here...

$(x + 2)(2x^2 - 3x - 2) = 2x^3 + x^2 - 8x - 4$

...and $-3x^2$ from here add together to give this x^2.

If this is okay, factorise the quadratic into two linear factors.

$2x^2 - 3x - 2 = (2x + 1)(x - 2)$

And so... $2x^3 + x^2 - 8x - 4 = (x + 2)(2x + 1)(x - 2)$

Factorising Cubics

1) Write down the **factor** $(x - k)$.

2) Put in the x^2 **term**.

3) Put in the **constant**.

4) Put in the x term by **comparing** the **number of x's** on both sides.

5) **Check** there are the same **number of x^2's** (or x's) on both sides.

6) **Factorise** the quadratic you've found — if that's possible.

You only need $-3x$ because it's going to be multiplied by 2 which makes $-6x$.

If every term in the cubic contains an 'x' (i.e. $ax^3 + bx^2 + cx$) then just take out x as your first factor before factorising the remaining quadratic as usual.

If you wanted to solve a cubic, you'd do it exactly the same way — put it in the form $ax^3 + bx^2 + cx + d = 0$ and factorise.

Use the Factor Theorem to factorise a cubic given No Factors

If the nasty examiner has given you **no factors**, you can find one using the Factor Theorem (see p.9) and then use the **method** above to factorise the rest. As if by magic, here's a reminder of the **Factor Theorem**:

If **f(x)** is a polynomial, and **f(k) = 0**, then **(x – k)** is a **factor** of f(x).

Example: Factorise $f(x) = 2x^3 + x^2 - 8x - 4$ fully.

Try small numbers until f(something) = 0:

For example, calculate f(1), f(–1), f(2), f(–2), etc.

$f(1) = 2(1^3) + 1^2 - 8(1) - 4 = -9$
$f(-1) = 2(-1)^3 + (-1)^2 - 8(-1) - 4 = 3$
$f(2) = 2(2^3) + 2^2 - 8(2) - 4 = 0$

Using the Factor Theorem:

$f(2) = 0$, so $(x - 2)$ is a factor.

Write down another set of brackets:

$(x - 2)($ $) = 2x^3 + x^2 - 8x - 4$

Use the method described above to get:

$2x^3 + x^2 - 8x - 4 = (x - 2)(2x + 1)(x + 2)$

This is actually the same example as above but the working will be slightly different because you're starting with the factor (x – 2).

Cubics

If you know the **Factors** of a cubic — the graph's easy to **Sketch**

All cubics have a similar shape: **'bottom-left to top-right'** if the coefficient of x^3 is **positive** or
'top-left to bottom-right' if the coefficient of x^3 is **negative**.

Once you know the **factors** of a cubic, the graph is easy to sketch — just find where the function is **zero**.

Example: Sketch the graphs of the following cubic functions:

a) $f(x) = x(x - 1)(2x + 1)$
b) $g(x) = (1 - x)(x^2 - 2x + 2)$
c) $m(x) = (x - 3)^2(x + 1)$
d) $n(x) = (2 - x)^3$

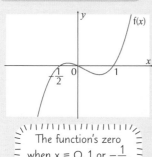
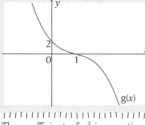
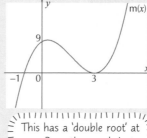
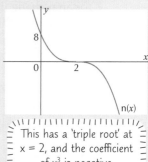

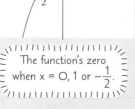
The function's zero when x = 0, 1 or $-\frac{1}{2}$.

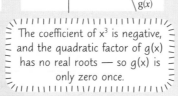
The coefficient of x^3 is negative, and the quadratic factor of g(x) has no real roots — so g(x) is only zero once.

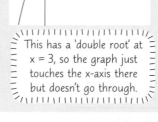
This has a 'double root' at x = 3, so the graph just touches the x-axis there but doesn't go through.

This has a 'triple root' at x = 2, and the coefficient of x^3 is negative.

Peter spent too much time sketching his cubic graph in the exam.

The **power** of a factor $(x - a)^n$ affects what happens at **x = a**:
even power $\Rightarrow$ the curve **touches** the x-axis but doesn't cross it
(e.g. the 'double root' in m(x) above)
odd power $\Rightarrow$ the curve **crosses** the x-axis
(e.g. the 'triple root' in n(x) above).

This is also true for other polynomials — e.g. quartics (p.24).

Practice Questions

Q1 Sketch these cubic graphs. Go on, this is the fun part.
  a) $y = (x - 4)^3$ b) $y = (3 - x)(x + 2)^2$ c) $y = (1 - x)(x^2 - 6x + 8)$ d) $y = (x - 1)(x - 2)(x - 3)$

Q2 Show that the expressions below are factors of the given functions. Hence factorise the functions fully.
  a) $(x - 1)$ is a factor of $f(x) = x^3 - x^2 - 2x + 2$ b) $(x + 4)$ is a factor of $g(x) = x^3 + 3x^2 - 10x - 24$
  c) $(2x - 1)$ is a factor of $h(x) = 2x^3 + 3x^2 - 8x + 3$ d) $(3x - 2)$ is a factor of $k(x) = 3x^3 + 10x^2 + 10x - 12$

Q3 Given that $(x + 5)$ is a factor of $f(x) = x^3 - 3x^2 - 33x + 35$, factorise $f(x)$ fully.

Exam Questions

Q1 The curve C has the equation $y = (2x + 1)(x - 2)^2$
   Sketch C, clearly showing the points at which the curve meets the x- and y-axes   [3 marks]

Q2 a) Show that $(2x + 1)$ is a factor of $f(x) = 6x^3 + 37x^2 + 5x - 6$ [2 marks]
   b) Hence, or otherwise, factorise $f(x)$ fully.   [2 marks]
   c) Sketch $y = f(x)$, clearly showing the points at which the curve meets the x- and y-axes.   [3 marks]

Q3 If $f(x) = 7x^3 - 26x^2 + 13x + 6$, solve $f(x) = 0$.   [4 marks]

Does your cubic have the x factor? Only if x is in every term...

Factorising cubics might seem daunting but once you're used to the method it gets easier. For sketches, always find where the cubic crosses the x- and y-axis — even if you're not sure what shape the curve will be. This goes for most other kinds of graph too, not just cubics. You'll be seeing some of these other curves very soon — happy sketching.

Graphs of Functions

A picture speaks a thousand words... and graphs are as close as you're going to get in maths. They're dead useful for getting your head round tricky questions, and time spent learning how to sketch graphs is time well spent.

The graph of $y = kx^n$ is a different **Shape** for different k and n

Usually, you only need a **rough** sketch of a graph — so just knowing the basic shapes of these graphs will do.

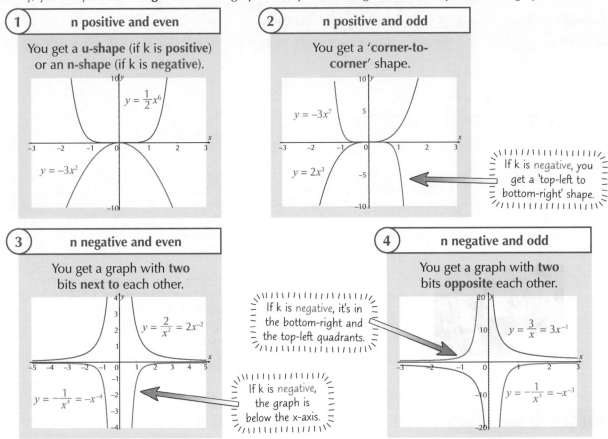

1 **n positive and even**

You get a **u-shape** (if k is **positive**) or an **n-shape** (if k is **negative**).

$y = \frac{1}{2}x^6$

$y = -3x^2$

2 **n positive and odd**

You get a '**corner-to-corner**' shape.

$y = -3x^7$

$y = 2x^3$

If k is negative, you get a 'top-left to bottom-right' shape.

3 **n negative and even**

You get a graph with **two** bits **next to** each other.

$y = \frac{2}{x^2} = 2x^{-2}$

$y = -\frac{1}{x^4} = -x^{-4}$

If k is negative, it's in the bottom-right and the top-left quadrants.

If k is negative, the graph is below the x-axis.

4 **n negative and odd**

You get a graph with **two** bits **opposite** each other.

$y = \frac{3}{x} = 3x^{-1}$

$y = -\frac{1}{x^3} = -x^{-3}$

An **asymptote** of a curve is a **line** which the curve gets **infinitely close** to, but **never touches**.
So graphs 3 and 4 both have asymptotes at $x = 0$ and $y = 0$.

Find where the curve **Crosses** the **x-axis** to sketch **Quartics**

A **quartic** has an x^4 term as the highest power. If you're asked to sketch one of these it's likely to be **factorised**, so you can easily work out where it **crosses** or **touches** the x-axis. Then you can figure out what the curve looks like.

Quartics with **positive coefficients** of x^4 are always positive for **very** positive and negative values of x. For **negative coefficients** of x^4 the curve is negative for **very** positive and negative x-values — this is similar to quadratics.

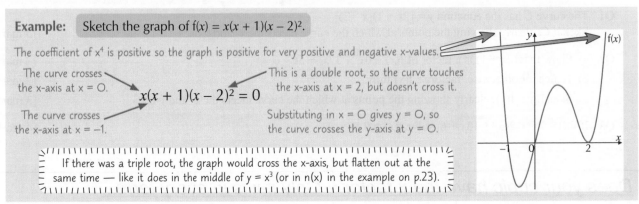

Example: Sketch the graph of $f(x) = x(x + 1)(x - 2)^2$.

The coefficient of x^4 is positive so the graph is positive for very positive and negative x-values.

The curve crosses the x-axis at x = 0.

$x(x + 1)(x - 2)^2 = 0$

The curve crosses the x-axis at x = –1.

This is a double root, so the curve touches the x-axis at x = 2, but doesn't cross it.

Substituting in x = 0 gives y = 0, so the curve crosses the y-axis at y = 0.

If there was a triple root, the graph would cross the x-axis, but flatten out at the same time — like it does in the middle of $y = x^3$ (or in n(x) in the example on p.23).

Graphs of Functions

There are **Four** main **Graph Transformations**

You'll have come across graph transformations before — **translations** (adding things to **shift** the graph vertically or horizontally) and **reflections** in the x- or y- axis. You also need to know **stretches** (either vertical or horizontal). Each transformation has the same effect on any function — here they're applied to f(x) = sin x:

y = f(x + c)

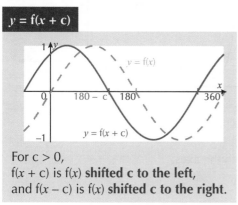

For c > 0,
f(x + c) is f(x) **shifted c to the left**,
and f(x – c) is f(x) **shifted c to the right**.

y = f(x) + c

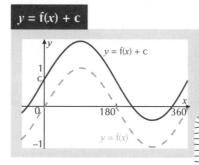

For c > 0, f(x) + c is
f(x) **shifted c upwards**,
and f(x) – c is
f(x) **shifted c downwards**.

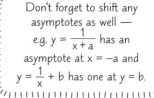
Don't forget to shift any asymptotes as well —
e.g. $y = \frac{1}{x + a}$ has an asymptote at x = –a and $y = \frac{1}{x} + b$ has one at y = b.

Reflections in the x-axis flip f(x) vertically and reflections in the y-axis flip f(x) horizontally.

y = f(ax)

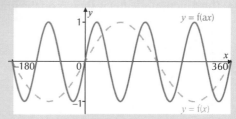

y = af(x)

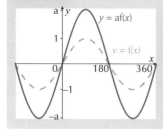

If a > 1 or a < –1, the graph of af(x) is f(x) **stretched vertically** by a factor of a.
If –1 < a < 1, the graph is **squashed vertically**.
And if a < 0, the graph is also **reflected** in the x-axis.

If a > 1 or a < –1 the graph of f(ax) is f(x) **squashed horizontally** by a factor of a.
If –1 < a < 1, the graph is **stretched horizontally**.
And if a < 0, the graph is also **reflected** in the y-axis.

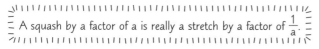
A squash by a factor of a is really a stretch by a factor of $\frac{1}{a}$.

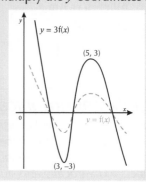
$\frac{1}{2}$f(orange) =

Transformations can be **Applied** to all sorts of **Functions**

You might be asked to find certain **coordinates** after a transformation has been applied to a function. These could include points of intersection with the x- and y-axes and turning points.

Example: The graph below shows the function y = f(x). Draw the graphs of y = f(x + 2) and y = 3f(x), showing the coordinates of the turning points.

First draw the graph of y = f(x + 2) and work out the coordinates of the turning points.

The graph is shifted left by 2 units, so subtract 2 from the x-coordinates.

Now draw the graph of y = 3f(x).

This is a stretch in the direction of the y-axis with scale factor 3, so multiply the y-coordinates by 3.

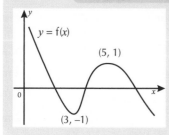

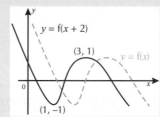

Graphs of Functions

Practice Questions

Q1 Four graphs, A, B, C and D, are shown below. Match each of the following functions to one of the graphs.

a) $y = \dfrac{4}{x^4}$ b) $y = -3x^6$ c) $y = -1.5x^3$ d) $y = \dfrac{2}{3x}$

A 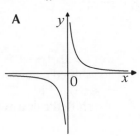   B 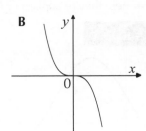   C 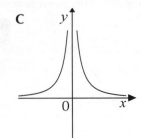   D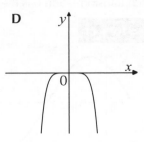

Q2 Sketch the following curves, labelling any points of intersection with the axes:

a) $y = -2x^4$ b) $y = \dfrac{7}{x^2}$ c) $y = -5x^3$ d) $y = -\dfrac{2}{x^5}$

Q3 Sketch the graph of $y = f(x)$, where $f(x) = x^2(x + 3)^2$.

Q4 The function $y = f(x)$ is shown on the graph below.

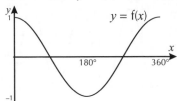

Sketch the graphs of the following:

a) $y = \dfrac{1}{4}f(x)$ b) $y = f(x) + 1$ c) $y = f(x + 180°)$

Exam Questions

Q1 $f(x) = (1 - x)(x + 4)^3$

Sketch the graph of $y = f(x)$, labelling the points where the curve intersects the x- and y-axes.   [4 marks]

Q2   The graph below shows the curve $y = f(x)$, and the intercepts of the curve with the x- and y-axes.

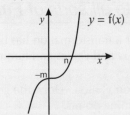

Sketch the graphs of the following transformations on separate axes, clearly labelling the points of intersection with the x- and y-axes in terms of m and n.

a) $y = f(3x)$ [2 marks]

b) $y = f(x) + m$ [2 marks]

c) $y = -3f(x)$ [2 marks]

d) $y = f\left(\dfrac{1}{3}x\right)$ [2 marks]

"Let's get graphical, graphical. I want to get graphical"...

Graphs of $y = kx^n$ and quartics are probably less likely to come up than quadratics or cubics. But if you're struggling to remember the right shape of any graph, test different x-values (e.g. positive values, negative values, values either side of any roots). For graph transformations you might find it useful to remember that stuff outside the brackets affects f(x) vertically and stuff inside affects f(x) horizontally. Now get out there and get sketching (graphs).

Proportion

Variables that are in proportion are closely related. Think of this page as like a daytime TV DNA test for variables.

Direct Proportion graphs are Straight Lines through the Origin

If two variables are in **direct proportion**, it means that changing one variable will change the other by the same scale factor. So multiplying or dividing by **any** constant will have the same effect on both variables.
To say that *"y is directly proportional to x"*, you can write:

$$y \propto x$$

which is equivalent to writing

$$y = kx$$

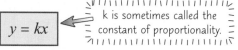
k is sometimes called the constant of proportionality.

Example: The circumference of a circle, C, is directly proportional to its radius, r.
a) Find the constant of proportionality and sketch the graph of C against r.
b) A circle with a radius of p cm has a circumference of 13 cm.
   Find the circumference of a circle with a radius of $2.5p$ cm.

y = kx is a straight line with gradient k that passes through the origin (0, 0).

a) The circumference of a circle is given by $2\pi r$:

   $C \propto r$ means $C = kr$. So $kr = 2\pi r \Rightarrow k = 2\pi$

   The graph is a straight line through the origin with gradient 2π:

b) You can do this without using the circumference formula. The radius of the second circle is 2.5 times the size of the first so the circumference will be 2.5 times the first as well:

   $C = 2.5 \times 13 = \textbf{32.5 cm}$

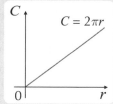

Inverse Proportion graphs are of the form y = k / x

If two variables are in **inverse proportion**, it means that changing one variable will change the other by the **reciprocal** of the scale factor. So **multiplying** one variable by **any** constant is the same as **dividing** the other by the same constant.
Saying that *"y is inversely proportional to x"* is the same as saying *"y is directly proportional to $\frac{1}{x}$"*, so you can write:

$$y \propto \frac{1}{x}$$

which is equivalent to writing

$$y = \frac{k}{x}$$

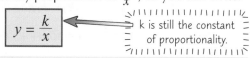
k is still the constant of proportionality.

Example: The pressure of a gas, P N/m², is modelled as being inversely proportional to the volume of its container, v m³.
a) A container with volume 12 m³ contains a gas with pressure 0.125 N/m². Find the constant of proportionality.
b) Sketch the graph of P against v.

a) $P \propto \frac{1}{v}$ is the same as saying $P = \frac{k}{v}$.

   Use the values from the question:

   When $v = 12$, $P = 0.125$, so $0.125 = \frac{k}{12}$

   $\Rightarrow k = 0.125 \times 12 = \textbf{1.5}$

b) $P = \frac{1.5}{v}$ is of the form $P = kv^n$
   with $k = 1.5$ and $n = -1$ (see p.24).
   But volume cannot be negative so you only need positive values of v.

There are asymptotes at v = 0 and P = 0.

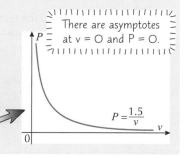

Practice Questions

Q1 If m is directly proportional to n and $m = 12$ when $n = 3$, find the constant of proportionality, k.

Q2 If p is inversely proportional to q and $p = 3$ when $q = 5$, find the constant of proportionality, k.

Exam Question

Q1 After a storm, the area of a small island was reduced by erosion in the following years. The area, A km², of the island is modelled as being inversely proportional to t, the time in years since the storm, for $t \geq 1$.

a) 5.5 years after the storm, the area of the island was 2.6 km². Find the constant of proportionality, k. [1 mark]

b) Sketch the graph of t against A, stating the equations of any asymptotes. [2 marks]

c) Suggest one reason why this model has the restriction $t \geq 1$. [1 mark]

Time spent checking your phone is inversely proportional to exam marks...

Watch out for other proportion relationships — e.g. you might come across relations such as $y \propto x^2$ or $y \propto 1/\sqrt{x}$.

Binomial Expansions

If you're feeling a bit stressed, just take a couple of minutes to relax before trying to get your head round this page — it's a bit of a stinker in places. Have a cup of tea and think about something else for a couple of minutes. Ready...

Writing **Binomial Expansions** is all about **Spotting Patterns**

Doing binomial expansions just involves **multiplying out** brackets. It would get nasty when you raise the brackets to **higher powers** — but once again I've got a **cunning plan**...

$$(1 + x)^0 = 1$$
$$(1 + x)^1 = 1 + x$$
$$(1 + x)^2 = 1 + 2x + x^2$$
$$(1 + x)^3 = 1 + 3x + 3x^2 + x^3$$
$$(1 + x)^4 = 1 + 4x + 6x^2 + 4x^3 + x^4$$

Anything to the power of O is 1.

$$(1 + x)^3 = (1 + x)(1 + x)^2$$
$$= (1 + x)(1 + 2x + x^2)$$
$$= 1 + 2x + x^2 + x + 2x^2 + x^3$$
$$= 1 + 3x + 3x^2 + x^3$$

A Frenchman named Pascal spotted the pattern in the coefficients and wrote them down in a **triangle**.
So it was called '**Pascal's Triangle**' (imaginative, eh?).
The pattern's easy — each number is the **sum** of the two above it.

So, the next line will be: **1 5 10 10 5 1**
giving $(1 + x)^5 = 1 + 5x + 10x^2 + 10x^3 + 5x^4 + x^5$.

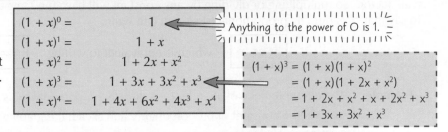

```
          1
       1     1
    1     2     1
  1    3     3   + 1
1    4     6   = 4    1
```

You **Don't** need to write out Pascal's Triangle for **Higher Powers**

There's a **formula** that gives you the numbers from the triangle. It looks **horrible** (take a glance at the next page — blegh...) but fortunately some kind soul has included it in your formula booklet. Make sure to say thank you.

Example: Expand $(1 + x)^{20}$, giving the first four terms in ascending powers of x.

This includes the x^0 term (i.e. the constant term).

Here's the basic expansion for $(1 + x)^n$. In this example $n = 20$.

$$(1 + x)^n = 1 + \frac{n}{1}x + \frac{n(n-1)}{1 \times 2}x^2 + \boxed{\frac{n(n-1)(n-2)}{1 \times 2 \times 3}x^3} + ... + x^n$$

This binomial expansion stuff will be really important in some of the stats chapters — see p.85.

Here's a closer look at the term in the blue box:

Start here. The power of x is 3 and everything else here is based on 3.

There are three things multiplied together on the top row. If n = 20, this would be 20 × 19 × 18.

$$\frac{n(n-1)(n-2)}{1 \times 2 \times 3}x^3$$

There are three integers here multiplied together. 1 × 2 × 3 is written as 3! and called 3 factorial.

This means, if $n = 20$ and you were asked for '**the term in x^7**' you should write $\frac{20 \times 19 \times 18 \times 17 \times 16 \times 15 \times 14}{1 \times 2 \times 3 \times 4 \times 5 \times 6 \times 7}x^7$.
This can be **simplified** to $\frac{20!}{7!13!}x^7$.

20 × 19 × 18 × 17 × 16 × 15 × 14 = $\frac{20!}{13!}$ because it's the numbers from 20 to 1 multiplied together, divided by the numbers from 13 to 1 multiplied together.

Believe it or not, there's an even **shorter** form: $\frac{20!}{7!13!}$ is written as $^{20}C_7$ or $\binom{20}{7}$

$$^nC_r = \binom{n}{r} = \frac{n!}{r!(n-r)!}$$
$$\binom{n}{0} = \binom{n}{n} = 1$$

Your calculator should have an nCr function for working this out.

So, to finish the example, $(1 + x)^{20} = 1 + \frac{20}{1}x + \frac{20 \times 19}{1 \times 2}x^2 + \frac{20 \times 19 \times 18}{1 \times 2 \times 3}x^3 + ...$

$$= 1 + \binom{20}{1}x + \binom{20}{2}x^2 + \binom{20}{3}x^3 + ...$$

$$= 1 + 20x + 190x^2 + 1140x^3 + ...$$

This is the way you'll normally see it written, since you'd usually just get your calculator to do all the hard work multiplying and dividing for you.

Binomial Expansions

There's a *General Formula* for *Expanding $(a + b)^n$*

So far, you've seen the expansion for $(1 + x)^n$. The **general formula** works on anything that looks like $(a + b)^n$, as long as n is a **positive integer**. This is the one that's given in your formula booklet, and it looks like this:

$$(a + b)^n = a^n + \binom{n}{1}a^{n-1}b + \binom{n}{2}a^{n-2}b^2 + \ldots + \binom{n}{r}a^{n-r}b^r + \ldots + b^n \quad n \in \mathbb{N}$$

This bit just means that n has to be a 'natural number' — basically, a positive integer.

If you set a = 1 and b = x, then you'd get your original binomial expansion formula. Go on — give it a go if you don't believe me.

These are those ^nC_r fellas that you met at the bottom of the last page.

Example: a) Find the first four terms in the expansion of $(2 - 3x)^6$, in ascending powers of x.

Here, $a = 2$, $b = (-3x)$ and $n = 6$. Using the formula:

$$(2 - 3x)^6 = 2^6 + \binom{6}{1}2^5(-3x) + \binom{6}{2}2^4(-3x)^2 + \binom{6}{3}2^3(-3x)^3 + \ldots$$
$$= 64 + (6 \times 32 \times -3x) + (15 \times 16 \times 9x^2) + (20 \times 8 \times -27x^3) + \ldots$$
$$= 64 - 576x + 2160x^2 - 4320x^3 + \ldots$$

b) Use your answer to give an estimate for the value of 1.7^6.

$(2 - 3x)^6 = 1.7^6$ when $x = 0.1$. Substitute this into your expansion:

$$1.7^6 \approx 64 - 576(0.1) + 2160(0.1)^2 - 4320(0.1)^3$$
$$= 64 - 57.6 + 21.6 - 4.32$$
$$= 23.68$$

The actual value of 1.7^6 is 24.137... so this is a pretty good estimate.

Estimates like this one work best when x is small, so that x^n gets tiny as n gets bigger — that way, the terms that you miss out won't affect the answer as much.

Example: Find the coefficient of x^9 in the expansion of $(4 - 2x)^{11}$.

You could work out the whole expansion up to x^9, but it's much quicker to just use one bit of the formula: $(a + b)^n = \ldots + \binom{n}{r}a^{n-r}b^r + \ldots$

$$(4 - 2x)^{11} = \ldots + \binom{11}{9}4^{11-9}(-2x)^9 + \ldots = \ldots + (55 \times 16 \times -512x^9) + \ldots = \ldots - 450\,560x^9 + \ldots$$

So the coefficient of x^9 is **-450 560**.

Watch out — the **term** is "-450 560x^9", but the **coefficient** is just "-450 560". Make sure you've checked what the question's asking for.

Practice Questions

Q1 Write down the sixth row of Pascal's triangle (hint: it starts with a '1').

Q2 Give the first four terms in the expansion of $(1 + x)^{12}$, in ascending powers of x.

Q3 What are the first four terms in the expansion of $(1 - 2x)^{16}$, in ascending powers of x?

Q4 Find the first four terms in the expansion of $(2 + 3x)^5$, in ascending powers of x.

Exam Questions

Q1 Find the first five terms in the binomial expansion of $(4 + 3x)^6$, in ascending powers of x. [5 marks]

Q2 The coefficient of the x^3 term in the binomial expansion of $(1 + px)^7$ is 280.
Find the value of p. [3 marks]

Pascal was great at maths but bad at music — he only played the triangle...

That nCr function is pretty bloomin' useful (remember that it could be called something else on your calculator) — it saves a lot of button pressing and errors. Just make sure you put your numbers in the right way round.

Geometry of Lines and Circles

You need to know about a billion things about lines, midpoints, circles, equations — all manner of geometrical goodies.
Okay, maybe not quite a billion, but enough to fill four whole pages, and that's more than enough for me.

Finding the **Equation of a Line**

You need to know three different ways of writing the equation of a straight line:

$$y - y_1 = m(x - x_1)$$ $$y = mx + c$$ $$ax + by + c = 0$$ where a, b and c are **integers**

You might be asked to write the equation of a line in **any** of these forms — but they're all similar.
Basically, if you find an equation in one form, you can easily **convert** it into either of the others.

The Easiest to find is $y - y_1 = m(x - x_1)$...

Equations of Lines

1) **LABEL** the points (x_1, y_1) and (x_2, y_2).
2) **GRADIENT** — find it and call it m.
3) **WRITE DOWN THE EQUATION** using $y - y_1 = m(x - x_1)$.
4) **CONVERT** to one of the other forms, if necessary.

Example: Find the equation of the line that passes through the points $(-3, 10)$ and $(1, 4)$, in the form $y - y_1 = m(x - x_1)$.

Label the points: $(x_1, y_1) = (-3, 10)$ and $(x_2, y_2) = (1, 4)$
It doesn't matter which way round you label them.

Find m, the gradient of the line: $m = \dfrac{y_2 - y_1}{x_2 - x_1} = \dfrac{4 - 10}{1 - (-3)} = \dfrac{-6}{4} = -\dfrac{3}{2}$

Be careful here — y goes on the top, x on the bottom.

Write down the equation of the line:

$$y - y_1 = m(x - x_1)$$
$$y - 10 = -\tfrac{3}{2}(x - (-3)) \quad \substack{x_1 = -3 \\ \text{and } y_1 = 10}$$
$$y - 10 = -\tfrac{3}{2}(x + 3)$$

> You might recognise this method for finding m from GCSE.

...and then you can **Rearrange**

Once you've got the equation in the form $y - y_1 = m(x - x_1)$, it's pretty easy to **convert** it to either of the other forms. Here's how you'd do it for the example above:

For the form $y = mx + c$, take **everything except the y** over to the right.

$$y - 10 = -\tfrac{3}{2}(x + 3)$$
$$\Rightarrow y = -\tfrac{3}{2}x - \tfrac{9}{2} + 10$$
$$\Rightarrow y = -\tfrac{3}{2}x + \tfrac{11}{2}$$

To find the form $ax + by + c = 0$, take **everything** over to one side — and then get rid of any fractions.

$$y = -\tfrac{3}{2}x + \tfrac{11}{2}$$
$$\Rightarrow \tfrac{3}{2}x + y - \tfrac{11}{2} = 0$$
$$\Rightarrow 3x + 2y - 11 = 0$$

a, b and c have to be integers, so multiply the whole equation by 2 to get rid of the 2s on the bottom of the fractions.

> If you end up with an equation like $\frac{3}{2}x - \frac{4}{3}y + 6 = 0$, where you've got a 2 and a 3 on the bottom of the fractions, multiply everything by the lowest common multiple of 2 and 3, i.e. 6.

You can find the **Midpoint** of a **Line Segment**

A **line segment** is just a straight line that goes between two points. Since it has a beginning and an end, it also has a middle (like all good books), and you can work out the coordinates of the **midpoint** using the formula:

$$\text{Midpoint (AB)} = \left(\frac{x_A + x_B}{2}, \frac{y_A + y_B}{2} \right)$$

You could think of this formula as the mean of the x-coordinates and the mean of the y-coordinates.

Example: Find the midpoint of the line segment between $(4, 3)$ and $(-2, 5)$.

Use the midpoint formula: $\text{Midpoint} = \left(\dfrac{4 + (-2)}{2}, \dfrac{3 + 5}{2} \right) = \left(\dfrac{2}{2}, \dfrac{8}{2} \right) = (1, 4)$

Geometry of Lines and Circles

Use **Pythagoras' Theorem** to find the **Length** of a line segment

To find the **length** of a line segment (or the **distance between two points**),
you can imagine a right-angled triangle, like in the diagram on the right.
Then it's just a matter of using Pythagoras' theorem:

$$\text{Length (AB)} = \sqrt{(x_B - x_A)^2 + (y_B - y_A)^2}$$

Example: Find the exact length of the segment of the line with equation
$y = 5x - 2$ between $x = 3$ and $x = 4$.

First, find the y-coordinates at $x = 3$ and $x = 4$:
When $x = 3$, $y = 5(3) - 2 \Rightarrow y = 15 - 2 = 13$ So: $(x_A, y_A) = (3, 13)$
When $x = 4$, $y = 5(4) - 2 \Rightarrow y = 20 - 2 = 18$ and $(x_B, y_B) = (4, 18)$

Now substitute these values into the formula:
$$\text{Length} = \sqrt{(4-3)^2 + (18-13)^2} = \sqrt{1 + 25} = \sqrt{26}$$
The question says "exact", so leave it as a surd.

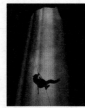

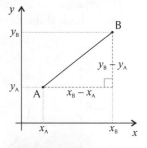

Pythagoras had to go to great lengths to discover his theorem.

Parallel Lines have equal **Gradient**

That's what makes them parallel — the fact that the gradients are the same.

Example: The equation of the line l_1 can be written as $y = \frac{3}{4}x - \frac{7}{4}$ or $3x - 4y - 7 = 0$.
Find the line parallel to l_1 that passes through the point $(3, -1)$.

Parallel lines have the same gradient.

The original equation is: $\quad y = \frac{3}{4}x - \frac{7}{4}$

So the new equation will be: $\quad y = \frac{3}{4}x + c$
We just need to find c.

We know that the line passes through $(3, -1)$,
so stick $x = 3$, $y = -1$ into the equation to find c.

At $(3, -1)$, $\quad -1 = \frac{3}{4} \times 3 + c \Rightarrow c = -1 - \frac{9}{4} = -\frac{13}{4}$

So the equation of the line is: $\quad y = \frac{3}{4}x - \frac{13}{4}$

Or with the ax + by + c = 0 form it's even easier:

The original line is: $\quad 3x - 4y - 7 = 0$

So the new line is: $\quad 3x - 4y + k = 0$

Then use the values of x and y at $(3, -1)$ to find k.
$$3 \times 3 - 4 \times (-1) + k = 0$$
$$\Rightarrow 9 + 4 + k = 0$$
$$\Rightarrow k = -13$$

So the equation is: $\quad 3x - 4y - 13 = 0$

The gradient of a **Perpendicular** line is **−1 ÷ the Other Gradient**

Finding **perpendicular** lines (or '**normals**') is just as easy as finding parallel lines — as long as
you remember the gradient of the perpendicular line is **−1 ÷ the gradient of the other one**.

Example: The equation of the line l_2 can be written as $y = \frac{1}{3}x - 1$ or $x - 3y - 3 = 0$.
Find the line perpendicular to l_2 that passes through the point $(-2, 4)$.

l_2 has equation: $y = \frac{1}{3}x - 1$

So if the equation of the new line is $y = mx + c$, then

$$m = -1 \div \frac{1}{3}$$
$$\Rightarrow m = -3$$
Since the gradient of a perpendicular line is −1 ÷ the other one.

At $x = -2$, $y = 4$: $\quad 4 = (-3) \times (-2) + c$
$$\Rightarrow c = 4 - 6 = -2$$

So the equation of the perpendicular line is $y = -3x - 2$

Or if you start with: $\quad l_2 \ x - 3y - 3 = 0$

To find a perpendicular line, swap these two numbers
around, and change the sign of **one of them**.
So here, 1 and −3 become 3 and 1.

So the new line has equation $\quad 3x + y + k = 0$

Or you could have used −3x − y + k = 0.

So at $x = -2$, $y = 4$: $\quad 3 \times (-2) + 4 + k = 0$
$$\Rightarrow k = 2$$

And so the equation of the perpendicular line is
$3x + y + 2 = 0$

Geometry of Lines and Circles

Equation of a circle: $(x - a)^2 + (y - b)^2 = r^2$

The equation of a circle looks complicated, but it's all based on Pythagoras' theorem.
Take a look at the circle below, with centre (6, 4) and radius 3.

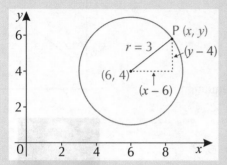

Joining a point P (x, y) on the circumference of the circle to its centre (6, 4), we can create a **right-angled triangle**.

Now let's see what happens if we use **Pythagoras' theorem**:

$$(x - 6)^2 + (y - 4)^2 = 3^2$$
$$\text{or:} \quad (x - 6)^2 + (y - 4)^2 = 9$$

← This is the equation for the circle. It's as easy as that.

In general, a circle with radius r and centre (a, b) has the equation:

$$(x - a)^2 + (y - b)^2 = r^2$$

Example: Find the centre and radius of the circle with equation $(x - 2)^2 + (y + 3)^2 = 16$.

Compare the equation... $\quad (x - 2)^2 + (y + 3)^2 = 16$
...with the general form: $\quad (x - a)^2 + (y - b)^2 = r^2$

So $a = 2$, $b = -3$ and $r = 4$.

So the centre (a, b) is **(2, –3)** and the radius r is **4**.

Example: Write down the equation of the circle with centre (–4, 2) and radius 6.

The question says, 'Write down...', so you know you don't need to do any working.

The centre of the circle is (–4, 2), so $a = -4$ and $b = 2$. The radius is 6, so $r = 6$.

Using the general equation $(x - a)^2 + (y - b)^2 = r^2$ you can write: $\quad (x + 4)^2 + (y - 2)^2 = 36$

Complete the Square to get into the Familiar Form

Not all circle equations look like $(x - a)^2 + (y - b)^2 = r^2$. If they don't, it can be a bit of a pain, because you can't immediately tell what the **radius** is or where the **centre** is. But all it takes is a bit of **rearranging**.

Example: Write the equation $x^2 + y^2 - 6x + 4y + 4 = 0$ in the form $(x - a)^2 + (y - b)^2 = r^2$.

Complete the square on the x and y terms.

$$x^2 + y^2 - 6x + 4y + 4 = 0$$
$$x^2 - 6x + y^2 + 4y + 4 = 0$$
$$(x - 3)^2 - 9 + (y + 2)^2 - 4 + 4 = 0$$
$$(x - 3)^2 + (y + 2)^2 = 9$$

Have a look at page 12 for more on completing the square.

Collect the x and y terms together...

...then find squares that give the terms you need, and add constants to balance things up.

This is the recognisable form, so the centre is **(3, –2)** and the radius is $\sqrt{9} = 3$.

Don't forget the Properties of Circles

You will have seen the circle properties at GCSE. You'll sometimes need to dredge them up from the darkest depths of your memory for these circle questions. Here's a reminder of the ones you need to know for this course.

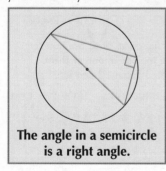

The angle in a semicircle is a right angle.

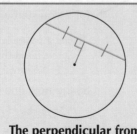

The perpendicular from the centre to a chord bisects the chord.

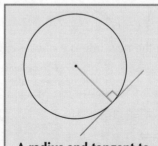

A radius and tangent to the same point will meet at right angles.

Bob thinks the Magic Circle rules. Bunnykin isn't so sure.

Geometry of Lines and Circles

Use the **Gradient Rule** for **Perpendicular Lines**

Remember that the tangent at a given point will be perpendicular to the radius at that same point.

Example: Point A $(6, 4)$ lies on a circle with the equation $(x - 2)^2 + (y - 1)^2 = 25$. Find the equation of the tangent to the circle at A.

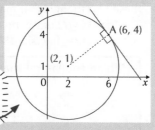

The equation of the circle tells you the centre is $(2, 1)$.
The tangent you're interested in is at right angles to the radius at $(6, 4)$.

The gradient of the **radius** at $(6, 4) = \dfrac{4 - 1}{6 - 2} = \dfrac{3}{4}$,

so the gradient of the **tangent** at $(6, 4) = \dfrac{-1}{\frac{3}{4}} = -\dfrac{4}{3}$.

It often helps with questions like this to use what you know at the start to sketch the graph.

So using $y - y_1 = m(x - x_1)$, the tangent at $(6, 4)$ is: $y - 4 = -\dfrac{4}{3}(x - 6) \Rightarrow 3y - 12 = -4x + 24 \Rightarrow \mathbf{3y + 4x - 36 = 0}$

Practice Questions

Q1 Find the equations of the lines that pass through the points: a) $(2, -1)$ and $(-4, -19)$, b) $\left(0, -\dfrac{1}{3}\right)$ and $\left(5, \dfrac{2}{3}\right)$.
Write each answer in the forms:
(i) $y - y_1 = m(x - x_1)$,   (ii) $y = mx + c$,   (iii) $ax + by + c = 0$, where a, b and c are integers.

Q2 The line l has equation $y = \dfrac{3}{2}x - \dfrac{2}{3}$. Find the equation of the line parallel to l, going through the point $(4, 2)$.

Q3 The line k passes through the point $(6, 1)$ and is perpendicular to $2x - y - 7 = 0$. What is the equation of k?

Q4 The coordinates of points R and S are $(-8, 15)$ and $(10, 3)$ respectively. Find, in the form $y = mx + c$, the equation of the line perpendicular to RS, passing through the midpoint of RS.

Q5 Write the equation of the circle with centre $(3, -1)$ and radius 7.

Q6 Give the radius and the coordinates of the centre of the circles with the following equations:
a) $x^2 + y^2 = 9$ b) $(x - 2)^2 + (y + 4)^2 = 4$ c) $x(x + 6) = y(8 - y)$

Exam Questions

Q1 The line segment PQ has equation $4x + 3y = 15$, where P has coordinates $(0, p)$ and Q has coordinates $(q, -3)$.
a) Find: (i) the gradient of PQ,   (ii) the length of PQ.   [3 marks]
b) The point R is the midpoint of PQ. Find the equation of the line which passes through the point R and is perpendicular to PQ, giving your answer in the form $y = mx + c$.   [3 marks]

Q2 The line l passes through the point S $(7, -3)$ and has gradient -2.
a) Find an equation of l, giving your answer in the form $y = mx + c$.   [2 marks]
b) The point T has coordinates $(5, 1)$. Show that T lies on l.   [1 mark]

Q3 The points J and K have coordinates $(-1, 4)$ and $(5, 8)$ respectively. The line l_1 passes through the midpoint, L, of the line segment JK, and is perpendicular to JK, as shown.
a) Find an equation for l_1 in the form $ax + by + c = 0$, where a, b, and c are integers.   [5 marks]
The line l_1 intersects the y-axis at the point M and the x-axis at the point N.
b) Find the coordinates of M.   [2 marks]
c) Find the coordinates of N.   [2 marks]

Q4 C is a circle with the equation: $x^2 + y^2 - 2x - 10y + 21 = 0$.
a) Find the centre and radius of C.   [5 marks]
b) The line joining P $(3, 6)$ and Q $(q, 4)$ is a diameter of C. Show that $q = -1$.   [3 marks]
c) Find the equation of the tangent to C at Q, giving your answer in the form $ax + by + c = 0$, where a, b and c are integers.   [3 marks]

A Geometry of Lines and Circles, Book 1 — A Game of Maths...

Well, that sure was a lot of geometry to deal with. Just make sure you've got all of these formulas and properties committed to memory for the exam. After all, when you play the Game of Maths, you win or you get no marks.

Trig Functions and Graphs

Questions on trigonometry quite often use the same common angles — so it pays to know the sin, cos and tan of them.

Draw Triangles to remember *sin*, *cos* and *tan* of the *Important Angles*

You should know the values of **sin**, **cos** and **tan** at 30°, 60° and 45°. But to help you remember, you can draw these two triangles. It may seem a complicated way to learn a few numbers, but it does make it easier. Honest. The idea is you draw the triangles below, putting in their angles and side lengths. Then you can use them to work out trig values like **sin 45°** or **cos 60°** more accurately than a calculator (which only gives a few decimal places).

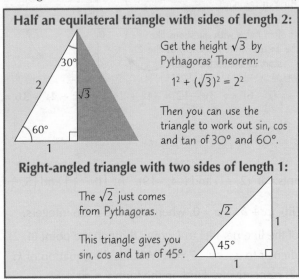

Half an equilateral triangle with sides of length 2:

Get the height $\sqrt{3}$ by Pythagoras' Theorem:

$$1^2 + (\sqrt{3})^2 = 2^2$$

Then you can use the triangle to work out sin, cos and tan of 30° and 60°.

Right-angled triangle with two sides of length 1:

The $\sqrt{2}$ just comes from Pythagoras.

This triangle gives you sin, cos and tan of 45°.

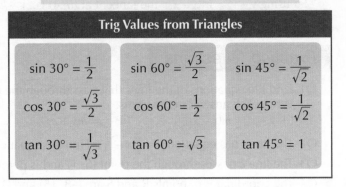

Remember: SOH CAH TOA...

$$\sin = \frac{\text{opp}}{\text{hyp}} \qquad \cos = \frac{\text{adj}}{\text{hyp}} \qquad \tan = \frac{\text{opp}}{\text{adj}}$$

Trig Values from Triangles

$\sin 30° = \dfrac{1}{2}$	$\sin 60° = \dfrac{\sqrt{3}}{2}$	$\sin 45° = \dfrac{1}{\sqrt{2}}$
$\cos 30° = \dfrac{\sqrt{3}}{2}$	$\cos 60° = \dfrac{1}{2}$	$\cos 45° = \dfrac{1}{\sqrt{2}}$
$\tan 30° = \dfrac{1}{\sqrt{3}}$	$\tan 60° = \sqrt{3}$	$\tan 45° = 1$

Find angles from the *Unit Circle*

The **unit circle** is a circle with **radius 1**, centred on the **origin**. For any point on the unit circle, the coordinates are **(cos θ, sin θ)**, where θ is the angle measured from the **positive** x-axis in an **anticlockwise** direction. The points on the **axes** of the unit circle give you the values of sin and cos of 0° and 90°. So at the point (1, 0): **cos 0° = 1**, **sin 0° = 0**. And at the point (0, 1): **cos 90° = 0**, **sin 90° = 1**.

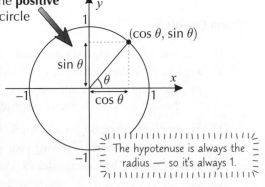

The hypotenuse is always the radius — so it's always 1.

Example: The coordinates of a point on the unit circle, given to 3 s.f., are (0.788, 0.616). Find θ to the nearest degree.

The point is on the unit circle, so you know that the coordinates are (cos θ, sin θ). So cos θ = 0.788 and sin θ = 0.616.

You only need one of these to find the value of θ.
cos θ = 0.788 ⇒ θ = cos⁻¹ (0.788) = **38°** (to the nearest degree).

sin x and *cos x* are always in the range *–1 to 1*

sin x and **cos x** are similar — they just bob up and down between –1 and 1.

They bounce up and down from –1 to 1 — they can *never* have a value outside this range.

sin x and cos x are both **periodic** (repeat themselves) with **period 360°**	$\cos(x + 360°) = \cos x$	$\sin(x + 360°) = \sin x$

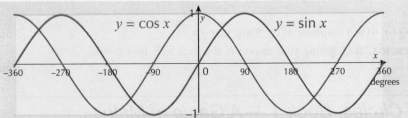

sin x goes through the **origin** — that means **sin 0 = 0**.

cos x crosses the y-axis at y = 1 — that means **cos 0 = 1**.

Symmetry in the **vertical axis**:	$\cos(-x) = \cos x$	$\sin(-x) = -\sin x$

Trig Functions and Graphs

tan x can be **Any Value** at all

tan x is **different** from sin x or cos x. It doesn't go up and down between –1 and 1 — it goes **between –∞ and +∞**.

| tan x is also periodic — but with **period 180°** | tan x is **undefined** at ±90°, ±270°, ±450°,... |

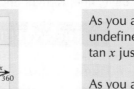

tan x goes from –∞ to +∞ **every 180°**

$$\tan(x + 180°) = \tan x$$

As you approach one of these undefined points from the left, tan x just shoots up to **infinity**.

As you approach from the right, it drops to **minus infinity**.

The graph never ever touches these lines. But it does get infinitely close, if you see what I mean... These are called **asymptotes**.

The easiest way to sketch sin, cos or tan graphs is to plot the **important points** which happen **every 90°** (i.e. **–180°, –90°, 0°, 90°, 180°, 270°, 360°**...) and then just join the dots up.

There are 3 basic types of **Transformed Trig Graph**

Transformed trigonometric graphs act just like the standard graph transformations on page 25.

$y = n \sin x$ — Vertical Stretch

If $n > 1$, the graph of $y = \sin x$ is **stretched vertically** by a factor of n.

If $0 < n < 1$, the graph is **squashed**.

And if $n < 0$, the graph is also **reflected** in the x-axis.

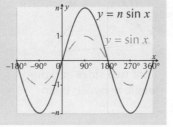

$y = \sin nx$ — Horizontal Stretch

If $n > 1$, the graph of $y = \sin x$ is **squashed horizontally** by a factor of n.

If $0 < n < 1$, the graph is **stretched**.

And if $n < 0$, the graph is also **reflected** in the y-axis.

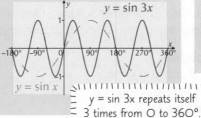

$y = \sin 3x$ repeats itself 3 times from O to 360°.

$y = \sin (x + c)$ — Horizontal Translation

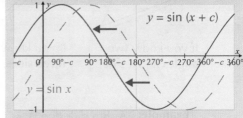

For $c > 0$, $\sin (x + c)$ is just sin x **translated** c **to the left.**

Similarly, $\sin (x – c)$ is just sin x **translated** c **to the right.**

Practice Questions

Q1 Write down the exact value of: a) cos 30°,   b) sin 45°,   c) tan 60°,   d) sin 30°.

Q2 Sketch: a) $y = \frac{1}{2} \cos x$ for $0° \leq x \leq 360°$,   b) $y = \sin (x + 30°)$ for $0 \leq x \leq 360$,   c) $y = \tan 3x$ for $0° \leq x \leq 180°$.

Exam Questions

Q1 The coordinates of a point on the unit circle are (0.914, –0.407), to 3 s.f. Find the angle measured in an anticlockwise direction, from the positive x-axis to the radius from the origin to (0.914, –0.407), to the nearest degree. [2 marks]

Q2 a) Sketch, for $0 \leq x \leq 360°$, the graph of $y = \cos (x + 60°)$. [2 marks]
   b) Write down all the values of x, for $0 \leq x \leq 360°$, where cos $(x + 60°) = 0$. [2 marks]

Q3 Sketch, for $0 \leq x \leq 180°$, the graph of $y = \sin 4x$. [2 marks]

Curling up on the sofa with 2 cos x — that's my idea of cosiness...

It's really really really really really important that you can draw and transform the trig graphs on these pages. Trust me.

Trig Formulas and Identities

There are some more trig formulas you need to know for the exam.
So here they are — learn them or you're seriously stuffed. Worse than an aubergine.

The **Sine Rule** and **Cosine Rule** work for **Any** triangle

Remember, these three formulas work for **ANY** triangle, not just right-angled ones.

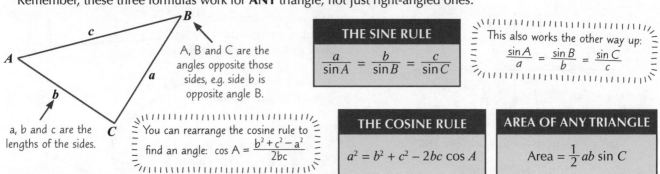

A, B and C are the angles opposite those sides, e.g. side b is opposite angle B.

a, b and c are the lengths of the sides.

You can rearrange the cosine rule to find an angle: $\cos A = \dfrac{b^2 + c^2 - a^2}{2bc}$

THE SINE RULE

$$\frac{a}{\sin A} = \frac{b}{\sin B} = \frac{c}{\sin C}$$

This also works the other way up:

$$\frac{\sin A}{a} = \frac{\sin B}{b} = \frac{\sin C}{c}$$

THE COSINE RULE

$$a^2 = b^2 + c^2 - 2bc \cos A$$

AREA OF ANY TRIANGLE

$$\text{Area} = \tfrac{1}{2}\, ab \sin C$$

Sine Rule *or* Cosine Rule *— which one is it...*

To decide which of these two rules you need to use, look at what you **already** know about the triangle.

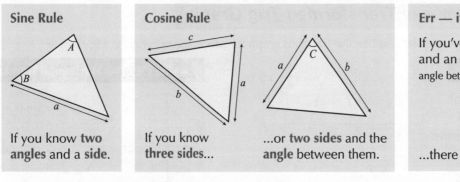

Sine Rule

If you know **two angles** and a **side**.

Cosine Rule

If you know **three sides**...

...or **two sides** and the **angle** between them.

Err — it doesn't work here...

If you've got two sides and an angle (but **not** the angle between them)...

...there are **two possible triangles**.

Example: A ship sails due West for 10 km before turning clockwise through an angle of 145° and sailing in a straight line for another 6.5 km. Find the shortest distance back to its starting point, and the angle it would need to turn through to get there.

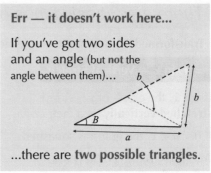

X is the angle the ship needs to turn through to get back.

1) First draw a sketch of the problem, labelling all the lengths and angles you know.

2) You know 2 sides and the angle between them, so you're going to need the **cosine rule** to find side a, the distance back to the start:

$$\boxed{a^2 = b^2 + c^2 - 2bc \cos A}$$

$$a^2 = 10^2 + 6.5^2 - 2(10)(6.5)\cos 35°$$
$$\Rightarrow a^2 = 142.25 - 130\cos 35°$$
$$\Rightarrow a^2 = 35.7602... \Rightarrow a = 5.9799... = \textbf{5.98 km} \text{ (3 s.f.)}$$

$A = 180° - 145° = 35°$

You need to work out angle A first from the question information.

$b = 10$ km

3) Now that you've got all the sides, you can use the **cosine rule** again to find angle B:

$$\cos B = \frac{a^2 + c^2 - b^2}{2ac} \Rightarrow \cos B = \frac{35.7602... + 42.25 - 100}{2 \times 5.9799... \times 6.5}$$

$$\Rightarrow \cos B = \frac{-21.979...}{77.739...} = -0.2828...$$

$$\Rightarrow B = \cos^{-1} -0.2828... = \textbf{106.43...}°$$

4) So the angle, *X*, that the ship needs to turn through is $180° - 106.43...° = \textbf{73.6°}$ (1 d.p.)

You could use the sine rule to find angle B, but watch out if you do — any value of $\sin \theta$ in the range $0 < \sin \theta < 1$ corresponds to two values of θ between 0° and 180°. Your calculator will give you the acute angle for B, but in this case you actually want the obtuse angle instead.

Section 3 — Trigonometry

Trig Formulas and Identities

Label the Angles and Sides carefully when Sketching triangles

Example: In the triangle ABC, $A = 40°$, $a = 27$ m and $B = 73°$.
Find the missing angles and sides, and calculate the area of the triangle.

1) Draw a quick sketch first — don't worry if it's not deadly accurate, though.

2) You're given 2 angles and a side, so you need the **sine rule**.

Make sure you put side a opposite angle A.
The angles in a triangle add up to 180°.

First of all, get the other angle: $\angle C = 180° - 40° - 73° = \mathbf{67°}$

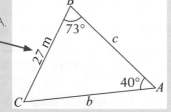

3) Then find the other sides, one at a time:

$\dfrac{a}{\sin A} = \dfrac{b}{\sin B} \Rightarrow \dfrac{27}{\sin 40°} = \dfrac{b}{\sin 73°}$

$\Rightarrow b = \dfrac{\sin 73°}{\sin 40°} \times 27 = 40.169... = \mathbf{40.2\ m}$ (1 d.p.)

$\dfrac{c}{\sin C} = \dfrac{a}{\sin A} \Rightarrow \dfrac{c}{\sin 67°} = \dfrac{27}{\sin 40°}$

$\Rightarrow c = \dfrac{\sin 67°}{\sin 40°} \times 27 = 38.665... = \mathbf{38.7\ m}$ (1 d.p.)

4) Now just use the formula to find its area: Area $\triangle ABC = \dfrac{1}{2}ab \sin C$

$= \dfrac{1}{2} \times 27 \times 40.169... \times \sin 67°$

$= \mathbf{499.2\ m^2}$ (1 d.p.)

Use a more accurate value for b here, rather than the rounded value 40.2.

The Best has been saved till last...

These two identities are really important. You'll need them **loads**.

$$\tan x \equiv \frac{\sin x}{\cos x} \qquad \sin^2 x + \cos^2 x \equiv 1$$

$\Rightarrow \sin^2 x \equiv 1 - \cos^2 x$
$\cos^2 x \equiv 1 - \sin^2 x$

Essential kit for maintaining two identities.

These two come up in exam questions **all the time**. Learn them.
Learnthemlearnthemlearnthemlearnthemlearnthemlear... okay, I'll stop now.

Work out these two using $\sin^2 x + \cos^2 x \equiv 1$.

Practice Questions

Q1 Find the missing sides and angles in: a) $\triangle ABC$, in which $A = 30°$, $C = 25°$, $b = 6$ m, and find its area.
b) $\triangle PQR$, in which $p = 3$ km, $q = 23$ km, $R = 10°$. (answers to 2 d.p.)

Q2 My pet triangle Freda has sides of length 10, 20 and 25. Find her angles (in degrees to 1 d.p.).

Exam Questions

Q1 For an angle x, $3 \cos x = 2 \sin x$. Find $\tan x$. [2 marks]

Q2 Two walkers, X and Y, walked in different directions from the same start position.
X walked due south for 150 m. Y walked 250 m on a bearing of 100°.

a) Calculate the final distance between the two walkers, in m to the nearest m. [2 marks]

b) θ is the final bearing of Y from X. Show that $\dfrac{\sin \theta}{\sin 80°} = 0.93$ to 2 decimal places. [3 marks]

Tri angles — go on... you might like them.

Formulas and trigonometry go together even better than Ant and Dec. I can count 7 formulas on these pages. That's not many, so please, make sure you know them. If you haven't learnt them I will cry for you. I will sob.

Solving Trig Equations

I used to really hate trig stuff like this. But once I'd got the hang of it, I just couldn't get enough. I stopped going out, lost interest in romance — the CAST method became my life. Learn it, but be careful. It's addictive.

There are **Two Ways** to find **Solutions** in an **Interval**

Example: Solve $\cos x = \frac{1}{2}$ for $-360° \leq x \leq 720°$.

Like I said — there are **two ways** to solve this kind of question. Just use the one you prefer...

You can draw a **graph**...

1) Draw the **graph** of $y = \cos x$ for the range you're interested in...

2) Get the first solution from your **calculator** and mark this on the graph,

3) Use the **symmetry of the graph** to work out what the other solutions are:

Your calculator gives you a solution of 60°...

...then the other solutions are 60° either side of the graph's peaks.

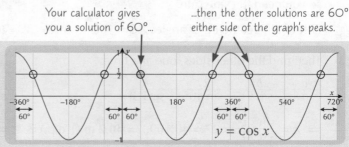

So the solutions are: **−300°, −60°, 60°, 300°, 420°** and **660°**.

...or you can use the **CAST** diagram

CAST stands for **COS**, **ALL**, **SIN**, **TAN** — and the CAST diagram shows you where these functions are **positive**:

Between 90° and 180°, only **S**in is positive.

Between 0 and 90°, **All** of sin, cos and tan are positive.

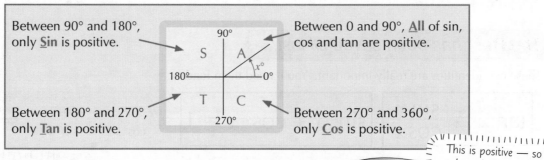

Between 180° and 270°, only **T**an is positive.

Between 270° and 360°, only **C**os is positive.

This is positive — so you're only interested in where cos is positive.

First, to find all the values of x between 0° and 360° where $\cos x = \frac{1}{2}$ — you do this:

Put the **first solution** onto the CAST diagram.	Find the **other angles** between 0° and 360° that might be solutions.	Ditch the ones that are the **wrong sign**.

The angle from your calculator goes anticlockwise from the x-axis (unless it's negative — then it would go clockwise into the 4th quadrant).	The other possible solutions come from making the same angle from the horizontal axis in the other 3 quadrants.	$\cos x = \frac{1}{2}$, which is positive. The CAST diagram tells you cos is positive in the 4th quadrant — but not the 2nd or 3rd — so ditch those two angles.

So you've got solutions 60° and 300° in the range 0° to 360°. But you need **all the solutions** in the range **−360° to 720°**. Get these by repeatedly **adding or subtracting 360°** onto each until you go out of range:

$$x = 60° \Rightarrow \text{(adding } 360°) \; x = 420°, 780° \text{ (too big)}$$
$$\text{and (subtracting } 360°) \; x = -300°, -660° \text{ (too small)}$$
$$x = 300° \Rightarrow \text{(adding } 360°) \; x = 660°, 1020° \text{ (too big)}$$
$$\text{and (subtracting } 360°) \; x = -60°, -420° \text{ (too small)}$$

So the solutions are: $x = $ **−300°, −60°, 60°, 300°, 420°** and **660°**.

Solving Trig Equations

Sometimes you end up with **sin kx = number**...

For these, you might find it easier to draw the **graph** rather than use the CAST method — that's one reason why being able to sketch trig graphs properly is so important.

Example: Solve: $\sin 3x = -\dfrac{1}{\sqrt{2}}$ for $0° \le x \le 360°$.

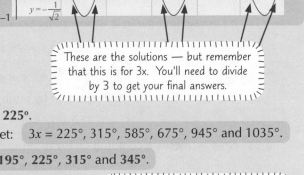

1) You've got $3x$ instead of x, which means the range you need to find solutions in is $\mathbf{0° \le 3x \le 1080°}$. So draw the graph of $y = \sin x$ between $0°$ and $1080°$.

2) Use your calculator to find the first solution. You'll get $\mathbf{3x = -45°}$. But this is **outside the range** for $3x$, so use the pattern of the graph to find a solution in the range. As the sin curve repeats every $360°$, there'll be a solution at $360 - 45 = \mathbf{315°}$.

These are the solutions — but remember that this is for 3x. You'll need to divide by 3 to get your final answers.

3) Now use your graph to find the other 5 solutions. You can see that there's another solution at $180 + 45 = \mathbf{225°}$. Then add on $360°$ and $720°$ to both $225°$ and $315°$ to get: $3x = 225°, 315°, 585°, 675°, 945°$ and $1035°$.

4) **Divide by 3** to get the solutions for x: $x = 75°, 105°, 195°, 225°, 315°$ and $345°$.

5) **Check** your answers by putting these values back into your calculator.

It really is mega-important that you check these answers — it's dead easy to make a silly mistake. They should all be in the range $0° \le x \le 360°$.

...or **sin (x + k) = number**

Example: Solve $\sin(x + 60°) = \dfrac{3}{4}$ for $-360° \le x \le 360°$, giving your answers to 1 d.p.

1) You've got $\sin(x + 60°)$ instead of $\sin x$ — so the range is $\mathbf{-300° \le x + 60° \le 420°}$.

2) Use your calculator to get the first solution: $x + 60° = \mathbf{48.6°}$ (1 d.p.)

3) Use a CAST diagram to get the second solution: $180° - 48.6° = \mathbf{131.4°}$

The red answers are outside $-300° \le x + 60° \le 420°$.

4) Add and subtract $360°$ to the first two solutions to find the rest: $48.6° + 360° = 408.6°$, $48.6° - 360° = -311.4°$, $131.4° + 360° = 491.4°$, $131.4° - 360° = -228.6°$

So, for $(x + 60°)$ the solutions to 1 d.p. are: $x + 60° = -228.6°, 48.6°, 131.4°, 408.6°$

5) Subtract $60°$ to get the solutions for x: $x = -288.6°, -11.4°, 71.4°$ and $348.6°$

Always check your answers.

Practice Question

Q1 a) Solve each of these equations for $0 \le \theta \le 360°$: (i) $\sin\theta = -\dfrac{\sqrt{3}}{2}$, (ii) $\tan\theta = -1$, (iii) $\cos\theta = -\dfrac{1}{\sqrt{2}}$

b) Solve each of these equations for $-180° \le \theta \le 180°$ (giving your answer to 1 d.p.):

(i) $\cos 4\theta = -\dfrac{2}{3}$ (ii) $\sin(\theta + 35°) = 0.3$ (iii) $\tan\left(\dfrac{1}{2}\theta\right) = 500$

Exam Question

Q1 a) Solve $2\cos(x - 45°) = \sqrt{3}$, for $0 \le x \le 360°$.   [3 marks]

b) Solve $\sin 2x = -\dfrac{1}{2}$, for $0° \le x \le 360°$.   [3 marks]

Trig equations are sinful (and cosful and tanful)...

Finding all the correct solutions can be tricky so take your time and make sure you check those answers for Pete's sake — or for your own sake if not for old Pete. You can use a trig graph or CAST diagram to find other solutions — just use whichever method you find most comfortable. With plenty of practice, these questions can be a banker in the exam.

Section 3 — Trigonometry

Using Trig Identities

Trig Identities *are useful for* **Solving Equations**...

$$\tan x \equiv \frac{\sin x}{\cos x}$$

$$\sin^2 x + \cos^2 x \equiv 1 \quad \Rightarrow \quad \begin{array}{l} \sin^2 x \equiv 1 - \cos^2 x \\ \cos^2 x \equiv 1 - \sin^2 x \end{array}$$

If you've got a trig equation with a **tan** in it, together with a sin or a cos —
chances are you'll be better off if you rewrite the tan using the first identity above.
The other identities are useful for getting rid of **sin² x** and/or **cos² x** (see next page).

Example: Solve: $3 \sin x - \tan x = 0$, for $0 \le x \le 360°$.

1) It's got **sin** and **tan** in it — so writing $\tan x$ as $\frac{\sin x}{\cos x}$ is probably a good move:

$$3 \sin x - \tan x = 0$$
$$\Rightarrow 3 \sin x - \frac{\sin x}{\cos x} = 0$$

2) Get rid of the **cos x** on the bottom by multiplying the whole equation by $\cos x$.

$$\Rightarrow 3 \sin x \cos x - \sin x = 0$$

3) Now — there's a **common factor** of $\sin x$. Take that outside a bracket.

$$\Rightarrow \sin x (3 \cos x - 1) = 0$$

4) And now you're almost there. You've got two things multiplying together
to make zero. That means either **one or both** of them is **equal to zero**.

$$\Rightarrow \sin x = 0 \ \text{ or } \ 3 \cos x - 1 = 0$$

*CAST gives any solutions in
the interval $0 \le x \le 360°$.*

$\sin x = 0$

The first solution is:
$$\sin 0 = 0$$

Now find the other points where $\sin x$ is
zero in the interval $0 \le x \le 360°$.

Remember the sin graph is zero every 180°.
$$\Rightarrow x = 0°, 180°, 360°$$

Having memorised the roots
of sin x, smug young Sherlock
had ample time to entertain his
classmates as they caught up.

$3 \cos x - 1 = 0$

Rearrange:
$$\cos x = \frac{1}{3}$$

So the first solution is:
$$\cos^{-1}\left(\frac{1}{3}\right) = 70.52877...°$$
$$= 70.5° \ (1 \text{ d.p.})$$

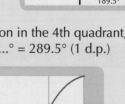

CAST (or the graph of $\cos x$)
gives another positive solution in the 4th quadrant,
where $x = 360° - 70.52877...° = 289.5°$ (1 d.p.)

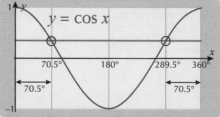

So altogether you've got **five** possible solutions:
$$\Rightarrow x = 0°, 70.5°, 180°, 289.5°, 360°$$

And the two solutions from this part are:
$$\Rightarrow x = 70.5°, 289.5°$$

Be warned — you might be tempted to simplify an equation by **dividing** by a trig function.
But you can **only** do this if the trig function you're dividing by is **never zero** in the range
the equation is valid for. Dividing by zero is not big or clever, or even possible.

Using Trig Identities

Use the identity $sin^2 x + cos^2 x = 1$ to get rid of $sin^2 x$ or $cos^2 x$

Example: Solve: $2 \sin^2 x + 5 \cos x = 4$, for $0° \le x \le 360°$.

1) You can't do much while the equation's got both sin's and cos's in it.
   So replace the $\sin^2 x$ bit with $1 - \cos^2 x$:

   $$2(1 - \cos^2 x) + 5 \cos x = 4 \longleftarrow \text{Now the only trig function is cos.}$$

2) Multiply out the bracket and rearrange it so that you've got zero on one side
   — and you get a **quadratic** in $\cos x$:

   $$\Rightarrow 2 - 2\cos^2 x + 5 \cos x = 4$$
   $$\Rightarrow 2\cos^2 x - 5 \cos x + 2 = 0$$

3) This is a quadratic in $\cos x$. It's easier to factorise this if you make the substitution $y = \cos x$.

   $$2y^2 - 5y + 2 = 0 \longleftarrow \quad 2y^2 - 5y + 2 = (2y\ ?)(y\ ?)$$
   $$\Rightarrow (2y - 1)(y - 2) = 0 \qquad\qquad = (2y - 1)(y - 2)$$
   $$\Rightarrow (2 \cos x - 1)(\cos x - 2) = 0$$

4) Now one of the brackets must be **0**. So you get 2 equations as usual:

   You did this example $2 \cos x - 1 = 0$ or $\cos x - 2 = 0$ *This is a bit weird. cos x is always*
   on page 38.   *between −1 and 1, so you don't get*
            $\cos x = \frac{1}{2} \Rightarrow x = 60°$ and $x = 300°$ and $\cos x = 2$ *any solutions from this bracket.*

   So at the end of all that, the only solutions you get are $x = 60°$ and $x = 300°$. How boring.

Use the **Trig Identities** to **Prove** something is the **Same** as something else

Example: Prove that $\dfrac{\cos^2 \theta}{1 + \sin \theta} \equiv 1 - \sin \theta$.

1) Play about with one side of the equation.   **Left-hand side:** $\dfrac{\cos^2 \theta}{1 + \sin \theta}$

                                             See page 37.

2) Replace $\cos^2 \theta$ with $1 - \sin^2 \theta$. $\equiv \dfrac{1 - \sin^2 \theta}{1 + \sin \theta} \longleftarrow$
                                                        $1 - a^2 = (1 + a)(1 - a)$

3) The top line is a **difference of two squares:** $\equiv \dfrac{(1 + \sin \theta)(1 - \sin \theta)}{1 + \sin \theta} \longleftarrow$

                                    $\equiv 1 - \sin \theta$, **the right-hand side.**

Practice Questions

Q1 Find all the solutions to $6 \sin^2 x = \cos x + 5$ in the range $0 \le x \le 360°$ (answers to 1 d.p. where appropriate).

Q2 Solve $3 \tan x + 2 \cos x = 0$ for $-90° \le x \le 90°$.

Q3 Simplify: $(\sin y + \cos y)^2 + (\cos y - \sin y)^2$.

Q4 Prove that $\dfrac{\sin^4 x + \sin^2 x \cos^2 x}{\cos^2 x - 1} \equiv -1$.

Exam Questions

Q1   a)   Show that the equation $2(1 - \cos x) = 3 \sin^2 x$ can be written as $3 \cos^2 x - 2 \cos x - 1 = 0$.   [2 marks]

     b)   Use this to solve the equation $2(1 - \cos x) = 3 \sin^2 x$ for $0 \le x \le 360°$, giving your answers to 1 d.p.   [6 marks]

Q2   Solve the equation $3 \cos^2 x = \sin^2 x$, for $-180° \le x \le 180°$.   [6 marks]

Always do trigonometry on holiday — you'll get a great tan...

You can bet your last penny that you'll need to use a trig identity in the exam. That substitution trick to get rid of a sin² or a cos² and end up with a quadratic in sin x or cos x is a real examiners' favourite. Remember to use CAST or graphs to find all the possible solutions in the given interval, not just the one on your calculator display, and check your answers.

Exponentials and Logs

Don't be put off by your parents or grandparents telling you that logs are hard. Logarithm (log for short) is just a fancy word for power, and once you know how to use them you can solve all sorts of equations.

You need to be able to **Switch** between **Different Notations**

Exponentials and **logs** can describe the same thing because they are **inverses** of each other.

$\log_a b = c$ means the same as $a^c = b$

That means that $\log_a a = 1$ and $\log_a 1 = 0$

> The little number 'a' after 'log' is called the **base**.
> Logs can be to any base, but **base 10** is the most common
> — this is usually left out, i.e. '$\log_{10}$' is just 'log'.

Example: Index notation: $10^2 = 100$ log notation: $\log_{10} 100 = 2$

So the **logarithm** of 100 to the **base 10** is 2, because 10 raised to the **power** of 2 is 100.

> Your calculator might have a 'log ■□' button and a 'log' button.

Examples: Write down the values of the following:
a) $\log_2 8$ b) $\log_5 5$

a) 8 is 2 raised to the power of 3,
   so $2^3 = 8$ and $\log_2 8 = 3$

b) Anything to the power of 1 is itself,
   so $\log_5 5 = 1$

Write the following using log notation:
a) $5^3 = 125$ b) $3^0 = 1$

a) 3 is the power or **logarithm** that 5
   (the **base**) is raised to to get 125,
   so $\log_5 125 = 3$

b) You'll need to remember this one:
   $\log_3 1 = 0$

The **Laws of Logarithms** are **Unbelievably Useful**

Whenever you have to deal with **logs**, you'll probably end up using the **laws** below.
That means it's not a bad idea to **learn them** by heart right now.

Laws of Logarithms

$\log_a x + \log_a y = \log_a (xy)$ $\log_a x - \log_a y = \log_a \left(\dfrac{x}{y}\right)$ $\log_a x^k = k \log_a x$

> So $\log_a \dfrac{1}{x} = -\log_a x$

Use the **Laws** to **Manipulate Logs**

Example: Write each expression in the form $\log_a n$, where n is a number.
a) $\log_a 5 + \log_a 4$ b) $2 \log_a 6 - \log_a 9$

a) $\log_a x + \log_a y = \log_a (xy)$ $\log_a 5 + \log_a 4 = \log_a (5 \times 4)$
                                                    $= \log_a 20$

b) $\log_a x^k = k \log_a x$ $2 \log_a 6 = \log_a 6^2 = \log_a 36$
                                    $\log_a 36 - \log_a 9 = \log_a (36 \div 9)$
                                                    $= \log_a 4$

You can use **Logs** to **Solve Equations**

Example: Solve $2^{4x} = 3$ to 3 significant figures.

You want x on its own, so take logs of both sides
(by writing 'log' in front of both sides): $\log 2^{4x} = \log 3$

Use $\log x^k = k \log x$: $4x \log 2 = \log 3$

Divide both sides by '4 log 2' to get x on its own: $x = \dfrac{\log 3}{4 \log 2}$

But $\dfrac{\log 3}{4 \log 2}$ is just a number you can find using a calculator: $x = 0.396$ (to 3 s.f.)

> Alternatively, you could do:
> $2^{4x} = 3 \Rightarrow \log_2 3 = 4x$
> $\Rightarrow x = \dfrac{1}{4}\log_2 3 = 0.396$ (to 3 s.f.)

Exponentials and Logs

Graphs of a^x never reach Zero

All the graphs of $y = a^x$ (**exponential graphs**) where $a > 1$ have the **same basic shape**. The graphs for $a = 2$, $a = 3$ and $a = 4$ are shown on the right.

- a is greater than 1 — so y **increases** as x **increases**.
- The **bigger** a is, the **quicker** the graphs increase.
- As x **decreases**, y **decreases** at a **smaller and smaller rate** — y will approach zero, but never actually get there.

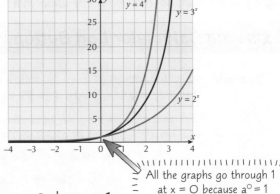

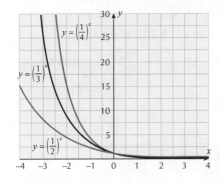

The graphs on the left are for $y = a^x$ where $a < 1$ (they're for $a = \frac{1}{2}$, $\frac{1}{3}$ and $\frac{1}{4}$).

All the graphs go through 1 at $x = 0$ because $a^0 = 1$ for any value of a.

- a is less than 1 — so y **decreases** as x **increases**.
- As x **increases**, y **decreases** at a **smaller and smaller rate** — again, y will approach zero, but never actually get there.

You can also use Exponentials and Logs to Solve Equations

Example: Solve $7 \log_{10} x = 5$ to 3 significant figures.

You want x on its own, so begin by dividing both sides by 7: $\log_{10} x = \frac{5}{7}$

You now need to take exponentials of both sides by doing '10 to the power of both sides' (since the log is to base 10): $10^{\log_{10} x} = 10^{\frac{5}{7}}$

Logs and exponentials are inverse functions, so they cancel out: $x = 10^{\frac{5}{7}}$

But $10^{\frac{5}{7}}$ is just a number you can find using a calculator: $x = 5.18$ (to 3 s.f.)

John's new shoes didn't improve his logarithm.

Practice Questions

Q1 Write down the values of the following: a) $\log_3 27$ b) $\log_3 \left(\frac{1}{27}\right)$ c) $\log_3 18 - \log_3 2$

Q2 Simplify the following: a) $\log 3 + 2 \log 5$ b) $\frac{1}{2}\log 36 - \log 3$ c) $\log 2 - \frac{1}{4}\log 16$

Q3 Simplify $\log_b (x^2 - 1) - \log_b (x - 1)$

Q4 Solve these jokers to 4 significant figures: a) $10^x = 240$ b) $\log_{10} x = 5.3$ c) $10^{2x+1} = 1500$

Exam Questions

Q1 Solve the equation $\log_7 (y + 3) + \log_7 (2y + 1) = 1$, where $y > 0$. [4 marks]

Q2 a) Solve the equation $3^x = 5$, giving your answer to 2 decimal places. [3 marks]

    b) Hence, or otherwise, solve the equation $3^{2x} - 14(3^x) = -45$ [4 marks]

It's sometimes hard to see the wood for the trees — especially with logs...

Tricky... I think of $\log_a b$ as 'the power I have to raise a to if I want to end up with b' — that's all it is. And the log laws make a bit more sense if you think of 'log' as meaning 'power'. For example, you know that $2^a \times 2^b = 2^{a+b}$ — this just says that if you multiply the two numbers, you add the powers. Well, the first law of logs is saying the same thing. Any road, even if you don't quite understand why they work, make sure you know the log laws like the back of your hand.

Using Exponentials and Logs

Now that you're familiar with the log laws, it's time to reveal their true power. Okay, maybe that's a slight exaggeration, but they are pretty useful in a variety of situations. Read on to find out more.

Use the **Calculator Log Button** whenever you can

Example: Use logarithms to solve the following for x, giving your answers to 4 s.f.
a) $10^{3x} = 4000$ b) $7^x = 55$ c) $\log_2 x = 5$

There's an unknown in the power, so take logs of both sides (if your calculator has a '$\log_{10}$' button, base 10 is usually a good idea):

a) $\log 10^{3x} = \log 4000$

You can choose any base, but use the same one for both sides.

Use one of the log laws: $\log x^k = k \log x$

$3x \log 10 = \log 4000$

Since $\log_{10} 10 = 1$, solve the equation to find x:

$3x = \log 4000$, so $x = \textbf{1.201 to 4 s.f.}$

Again, take logs of both sides, and use the log rules:

b) $x \log_{10} 7 = \log_{10} 55$, so $x = \dfrac{\log_{10} 55}{\log_{10} 7} = \textbf{2.059 to 4 s.f.}$

To get rid of a log, you 'take exponentials', meaning you do '2 (the base) to the power of each side'.

c) $2^{\log_2 x} = 2^5$,
so $x = 2^5 = \textbf{32}$

Or using base 7 for b):
$x = \log_7 55 = 2.059$ (4 s.f.)

You might have to **Combine** the **Laws of Logs** to **Solve** equations

If the examiners are feeling particularly mean, they might make you use **more than one** law to solve an equation.

Example: Solve the equation $\log_3(2 - 3x) - 2\log_3 x = 2$.

First, combine the log terms into one term (you can do this because they both have the same base):

$\log_3 \dfrac{2 - 3x}{x^2} = 2$

Remember that $a \log x = \log x^a$.

Then take exponentials of both sides:

$3^{\log_3 \frac{2-3x}{x^2}} = 3^2 \Rightarrow \dfrac{2 - 3x}{x^2} = 9$

Ignore the negative solution because you can't take logs of a negative number.

Finally, rearrange the equation and solve for x:

$2 - 3x = 9x^2 \Rightarrow 0 = 9x^2 + 3x - 2$

$\Rightarrow 0 = (3x - 1)(3x + 2) \Rightarrow x = \dfrac{1}{3}$

Exponential Growth and **Decay** applies to **Real-life** problems

Logs can even be used to model **real-life** situations — see pages 48-49 to see more of this.

Example: The radioactivity of a substance decays by 20 percent over a year. The initial level of radioactivity is 400. Find the time taken for the radioactivity to fall to 200 (the half-life).

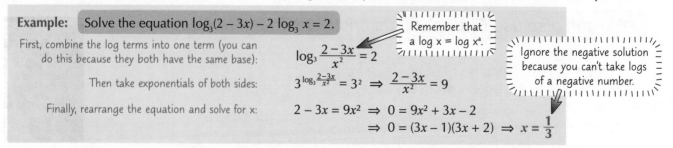

$R = 400 \times 0.8^T$ where R is the **level of radioactivity** at time T years.
We need $R = 200$, so solve $200 = 400 \times 0.8^T$

The 0.8 comes from 100% − 20% decay.

$0.8^T = \dfrac{200}{400} = 0.5 \Rightarrow T \log 0.8 = \log 0.5 \Rightarrow T = \dfrac{\log 0.5}{\log 0.8} = \textbf{3.106 years}$ (4 s.f.)

Exponential **models** often have a **time restriction** — for larger times the numbers get too big or small.

Exponential equations can be **Reduced to Linear Form**

Equations like $y = ax^n$ and $y = ab^x$ can be a bit awkward to use. Fortunately, using the **laws of logs**, they can be rewritten to look like a form you've seen before — good old $y = mx + c$. Just take **logs** of both sides and rearrange:

$$y = ax^n \Rightarrow \log y = n \log x + \log a$$

$$y = ab^x \Rightarrow \log y = x \log b + \log a$$

The equations look pretty horrendous now, I'll admit. But look at them carefully — they're just a nasty-looking version of y = mx + c.

Once the equations are in this form you can draw their **straight line graphs** — you just need to **label** the axes **log x** (top) or **x** (bottom) against **log y**. Now your graph is **easier** to work with than the exponential graph.

Using Exponentials and Logs

Example: The number of employees, p, working for a company t years after it was founded can be modelled by the equation $p = at^b$. The table below shows the number of employees the company has:

Age of company (t years)	2	5	8	13	25
Number of employees (p)	3	7	10	16	29

a) Show that $p = at^b$ can be written in the form $\log p = b \log t + \log a$.

b) Plot a graph of $\log t$ against $\log p$ and draw a line of best fit for your graph.

c) Use your graph to estimate the values of a and b in the equation $p = at^b$.

Starting with $p = at^b$, take logs of both sides:

Now use the laws of logs to rearrange into required form:

Make a table of the values of $\log t$ and $\log p$ using p and t as given in the question:

a) $\log p = \log at^b$

$\log p = \log a + \log t^b = b \log t + \log a$

b)

$\log t$	0.301	0.699	0.903	1.114	1.398
$\log p$	0.477	0.845	1.000	1.204	1.462

Now plot a graph of $\log t$ against $\log p$ and draw a line of best fit:

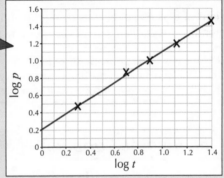

c) From part a), the graph has equation $\log p = b \log t + \log a$.
Compare this to $y = mx + c$:
b is the gradient of the line and
$\log a$ is the vertical intercept of the line.

Use the coordinates of two points on the line to find the gradient:
E.g. use coordinates (1.0, 1.1) and (0, 0.2):
$$b = \frac{y_2 - y_1}{x_2 - x_1} = \frac{1.1 - 0.2}{1.0 - 0} = \mathbf{0.9}$$

You can also read the vertical intercept off the graph — 0.2.
BUT this value is equal to $\log a$, so take exponentials of both sides:
$a = 10^{0.2} = \mathbf{1.585}$ to 3 d.p.
So $b = 0.9$ and $a = 1.585$, and the original equation $p = at^b$ is $p = 1.585t^{0.9}$.

> Be careful when using models like this to predict values outside the range of the given data — this is extrapolation (see p.77).

Practice Questions

Q1 If $6^{(3x + 2)} = 9$, find x to 3 significant figures.

Q2 If $3^{(y^2 - 4)} = 7^{(y + 2)}$, find y. Give your answer to 3 significant figures where appropriate.

Q3 The value of a painting is modelled as increasing by 5% each year. If the initial price of the painting is £1000, find the time taken in years for the price to reach £2000. Give your answer to 1 d.p.

Exam Question

Q1 The yearly income from book sales of a particular author has tended to increase with time.
The table below shows his income from book sales over the first five years after his book was published.

Number of years after book published (t)	1	2	3	4	5
Income (£p thousand)	10	13	17	24	35

The relationship is modelled by the equation $p = ab^t$, where a and b are constants to be found.

a) Plot a graph of t against $\log_{10} p$. Draw, by eye, a line of best fit for your graph. [2 marks]

b) State, in terms of a and b, the gradient and vertical-axis intercept of your graph.
Hence use your graph to find the values of a and b. [4 marks]

c) Predict the author's income 10 years after his book was published. [1 mark]

d) Suggest one reason why the prediction in part c) might not be accurate. [1 mark]

Reducing to linear form is hard work — you'll sleep like a log tonight...

The results you get with the method shown in the example will depend on your line of best fit, so make sure you draw it carefully. It doesn't hurt to check your final answer using the values in the original table to see how well it fits the data. And don't forget that the vertical intercept is a log — you'll need to take exponentials to get the value you want.

e^x and ln x

Of all the exponential functions in the world (and there are infinite exponential functions), only one can be called the exponential function. The most powerful, most incredible — e^x. Wait, what do you mean, "anticlimactic"?

The **Gradient** of the **Exponential Function** $y = e^x$ is e^x

There is a value of 'a' for which the **gradient** of $y = a^x$ is **exactly the same as** a^x. That value is known as **e**, an **irrational number** around **2.7183** (it's stored in your calculator, just like π). Because e is just a number, the graph of $y = \mathbf{e^x}$ has all the properties of $y = a^x$...

1) $y = \mathbf{e^x}$ crosses the y-axis at **(0, 1)**.
2) As $x \to \infty$, $e^x \to \infty$ and as $x \to -\infty$, $e^x \to 0$.
3) $y = e^x$ **does not exist** for $y \leq 0$ (i.e. e^x **can't be zero** or **negative**).

The **gradient** of e^x is e^x (i.e. e^x is its own gradient). More generally, the gradient of e^{kx} is ke^{kx} for any number, k.

> $y = e^{ax+b} + c$ is a **transformation** (see p.25) of $y = e^x$. The value of a stretches the graph horizontally, b shifts it horizontally and c shifts it vertically.

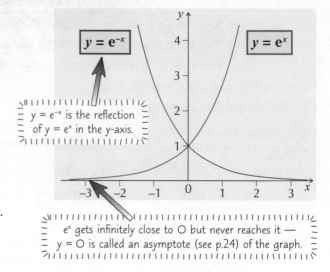

$y = e^{-x}$ $y = e^x$

~ $y = e^{-x}$ is the reflection of $y = e^x$ in the y-axis. ~

e^x gets infinitely close to O but never reaches it — $y = O$ is called an asymptote (see p.24) of the graph.

ln x is the **Inverse Function** of e^x

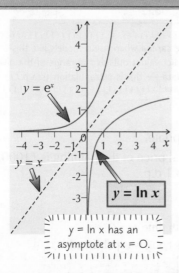

$y = e^x$

$y = x$

$y = \ln x$

~ $y = \ln x$ has an asymptote at $x = O$. ~

$\ln x$ (also known as $\log_e x$, or '**natural log**'*) is the **inverse function** of $\mathbf{e^x}$:

1) $y = \ln x$ is the **reflection** of $y = e^x$ in the line $y = x$.
2) It crosses the x-axis at **(1, 0)** (so **ln 1 = 0**).
3) As $x \to \infty$, $\ln x \to \infty$ (but slowly), and as $x \to 0$, $\ln x \to -\infty$.
4) $\ln x$ **does not exist** for $x \leq 0$ (i.e. x **can't be zero** or **negative**).

Because $\ln x$ is a logarithmic function and the inverse of e^x, we get these juicy **formulas** and **log laws**...

$$e^{\ln x} = x$$
$$\ln(e^x) = x$$

~ i.e. doing one function then the other to x takes you back to x. ~

These formulas are **extremely useful** for dealing with **equations** containing 'e^x's or '$\ln x$'s.

'Log laws' for $\ln x$

$$\ln x + \ln y = \ln xy$$
$$\ln x - \ln y = \ln\left(\frac{x}{y}\right)$$
$$\ln x^k = k \ln x$$

~ These are the same old log laws from p.42, applied to ln x. ~

Use **Inverses** and **Log Laws** to **Solve Equations**

Just as with other logs and exponentials (p.42), you can use e^x and $\ln x$ to cancel each other out.

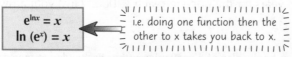

Example: If $e^{2x} = 9$, find the exact value of x.

Take ln of both sides: $\ln e^{2x} = \ln 9$
Using $\ln x^k = k \ln x$: $2x \ln e = \ln 9 \Rightarrow 2x = \ln 9$
$$\Rightarrow x = \frac{1}{2}\ln 9 = \ln 9^{\frac{1}{2}} = \mathbf{\ln 3}$$

~ The 'exact value of x' means 'leave x in terms of e and/or ln.' ~

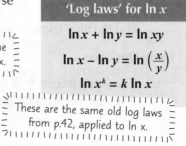

Example: If $\ln(x - 5) = 3$, find the exact value of x.

Take exponentials of both sides: $e^{\ln(x-5)} = e^3$
$$x - 5 = e^3$$
$$\Rightarrow x = 5 + e^3$$

All logs and no play makes Jill a dull girl.

*Certified organic

e^x and $\ln x$

Example: a) Solve the equation $2 \ln x - \ln 2x = 6$, giving your answer as an exact value of x.

Use the log laws to simplify:

$2 \ln x - \ln 2x = 6$

$\Rightarrow \ln x^2 - \ln 2x = 6 \;\Rightarrow\; \ln (x^2 \div 2x) = 6 \;\Rightarrow\; \ln \left(\dfrac{x}{2}\right) = 6$

Now apply the inverse function e^x to both sides
— this will remove the $\ln \left(\dfrac{x}{2}\right)$:

$e^{\ln\left(\frac{x}{2}\right)} = e^6 \;\Rightarrow\; \dfrac{x}{2} = e^6 \;\Rightarrow\; x = 2e^6$

Using $e^{\ln x} = x$ from the last page.

b) Find the exact solutions of the equation $e^x + 5e^{-x} = 6$.

When you're asked for more than one solution think quadratics.
Multiply each part of the equation by e^x to get rid of that e^{-x}:

$e^x + 5e^{-x} = 6$

$\Rightarrow e^{2x} + 5 = 6e^x \;\Rightarrow\; e^{2x} - 6e^x + 5 = 0$

It starts to look a bit nicer if you substitute y for e^x:

$y^2 - 6y + 5 = 0$

Basic power laws — $(e^x)^2 = e^{2x}$ and $e^{-x} \times e^x = e^0 = 1$.

Factorise to find solutions:

$(y - 1)(y - 5) = 0 \;\Rightarrow\; y = 1$ and $y = 5$

Put e^x back in:

$e^x = 1$ and $e^x = 5$

Using $\ln e^x = x$.

Take 'ln' of both sides to solve:

$\ln e^x = \ln 1 \;\Rightarrow\; x = \ln 1 = \mathbf{0}$ and $\ln e^x = \ln 5 \;\Rightarrow\; \boldsymbol{x = \ln 5}$

Practice Questions

Q1 Four graphs, A, B, C and D, are shown below. Match the graphs to each of the following equations:
a) $y = 4e^x$ b) $y = 4e^{-x}$ c) $y = 4 \ln x$ d) $y = \ln 4x$

A 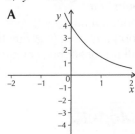   **B** 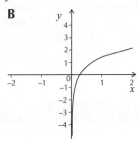   **C** 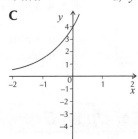   **D**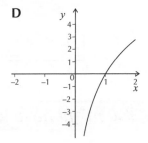

Q2 Find the value of x, to 4 decimal places, when:
a) $e^{2x} = 6$ b) $\ln (x + 3) = 0.75$ c) $3e^{-4x+1} = 5$ d) $\ln x + \ln 5 = \ln 4$

Q3 Solve the following equations, giving your solutions as exact values:
a) $\ln (2x - 7) + \ln 4 = -3$ b) $2e^{2x} + e^x = 3$

Exam Questions

Q1 a) Given that $6e^x = 3$, find the exact value of x.   [2 marks]

b) Find the exact solutions to the equation $e^{2x} - 8e^x + 7 = 0$.   [4 marks]

c) Given that $4 \ln x = 3$, find the exact value of x.   [2 marks]

d) Solve the equation $\ln x + \dfrac{24}{\ln x} = 10$, giving your answers as exact values of x.   [4 marks]

Q2 Solve the following equations, giving your answers as exact values of x.

a) $2e^x + 18e^{-x} = 20$ [4 marks]

b) $2 \ln x - \ln 3 = \ln 12$ [3 marks]

No problems — only solutions...

All the individual steps to solving these equations are easy — the hard bit is spotting what combination of things to try. A good thing to look for is hidden quadratics, so try and substitute for e^x or $\ln x$ to make things look a bit nicer.

Modelling with e^x and $\ln x$

This page is all about models. Except they're modelling exponential growth and decay in real-world applications rather than the Chanel Autumn/Winter collection. Unless Chanel's lineup is growing exponentially, I suppose.

Use **Exponential Functions** to **Model** real-life **Growth and Decay**

In the **exam** you might be given a background story to an exponential equation.
They may then ask you to **find some values**, work out a **missing part** of the equation, or even **sketch a graph**.
There's nothing here you haven't seen before — you just need to know how to deal with all the **wordy** bits.

Example: The exponential growth of a colony of bacteria can be modelled by the equation $B = 60e^{0.03t}$, where B is the number of bacteria, and t is the time in hours from the point at which the colony is first monitored ($t \geq 0$). Use the model to predict:

a) the number of bacteria after 4 hours,

You need to find B when $t = 4$,
so put the numbers into the equation:
$B = 60 \times e^{(0.03 \times 4)}$
$= 60 \times 1.1274...$
$= 67.6498...$
So $B =$ **67 bacteria**

You shouldn't round up here — there are only 67 whole bacteria, not 68.

b) the time taken for the colony to grow to 1000.

- You need to find t when $B = 1000$,
  so put the numbers into the equation:
  $1000 = 60e^{0.03t}$
  $\Rightarrow e^{0.03t} = 1000 \div 60 = 16.6666...$

- Now take 'ln' of both sides as usual:
  $\ln e^{0.03t} = \ln (16.6666...)$
  $\Rightarrow 0.03t = 2.8134...$
  $\Rightarrow t = 2.8134... \div 0.03 =$ **93.8 hours** (3 s.f.)

c) Explain why this model may be unrealistic for large t.

A sketch of the graph of the function can help here.
As t increases, B gets larger and larger without a limit.
In reality, the population will eventually stop increasing (e.g. due to limited food or space etc.) so the model will no longer be accurate.

You might have to **Set Up** an **Exponential Growth/Decay Model**

Exponential models are incredibly useful, but they're a bit of a pain to get started with.
Here are some handy tips to help you on your way:

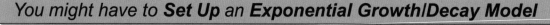

1) "The **rate of change** of y is **proportional** to y" — this is your hint that you should use an **exponential model** i.e. $y = Ae^{kx}$ or similar. In the example above, the **rate of growth** of the population at time t, is **proportional** to B, the size of the population at time t.

   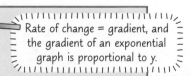
   Rate of change = gradient, and the gradient of an exponential graph is proportional to y.

2) "The **initial value** of y is P_0" — where P_0 is a number. This means you can set $y = P_0$ at the point where the model starts, which usually means $t = 0$. More often than not, your model will look like this: $y = P_0 e^{kt}$ (where k is another constant). In the previous example, the initial value of B is 60 — i.e. there were 60 bacteria when the colony was first monitored.

3) "y is exponentially **growing/decaying**" — you can tell whether y is increasing or decreasing by the **sign** of the **coefficient** of the other variable (x/t/etc.). So $y = 2e^{4x}$ will **grow exponentially** as x increases, while $y = 2e^{-4x}$ will **exponentially decay**. The population of bacteria in the example is **growing** (as the coefficient of t is **0.03**).

4) "Find the value of x for which y has **tripled/halved**/etc." — these are classic exponential modelling questions. Set $y = 3P_0$ or $\frac{1}{2}P_0$ or whatever you need, and then solve for x.
   Be careful with the final answer — depending on the context, you might have to figure out whether to round up or down. Just think logically about what you're modelling — you can have '0.4 days', but you can't have '0.4 people'.

Modelling with e^x and $\ln x$

Example: The concentration (C) of a drug in the bloodstream, t hours after taking an initial dose, decreases exponentially according to $C = Ae^{-kt}$, where k is a constant. If the initial concentration is 0.72, and this halves after 5 hours, find the values of A and k and sketch the graph of C against t.

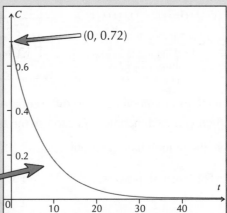

- The 'initial concentration' is 0.72 when $t = 0$, so put this information into the equation to find A:
  $0.72 = A \times e^0 \Rightarrow 0.72 = A \times 1 \Rightarrow \mathbf{A = 0.72}$

- The question also says that when $t = 5$ hours, C is half of 0.72. So using the value for A found above:
  $C = 0.72e^{-kt}$
  $0.72 \div 2 = 0.72 \times e^{(-k \times 5)}$
  $\Rightarrow 0.36 = 0.72 \times e^{-5k} \Rightarrow 0.36 = \dfrac{0.72}{e^{5k}} \Rightarrow e^{5k} = \dfrac{0.72}{0.36} = 2$

- Now take 'ln' of both sides to solve:
  $\ln e^{5k} = \ln 2 \Rightarrow 5k = \ln 2$
  $\Rightarrow k = \ln 2 \div 5 = \mathbf{0.139}$ **(3 s.f.)**

- So the equation is $C = 0.72e^{-0.139t}$.
  You still need to do a **sketch** though, so find the **intercepts** and **asymptotes**:
  When $t = 0$, $C = 0.72$. As $t \to \infty$, $e^{-0.139t} \to 0$, so $C \to 0$.

The sketch should make sense for the situation in the question — here t can only be positive as it is the time after an event, so only sketch the graph for t ≥ O.

Practice Question

Q1 The value of a motorbike (£V) varies with age (in t years from new) according to $V = 7500e^{-0.2t}$.

a) How much did it originally cost?

b) What will its value be after 10 years (to the nearest £)?

c) After how many years will the motorbike's value have fallen to £500? Give your answer to 1 d.p.

d) Sketch a graph showing how the value of the motorbike varies with age, labelling all key points.

Exam Questions

Q1 A breed of mink is introduced to a new habitat.
The number of mink, M, after t years in the habitat, is modelled by: $M = 74e^{0.6t}$ $(t \geq 0)$

a) State the number of mink that were introduced to the new habitat originally. [1 mark]

b) Predict the number of mink after 3 years in the habitat. [2 marks]

c) Predict the number of complete years it would take for the population of mink to exceed 10 000. [2 marks]

d) Sketch a graph to show how the mink population varies with time in the new habitat. [2 marks]

Q2 A radioactive substance decays exponentially so that its activity, A, can be modelled by $A = Be^{-kt}$, where t is the time in days, and $t \geq 0$.
Some experimental data is shown in the table.

t	0	5	10
A	50	42	

a) State the value of B. [1 mark]

b) Find the value of k, to 3 significant figures. [2 marks]

c) Estimate the missing value from the table, to the nearest whole number. [2 marks]

d) The half-life of a substance is the time it takes for the activity to halve.
Find the half-life of this substance, in days. Give your answer to the nearest day. [3 marks]

Learn this and watch your knowledge grow exponentially...

For these wordy problems, the key is just to extract the relevant information and solve like you did on the previous pages. The more you practise, the more familiar they'll become — soon you'll be able to do them with your eyes shut.

Differentiation

Differentiation is a great way to work out gradients of graphs. You take a function, differentiate it, and you can quickly tell how steep a graph is. It's magic. No, wait, the other thing — it's <u>calculus</u>.

Use this **Formula** to **Differentiate Powers of x**

For a function $f(x) = x^n$, the **derivative** $f'(x)$ can be found using this formula:

'Derivative' just means 'the thing you get when you differentiate something'.

$\frac{d}{dx}$ *just means 'the derivative of the thing in the brackets with respect to x'.*

$$f'(x) = \frac{d}{dx}(x^n) = nx^{n-1}$$

If you have y = (some function of x), its derivative is written $\frac{dy}{dx}$, which means 'the rate of change of y with respect to x'.

Functions are much easier to **differentiate** when they're written as **powers of x** — like writing $\sqrt{x}$ as $x^{\frac{1}{2}}$ (see p.4). When you've done this, you can use the formula in the box above to differentiate the function.

Use the differentiation formula:

For '**normal**' powers:	For **negative** powers:	For **fractional** powers:
E.g. $f(x) = x^2$	E.g. $f(x) = \frac{1}{x^2} = x^{-2}$	E.g. $f(x) = \sqrt{x} = x^{\frac{1}{2}}$.
n is just the power of x.	*Always rewrite the function as a power of x.*	*Write the square root as a power of x.*
Here, $n = 2$, so:	Here $n = -2$, so:	Here, $n = \frac{1}{2}$, so:
$f'(x) = nx^{n-1} = 2x^1 = 2x$	$f'(x) = nx^{n-1} = -2x^{-3} = -\frac{2}{x^3}$	$f'(x) = \frac{1}{2}x^{-\frac{1}{2}} = \frac{1}{2\sqrt{x}}$

Differentiate each term **Separately**

Even if there are loads of terms in the function, it doesn't matter.
Differentiate each bit **separately** and you'll be fine. Here are a couple of examples:

Example: Differentiate $y = 3\sqrt{x} = 3x^{\frac{1}{2}}$

If the function is being multiplied by a constant (3 in this case)...

$$\frac{dy}{dx} = 3\left(\frac{1}{2}x^{-\frac{1}{2}}\right)$$

...multiply the derivative by the same number.

$$\frac{dy}{dx} = \frac{3}{2} \times x^{-\frac{1}{2}} = \frac{3}{2\sqrt{x}}$$

Example: Differentiate $y = 6x^2 + \frac{4}{\sqrt[3]{x}} - \frac{2}{x^2} + 1$

Write each term as a power of x, including the constants: $1 = x^0$

Differentiate each bit separately and add or subtract the results.

$$y = 6x^2 + 4x^{-\frac{1}{3}} - 2x^{-2} + x^0$$

$$\frac{dy}{dx} = 6(2x) + 4\left(-\frac{1}{3}x^{-\frac{4}{3}}\right) - 2(-2x^{-3}) + 0x^{-1}$$

$$\frac{dy}{dx} = 12x - \frac{4}{3\sqrt[3]{x^4}} + \frac{4}{x^3}$$

A constant always differentiates to O.

You can **Differentiate** to find **Gradients**

Differentiating tells you the **gradient** of a curve at any given point, which is the same as the gradient of the **tangent** to the curve at that point. Tangents will become a lot more important on the next page, so stay tuned...

Example: Find the gradient of the graph $y = x^2$ at $x = 1$ and $x = -2$.

You need the **gradient** of the graph of: $\quad y = x^2$

So **differentiate** this function to get: $\quad \frac{dy}{dx} = 2x$

When $x = 1$, $\frac{dy}{dx} = 2(1) = 2$, so the gradient at $x = 1$ is **2**.

When $x = -2$, $\frac{dy}{dx} = 2(-2) = -4$, so the gradient at $x = -2$ is **−4**.

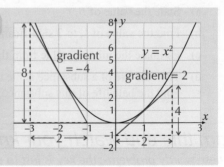

Differentiation

You can find the *Equation* of a *Tangent* or a *Normal* to a curve

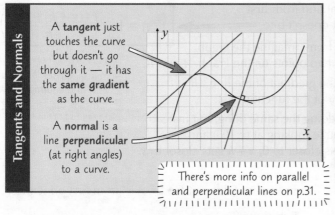

Tangents and Normals

A **tangent** just touches the curve but doesn't go through it — it has the **same gradient** as the curve.

A **normal** is a line **perpendicular** (at right angles) to a curve.

There's more info on parallel and perpendicular lines on p.31.

Finding Tangents and Normals

1) Differentiate the function.

2) Find the gradient of the tangent or normal. For a **tangent**, this is the gradient of the curve. For a **normal**, this is $\dfrac{-1}{\text{gradient of the curve}}$.

3) Write the equation of the tangent or normal in the form $y - y_1 = m(x - x_1)$ or $y = mx + c$.

4) Use the coordinates of a point on the line to complete the equation of the line .

Tangents have the *Same Gradient* as the curve

Example: Find the tangent to the curve $y = (4 - x)(x + 2)$ at the point (2, 8).

To find the **gradient** of the curve (and the tangent), first write the equation in a **form** you can differentiate:
$$y = (4 - x)(x + 2) = 8 + 2x - x^2$$

Then **differentiate** it: $\dfrac{dy}{dx} = 2 - 2x$

The **gradient** of the tangent at (2, 8) will be the gradient of the curve at $x = 2$.

$$\text{At } x = 2, \dfrac{dy}{dx} = -2$$

You could also use $y = mx + c$ here.

So the tangent has equation $y - y_1 = -2(x - x_1)$,

and since it passes through the point (2, 8), this becomes:

$$y - 8 = -2(x - 2) \text{ or } y = 12 - 2x$$

You can give your answer in any of the forms from p.30.

"Sir, I'm picking up something abnormal in the system..."

Normals are *Perpendicular* to the curve

Example: Find the normal to the curve $y = \dfrac{(x + 2)(x + 4)}{6\sqrt{x}}$ at the point (4, 4).

Write the equation of the curve in a **form** you can differentiate:

$$y = \dfrac{x^2 + 6x + 8}{6x^{\frac{1}{2}}} = \dfrac{1}{6}x^{\frac{3}{2}} + x^{\frac{1}{2}} + \dfrac{4}{3}x^{-\frac{1}{2}}$$

Divide everything on the top line by everything on the bottom line.

Then **differentiate** it:
$$\dfrac{dy}{dx} = \dfrac{1}{6}\left(\dfrac{3}{2}x^{\frac{1}{2}}\right) + \dfrac{1}{2}x^{-\frac{1}{2}} + \dfrac{4}{3}\left(-\dfrac{1}{2}x^{-\frac{3}{2}}\right)$$
$$= \dfrac{1}{4}\sqrt{x} + \dfrac{1}{2\sqrt{x}} - \dfrac{2}{3\sqrt{x^3}}$$

Find the **gradient** at (4, 4): At $x = 4$, $\dfrac{dy}{dx} = \dfrac{1}{4} \times 2 + \dfrac{1}{2 \times 2} - \dfrac{2}{3 \times 8} = \dfrac{2}{3}$

So the **gradient** of the **normal** is $-1 \div \dfrac{2}{3} = -\dfrac{3}{2}$

Because the gradients of perpendicular lines multiply to give −1.

And the **equation** of the normal is $y - y_1 = -\dfrac{3}{2}(x - x_1)$,

and since it passes through the point (4, 4), this becomes:

$$y - 4 = -\dfrac{3}{2}(x - 4) \text{ or } 3x + 2y - 20 = 0$$

Differentiation

You can also Differentiate from First Principles

You can use this **formula** to find the derivative of a function from **first principles**. I know it looks nasty, but don't worry — it doesn't bite. ⟹

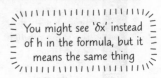

$$f'(x) = \lim_{h \to 0}\left(\frac{f(x+h) - f(x)}{h}\right)$$

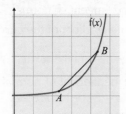

- To see where this comes from, imagine the graph of f(x), and a line joining two points on the graph, A and B.
- As B moves closer to A, the gradient of the line AB gets closer to the gradient of the function at A.
- The formula is basically doing the same thing, but instead of the points A and B, you're looking at $(x, f(x))$ and $(x + h, f(x + h))$ — as h gets closer to 0, $x + h$ gets closer to x.

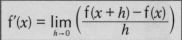
You might see 'δx' instead of h in the formula, but it means the same thing

Here's one of our classic step-by-step guides on how to tackle a question like this:

1) Find $\dfrac{f(x+h) - f(x)}{h}$ and **simplify** (you need to **remove** h from the **denominator** when you're simplifying).

2) Find the **limit** of the expression as h tends to zero (written $\lim\limits_{h \to 0}$) by setting $h = 0$ and simplifying.

3) If needed, put the **x-value** for your given point into the expression to find the **gradient** of f(x) at that point.

Example: Differentiate f(x) = x^2 from first principles.

Substitute f(x) = x^2 into the formula: ⟶ $f'(x) = \lim\limits_{h \to 0}\left(\dfrac{(x+h)^2 - x^2}{h}\right)$

The x^2s cancel on the top, and then you can cancel h from the bottom too.
$$= \lim_{h \to 0}\left(\frac{x^2 + 2hx + h^2 - x^2}{h}\right)$$
$$= \lim_{h \to 0}\left(\frac{2hx + h^2}{h}\right)$$

Now you can set $h = 0$ (without dividing by 0) to find the derivative: ⟶ $= \lim\limits_{h \to 0}(2x + h)$
$$= 2x \quad \text{what a shocker...}$$

Practice Questions

Q1 Differentiate these functions with respect to x: a) $y = x^2 + 2$ b) $y = x^4 + \sqrt{x}$ c) $y = \dfrac{7}{x^2} - \dfrac{3}{\sqrt{x}} + 12x^3$

Q2 Find the gradient of the graph of $y = x^3 - 7x^2 - 1$ at $x = 2$.

Q3 Find the equations of the tangent and the normal to the curve $y = \sqrt{x^3} - 3x - 10$ at $x = 16$.

Q4 Use differentiation from first principles to find the derivative of f(x) = 5x.

Exam Questions

Q1 Find the gradient of the curve $y = \dfrac{1}{\sqrt{x}} + \dfrac{1}{x}$ at the point $\left(4, \dfrac{3}{4}\right)$. [2 marks]

Q2 The curve C is given by the equation $y = mx^3 - x^2 + 8x + 2$, for a constant m.

a) Find $\dfrac{dy}{dx}$. [1 mark]

The point P lies on C, and has an x-coordinate of 5.
The normal to C at P is parallel to the line given by the equation $y + 4x - 3 = 0$.

b) Find the gradient of curve C at P. [2 marks]

c) Hence or otherwise, find: (i) the value of m, [3 marks]

(ii) the y-coordinate of P. [2 marks]

Q3 Show that the lines $y = \dfrac{x^3}{3} - 2x^2 - 4x + \dfrac{86}{3}$ and $y = \sqrt{x}$ both go through the point (4, 2), and are perpendicular at that point. [6 marks]

Q4 Use a binomial expansion to differentiate f(x) = x^4 from first principles. [5 marks]

---

f(x) and g(x) are like identical twins — it can be hard to differentiate them...

This is where AS Maths really kicks off, but don't get carried away and forget the basics. Always write out your working really clearly, particularly when differentiating from first principles. I mean, I know the answer's obvious, and I know you know the answer's obvious, but if they've asked you to use the formula then you'd better do it properly.

Stationary Points

Let me tell you about a special place — it's a magical point called a stationary point, where the gradient of the graph is zero, and there's a pot of g- oh no, wait, it's actually just the gradient thing. Turns out they're pretty ordinary, really.

Stationary Points are when the gradient is Zero

Stationary points are points on a graph where the curve **flattens out** — i.e. the **gradient is zero**.

A stationary point could be...

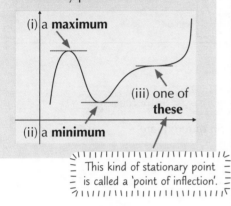

(i) a **maximum**

(iii) one of **these**

(ii) a **minimum**

This kind of stationary point is called a 'point of inflection'.

Example: Find the coordinates of the stationary points of the curve $y = 2x^3 - 3x^2 - 12x + 5$, and determine the nature of each.

You need to find where $\frac{dy}{dx} = 0$. So first, **differentiate** the function.

$$y = 2x^3 - 3x^2 - 12x + 5 \Rightarrow \frac{dy}{dx} = 6x^2 - 6x - 12$$

Then set this derivative equal to **zero** and solve for x:

$$6x^2 - 6x - 12 = 0 \Rightarrow x^2 - x - 2 = 0$$
$$\Rightarrow (x + 1)(x - 2) = 0 \Rightarrow x = -1 \text{ or } x = 2$$

So the graph has **two** stationary points, at $x = -1$ and $x = 2$.

When $x = -1$, $y = 2(-1)^3 - 3(-1)^2 - 12(-1) + 5$
$$= -2 - 3 + 12 + 5 = 12$$

When $x = 2$, $y = 2(2)^3 - 3(2)^2 - 12(2) + 5$
$$= 16 - 12 - 24 + 5 = -15$$

So the stationary points are at **(-1, 12)** and **(2, -15)**. To be continued...

Decide if it's a Maximum or a Minimum by differentiating Again

Once you've found where the stationary points are, you have to decide whether each one is a **maximum** or a **minimum** — that's all a question means when it says, '...determine the nature of the turning points' (a '**turning point**' is either a maximum or minimum — points of inflection don't count).

To decide whether a stationary point is a **maximum** or a **minimum**, differentiate again to find $\frac{d^2y}{dx^2}$, or f''(x). f''(x) is called the **second order derivative**, and is the **rate of change** of the gradient.

$\frac{d^2y}{dx^2}$ is read 'd 2 y by dx squared'.

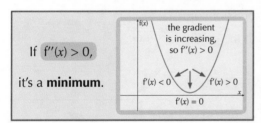

If f''(x) > 0, it's a **minimum**.

the gradient is increasing, so f''(x) > 0

f'(x) < 0   f'(x) > 0

f'(x) = 0

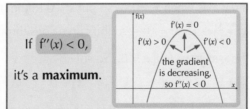

If f''(x) < 0, it's a **maximum**.

f'(x) = 0

f'(x) > 0   f'(x) < 0

the gradient is decreasing, so f''(x) < 0

If $\frac{d^2y}{dx^2} = 0$, then it could be any type of stationary point.

Last time, on 'Strictly Come Differentiating'...

...you found that the stationary points were at **(-1, 12)** and **(2, -15)**.

$\frac{dy}{dx} = 6x^2 - 6x - 12$, so differentiate again: $\frac{d^2y}{dx^2} = 12x - 6$

Now find the value of $\frac{d^2y}{dx^2}$ at the stationary points:

At $x = -1$, $\frac{d^2y}{dx^2} = 12(-1) - 6 = -18$

This is **negative**, so **(-1, 12) is a maximum**.

At $x = 2$, $\frac{d^2y}{dx^2} = 12(2) - 6 = 18$

This is **positive**, so **(2, -15) is a minimum**.

Finding the maximum and minimum points of a function makes it a lot easier to sketch the graph — check out the stuff on the next two pages.

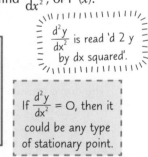

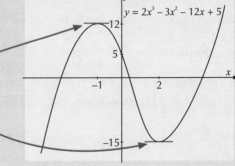

$y = 2x^3 - 3x^2 - 12x + 5$

Stationary Points

Find out if a function is Increasing or Decreasing

You can use differentiation to work out exactly where a function is **increasing** or **decreasing** — and how quickly.

A function is **increasing** if the gradient is **positive**.	A function is **decreasing** if the gradient is **negative**.	The **bigger** the gradient, the **quicker** y changes as x changes.
y gets bigger... ...as x gets bigger.	y gets smaller... ...as x gets bigger.	small positive gradient small negative gradient large positive gradient large negative gradient

Example: Find the range of x-values for which the graph of $f(x) = 4 + 3x - 2x^2$ is increasing.

You want to find where the gradient is positive, i.e. where $f'(x) > 0$. So differentiate:

$$f(x) = 4 + 3x - 2x^2 \implies f'(x) = 3 - 4x$$

Now find where $f'(x) > 0$: $\quad 3 - 4x > 0 \implies 4x < 3 \implies x < \frac{3}{4}$

Use differentiation to make Curve Sketching easier

Now, you might be wondering where I'm going with all of this stuff about increasing functions and stationary points and gradients... Well, as it happens, it's all really helpful for sketching graphs of complicated functions. So sit tight — here comes one mega-example that you won't soon forget:

1) Find where the curve crosses the Axes

Example: Sketch the graph of $f(x) = \frac{x^2}{2} - 2\sqrt{x}$ for $x \geq 0$.

The curve crosses the **y-axis** when $x = 0$ — so put $x = 0$ in the expression for y.

When $x = 0$, $f(x) = \frac{0^2}{2} - 2\sqrt{0} = 0$ — so the curve goes through the **origin**.

The curve crosses the **x-axis** when $f(x) = 0$. So solve:

$$\frac{x^2}{2} - 2\sqrt{x} = 0 \implies x^2 - 4x^{\frac{1}{2}} = 0 \implies x^{\frac{1}{2}}\left(x^{\frac{3}{2}} - 4\right) = 0$$

$$x^{\frac{1}{2}} = 0 \implies x = 0 \quad \text{and} \quad x^{\frac{3}{2}} - 4 = 0 \implies x^{\frac{3}{2}} = 4 \implies x = 4^{\frac{2}{3}} \ (\approx 2.5)$$

So the curve crosses the x-axis when $x = 0$ and when $x \approx 2.5$.

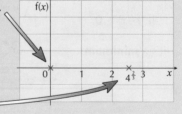

2) Differentiate to find information about the Gradient and Stationary Points

Differentiating the function gives: $f'(x) = \frac{1}{2}(2x) - 2\left(\frac{1}{2}x^{-\frac{1}{2}}\right) = x - x^{-\frac{1}{2}} = x - \frac{1}{\sqrt{x}}$

Find any **stationary points**: $x - \frac{1}{\sqrt{x}} = 0 \implies x = \frac{1}{\sqrt{x}} \implies x^{\frac{3}{2}} = 1 \implies x = 1 \longrightarrow$ At $x = 1$,
$f(x) = \frac{1}{2} - 2 = -\frac{3}{2}$

The gradient is **positive** when: $x - \frac{1}{\sqrt{x}} > 0 \implies x > \frac{1}{\sqrt{x}} \implies x^{\frac{3}{2}} > 1 \implies x > 1$

and it's **negative** when $x < 1$ — so the function is decreasing for $0 < x < 1$, then increasing for $x > 1$.

So you know that $\left(1, -\frac{3}{2}\right)$ is a **minimum**. You can check this by differentiating again:

$$f''(x) = 1 - \left(-\frac{1}{2}x^{-\frac{3}{2}}\right) = 1 + \frac{1}{2\sqrt{x^3}} \qquad f''(1) = 1 + \frac{1}{2\sqrt{1^3}} = 1 + \frac{1}{2} > 0 \text{ so } x = 1 \text{ is a minimum.}$$

Stationary Points

3) Find out what happens when x gets Big

You can also try and decide what happens as x gets very **big** — in both the positive and negative directions. There's a handy trick you can use to help with this when your function is made up of **powers of x** — **factorise** to take out the **highest power of x** from every term.

> If the highest power of x is negative, then the graph will flatten out as x gets larger — see p.24 for more.

Factorise f(x) by taking the **biggest** power outside the brackets...

$$\frac{x^2}{2} - 2\sqrt{x} = x^2\left(\frac{1}{2} - 2x^{-\frac{3}{2}}\right) = x^2\left(\frac{1}{2} - \frac{2}{x^{\frac{3}{2}}}\right)$$

As x gets large, the $\frac{2}{x^{\frac{3}{2}}}$ gets smaller and smaller — so the bit in brackets gets closer to $\frac{1}{2}$.

So as x gets larger, f(x) gets closer and closer to $\frac{1}{2}x^2$ — and this just keeps growing and growing.

So the final graph looks like this:

It passes through **(0, 0)** and **($4^{\frac{2}{3}}$, 0)**,

has a minimum point at $\left(1, -\frac{3}{2}\right)$,

and gets larger and larger as x increases.

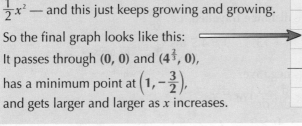

You should normally also think about what happens when x is big and negative, but you don't have to here as the graph is for x ≥ 0.

Practice Questions

Q1 Find the stationary points of the graph of $y = x^3 - 6x^2 - 63x + 21$.

Q2 Find the stationary points of the function $y = x^3 + \frac{3}{x}$.
Decide whether each stationary point is a minimum or a maximum.

Q3 Find when these functions are increasing and decreasing:
a) $y = 6(x + 2)(x - 3)$ b) $y = \frac{1}{x^2}$

Q4 Sketch the graph of $y = x^3 - 4x$, clearly showing the coordinates of any turning points.

Exam Questions

Q1 a) Find $\frac{dy}{dx}$ for the curve $y = 6 + \frac{4x^3 - 15x^2 + 12x}{6}$.   [2 marks]

    b) Hence find the coordinates of the stationary points of the curve.   [3 marks]

    c) Determine the nature of each stationary point.   [3 marks]

Q2 a) Find the coordinates of the stationary points for the curve $y = (x - 1)(3x^2 - 5x - 2)$.   [4 marks]

    b) Determine whether each of these points is a maximum or minimum.   [3 marks]

    c) Sketch the graph of $y = (x - 1)(3x^2 - 5x - 2)$.   [3 marks]

Q3 The function $f(x) = \frac{1}{2}x^4 - 3x$ has a single stationary point.

    a) Find the coordinates of the stationary point.   [3 marks]

    b) Determine the nature of the stationary point.   [2 marks]

    c) State the range of values of x for which f(x) is:
       (i) increasing   [1 mark]
       (ii) decreasing   [1 mark]

    d) Sketch the graph of $y = $ f(x).   [2 marks]

Curve sketching's important — but don't take my word for it...

Curve sketching — an underrated skill, in my opinion. As Shakespeare once wrote, 'Those who can do fab sketches of graphs and stuff are likely to get pretty good grades in maths exams, no word of a lie'. Well, he probably would've written something like that if he was into maths. And he would've written it because graphs are helpful when you're trying to work out what a question's all about — and once you know that, you can decide the best way forward. And if you don't believe me, remember the saying of the ancient Roman Emperor Julius Caesar, 'If in doubt, draw a graph'.

Using Differentiation

Differentiation isn't just mathematical daydreaming. It can be applied to real-life problems. For instance, you can use differentiation to find out the maximum possible volume of a box, given a limited amount of cardboard. Thrilling.

Differentiation is used to find **Rates of Change** in **Mechanics**...

Rates of change are particularly important in **mechanics** (you'll see more of this in Section 12) — and that means **differentiation** is important. You should know that **speed** is the rate of change of **distance travelled**, and **acceleration** is the rate of change of **speed** (see p.100 for more).

Example: The distance travelled by a car, s (in m), t seconds after it moves off, is given by: $s = \frac{9}{4}t^2 - \frac{1}{3}t^3$
for $0 \le t \le 4$. Find: a) the car's speed after 3 seconds, b) when the car is decelerating.

a) The **speed** of the car is the **rate of change** of the **distance travelled**, i.e. $\frac{ds}{dt}$:

$\frac{ds}{dt} = \frac{9}{2}t - t^2$ When $t = 3$, $\frac{ds}{dt} = \frac{9}{2}(3) - (3)^2 = 13.5 - 9 = \textbf{4.5 ms}^{-1}$

The units of $\frac{ds}{dt}$ are $\frac{\text{units of } s}{\text{units of } t}$, which are $\frac{m}{s}$, or ms⁻¹.

b) If the car is **decelerating**, then its acceleration is **negative**.

Acceleration is the **rate of change** of speed, i.e. $\frac{d}{dt}\left(\frac{ds}{dt}\right)$ or $\frac{d^2s}{dt^2}$:

$\frac{d^2s}{dt^2} = \frac{9}{2} - 2t$ $\frac{d^2s}{dt^2} < 0 \Rightarrow \frac{9}{2} - 2t < 0 \Rightarrow 4t > 9 \Rightarrow t > 2.25$ s

So the car is decelerating for **2.25 < $t \le$ 4.**

Remember that the equation given is only valid up to t = 4.

...and for finding **Maximum** or **Minimum Values** for **Volume** and **Area**

To find the maximum for a shape's volume, all you need is an equation for the volume **in terms of only one variable** — then just **differentiate as normal**. But examiners don't hand it to you on a plate — there's usually one too many variables chucked in. So you need to know how to manipulate the information to get rid of that unwanted variable.

Example: A jewellery box with a lid and dimensions $3x$ cm by x cm by y cm is made using a total of 450 cm² of wood.
a) Show that the volume of the box can be expressed as: $V = \frac{675x - 9x^3}{4}$.
b) Use calculus to find the maximum possible volume.

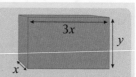

a) You know the basic equation for **volume**: $V = \text{width} \times \text{depth} \times \text{height} = 3x \times x \times y = 3x^2y$

But the question asks for volume in terms of x only — you don't want that pesky y in there. So you need to find y **in terms of** x and substitute that in.

Write an expression for the **surface area**:

$A = 2[(3x \times x) + (3x \times y) + (x \times y)] = 450 \Rightarrow 3x^2 + 4xy = 225$

Be careful when finding the surface area — here there's a lid so there are two of each side, but sometimes you'll get an open-topped shape.

Then rearrange to find an expression for y:

$4xy = 225 - 3x^2 \Rightarrow y = \frac{225 - 3x^2}{4x}$

Finally, **substitute** this into the equation for the volume: $V = 3x^2y = 3x^2 \times \frac{225 - 3x^2}{4x} = \frac{3x(225 - 3x^2)}{4}$

$$\Rightarrow V = \frac{675x - 9x^3}{4} \text{ as required}$$

b) You want to find the **maximum** value of V, so **differentiate** and set $\frac{dV}{dx} = 0$:

$\frac{dV}{dx} = \frac{675 - 27x^2}{4}$, $\frac{dV}{dx} = 0 \Rightarrow \frac{675 - 27x^2}{4} = 0 \Rightarrow 675 = 27x^2 \Rightarrow x^2 = 25 \Rightarrow \textbf{x = 5}$

Ignore the other solution, $x = -5$, since you can't have a negative length.

(You could check that this is a maximum by finding $\frac{d^2V}{dx^2}$ when $x = 5$: $\frac{d^2V}{dx^2} = -\frac{27}{2}x = -\frac{135}{2} < 0$)

So the maximum volume is: $V = \frac{(675 \times 5) - (9 \times 5^3)}{4} = \textbf{562.5 cm}^3$

$\frac{d^2V}{dx^2}$ is negative — so it's a maximum.

Using Differentiation

Another example? Coming right up. You want pie in this one? No probl- oh hang on — do you mean pie, or pi?
I'll use both, just to make sure — I wouldn't want you to be disappointed. I really spoil you, don't I...

Example: Ned uses a circular tin to bake his pies in. The tin is t cm high with a d cm diameter. The volume of the pie tin is 1000 cm³.
a) Prove that the surface area of the tin, $A = \frac{\pi}{4}d^2 + \frac{4000}{d}$.
b) Find the minimum surface area.

a) A = area of tin's base + area of tin's curved face = $\pi\left(\frac{d}{2}\right)^2 + (\pi d \times t) = \frac{\pi}{4}d^2 + \pi dt$ This shape is open-topped, so only count the area of the circle once.

You want to get rid of the t, so use the given value of volume to find an expression for t in terms of d:

$$V = \pi\left(\frac{d}{2}\right)^2 t = 1000 \Rightarrow \pi d^2 t = 4000 \Rightarrow t = \frac{4000}{\pi d^2}$$

Substitute your expression for t into the equation for surface area:

$$A = \frac{\pi}{4}d^2 + \left(\pi d \times \frac{4000}{\pi d^2}\right) \Rightarrow A = \frac{\pi}{4}d^2 + \frac{4000}{d} \text{ as required.}$$

b) Differentiate and find the stationary point:

$$\frac{dA}{dd} = \frac{\pi}{2}d - \frac{4000}{d^2} \Rightarrow \frac{\pi}{2}d - \frac{4000}{d^2} = 0 \Rightarrow d^3 = \frac{8000}{\pi} \Rightarrow d = \frac{20}{\sqrt[3]{\pi}}$$

Check it's a minimum: $\frac{d^2A}{dd^2} = \frac{\pi}{2} + \frac{8000}{d^3} = \frac{\pi}{2} + \frac{8000}{\left(\frac{8000}{\pi}\right)} = \frac{3\pi}{2}$ $\frac{d^2A}{dd^2}$ is positive — so it's a minimum.

Calculate the area for this value of d: $A = \frac{\pi}{4}\left(\frac{20}{\sqrt[3]{\pi}}\right)^2 + \left(\frac{4000}{\left(\frac{20}{\sqrt[3]{\pi}}\right)}\right) = \textbf{439 cm}^2$ (3 s.f.)

Practice Questions

Q1 1 litre of water is poured into a bowl. The volume (v) of water in the bowl (in ml) is modelled by the function: $v = 17t^2 + 10t$. Find the rate at which water is poured into the bowl when $t = 4$ seconds.

Q2 The height (h m) a firework can reach is related to the mass (m g) of fuel it carries by: $h = \frac{m^2}{10} - \frac{m^3}{800}$
Find the mass of fuel required to achieve the maximum height and state what the maximum height is.

Exam Questions

Q1 A steam train travels between Haverthwaite and Eskdale at a speed of x miles per hour and burns y units of coal, where y is modelled by: $2\sqrt{x} + \frac{27}{x}$, for $x > 2$.
a) Find the speed that gives the minimum coal consumption. [4 marks]
b) Find $\frac{d^2y}{dx^2}$, and hence show that this speed gives the minimum coal consumption. [2 marks]
c) Calculate the minimum coal consumption. [1 mark]

Q2 Ayesha is building a closed-back bookcase. She uses a total of 72 m² of wood (not including shelving) to make a bookcase that is x metres high, $\frac{x}{2}$ metres wide and d metres deep, as shown.
a) Show that the full capacity of the bookcase is given by: $V = 12x - \frac{x^3}{12}$. [4 marks]
b) Find the value of x for which V is stationary. Leave your answer in surd form. [3 marks]
c) Show that this is a maximum point and hence calculate the maximum V. [4 marks]

All this page has done is maximise my hunger for pie...

I hope I've managed to convince you that differentiation can pop up pretty much anywhere — those cheeky examiners can make a whole question about it without so much as a single 'd'. Don't fall for their evil schemes.

Integrating f(x) = xⁿ

Integration is the 'opposite' of differentiation — and so if you can differentiate, you can be pretty confident you'll be able to integrate too. There's just one extra thing you have to remember — the constant of integration...

The Fundamental Theorem of Calculus

When you differentiate y, you get $\dfrac{dy}{dx}$.

And when you integrate $\dfrac{dy}{dx}$, you get y plus a **constant of integration**.

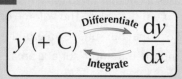

$$y\,(+\,C) \underset{\text{Integrate}}{\overset{\text{Differentiate}}{\rightleftharpoons}} \frac{dy}{dx}$$

You need the constant because there's **More Than One** right answer

When you **integrate** something, you're trying to find a function that differentiates to give what you started with. You add the **constant of integration** to allow for the fact that there's **more than one** possible function that does this...

This means the **integral** of 2x **with respect to** x.

$$\int 2x\,dx = \begin{array}{l} x^2 - 207.253 \\ x^2 - 1 \\ x^2 \\ x^2 + \pi \end{array}$$

If you differentiate any of these functions, you get the thing on the left — they're **all** possible answers.

So the answer to this integral is actually...

$$\int 2x\,dx = x^2 + C$$

The '**C**' just means '**any number**'. This is the **constant of integration**.

You only need to add a constant of integration to **indefinite integrals** like these ones. Definite integrals are just integrals with **limits** (or little numbers) next to the integral sign (see p.60).

Up the power by **One** — then **Divide** by it

The formula below tells you how to integrate **any** power of x (except x^{-1}).

This is an indefinite integral — it doesn't have any limits (numbers) next to the integral sign.

$$\int x^n\,dx = \frac{x^{n+1}}{n+1} + C$$

You can't do this to $\frac{1}{x} = x^{-1}$. When you increase the power by 1 (to get **zero**) you end up dividing by zero — and that's a big problem.

In a nutshell, this says:

> To integrate a power of x: (i)   increase the power by one — then divide by it,
>
> and   (ii)   stick a constant on the end.

Examples: Use the integration formula...

1   **For 'normal' powers**

$$\int x^3\,dx = \frac{x^4}{4} + C$$

Increase the power to 4... ...and then divide by 4.

2   **For negative powers**

$$\int \frac{1}{x^3}\,dx = \int x^{-3}\,dx$$
$$= \frac{x^{-2}}{-2} + C$$
$$= -\frac{1}{2x^2} + C$$

Increase the power by 1 to −2... ...and then divide by −2.

3   **For fractional powers**

$$\int \sqrt[3]{x^4}\,dx = \int x^{\frac{4}{3}}\,dx$$
$$= \frac{x^{\frac{7}{3}}}{(7/3)} + C$$
$$= \frac{3\sqrt[3]{x^7}}{7} + C$$

Add 1 to the power... ...then divide by this new power.

4   **And for complicated looking stuff...**

$$\int \left(3x^2 - \frac{2}{\sqrt{x}} + \frac{7}{x^2}\right) dx = \int \left(3x^2 - 2x^{-\frac{1}{2}} + 7x^{-2}\right) dx$$
$$= \frac{3x^3}{3} - \frac{2x^{\frac{1}{2}}}{(1/2)} + \frac{7x^{-1}}{-1} + C$$
$$= x^3 - 4\sqrt{x} - \frac{7}{x} + C$$

Do each of these bits separately.

CHECK YOUR ANSWERS:
You can check you've integrated properly by **differentiating** the **answer** — you should end up with the thing you started with.

Integrating f(x) = xⁿ

You sometimes need to find the **Value** of the **Constant of Integration**

When they tell you something else about the curve in addition to its derivative, you can work out the value of that **constant of integration**. Usually the something is the **coordinates** of one of the points the curve goes through.

Example: The curve $y = f(x)$ goes through the point (2, 8) and $f'(x) = 6x(x - 1)$. Find $f(x)$.

You know the derivative $f'(x)$ and need to find the function $f(x)$ — so **integrate**.

$$f'(x) = 6x(x - 1) = 6x^2 - 6x$$

So integrating both sides gives...

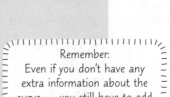
$f'(x)$ is just another way of saying $\frac{dy}{dx}$. So when you integrate $f'(x)$ you get $f(x)$.

$$f(x) = \int (6x^2 - 6x)\, dx$$
$$\Rightarrow\ f(x) = 6\int (x^2 - x)\, dx \quad \text{← 6 is a constant factor of both terms, so you can take it outside the integral.}$$
$$\Rightarrow\ f(x) = 6\left(\frac{x^3}{3} - \frac{x^2}{2} + C\right) \quad \text{← You don't need to write 6C here, as C is just 'some unknown number'.}$$
$$\Rightarrow\ \mathbf{f(x) = 2x^3 - 3x^2 + C}$$

Check this is correct by **differentiating** it and making sure you get what you started with.

$$f(x) = 2x^3 - 3x^2 + C = 2x^3 - 3x^2 + C$$
$$f'(x) = 2(3x^2) - 3(2x^1) + O$$
$$\mathbf{f'(x) = 6x^2 - 6x}$$

A constant always differentiates to zero.

Remember: Even if you don't have any extra information about the curve — you still have to add a constant when you work out an integral without limits.

So this function's got the **correct derivative** — but you now need to **find C**.

You do this using the fact that the curve goes through (2, 8). Putting $x = 2$ and $f(x) = 8$ into the equation above gives:

$$8 = (2 \times 2^3) - (3 \times 2^2) + C$$
$$\Rightarrow 8 = 16 - 12 + C$$
$$\Rightarrow C = 4$$

So the answer you need is this one:

$$\mathbf{f(x) = 2x^3 - 3x^2 + 4}$$

It's a cubic equation — and the graph looks like this...

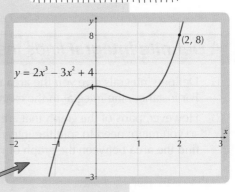
$y = 2x^3 - 3x^2 + 4$

Practice Questions

Q1 Integrate: a) $\int 10x^4\, dx$, b) $\int (3x + 5x^2)\, dx$, c) $\int x^2(3x + 2)\, dx$

Q2 Find the equation of the curve that has derivative $\frac{dy}{dx} = 6x - 7$ and goes through the point (1, 0).

Q3 $f(x)$ passes through (1, 0) and $f'(x) = 3x^3 + 2$. Work out the equation of $f(x)$.

Exam Questions

Q1 a) Show that $(5 + 2\sqrt{x})^2$ can be written in the form $a + b\sqrt{x} + cx$, stating the values of the constants a, b and c. [3 marks]

   b) Hence find $\int (5 + 2\sqrt{x})^2\, dx$. [3 marks]

Q2 Curve C has equation $y = f(x)$, $x \neq 0$, where the derivative is given by $f'(x) = x^3 - \frac{2}{x^2}$. The point P (1, 2) lies on C.

   a) Find an equation for the tangent to C at the point P, giving your answer in the form $y = mx + c$, where m and c are integers. [4 marks]

   b) Find $f(x)$. [4 marks]

Indefinite integrals — joy without limits...

This integration lark isn't so bad then — there are only a couple of things to remember and then you can do it no problem. But that constant of integration catches loads of people out — it's so easy to forget — and you'll definitely lose marks if you do forget it. You have been warned. Other than that, there's not much to it. Hurray.

Definite Integrals

Some integrals have limits (i.e. little numbers) next to the integral sign. You integrate them in exactly the same way — but you don't need a constant of integration. Much easier. And scrummier and yummier too.

Definite Integrals are like regular integrals, but with Limits

Definite integrals are ones that have little numbers on the top and bottom called **limits**. These are the values of x that you're 'integrating between'.

Finding a definite integral isn't really any harder than an indefinite one — there's just an **extra** stage you have to do. After you've integrated the function, you have to work out the value of this new function by **sticking in** the limits, and **subtracting** what the **bottom** limit gave you from what the **top** limit gave you.

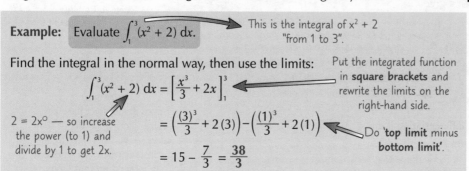

Example: Evaluate $\int_1^3 (x^2 + 2)\, dx$. This is the integral of x² + 2 "from 1 to 3".

Find the integral in the normal way, then use the limits: Put the integrated function in **square brackets** and rewrite the limits on the right-hand side.

$$\int_1^3 (x^2 + 2)\, dx = \left[\frac{x^3}{3} + 2x\right]_1^3$$

$2 = 2x^0$ — so increase the power (to 1) and divide by 1 to get 2x.

$$= \left(\frac{(3)^3}{3} + 2(3)\right) - \left(\frac{(1)^3}{3} + 2(1)\right)$$

Do 'top limit minus bottom limit'.

$$= 15 - \frac{7}{3} = \frac{38}{3}$$

You don't need a constant of integration with a **definite** integral.

"I'm looking for a loan to start my business — Integrals, Ltd."

A Definite Integral finds the Area Under a Curve

1) Definite integrals give you the **area under the graph** of the function you're integrating. For instance, the integral in the example above gives this area:

2) However, parts of the graph that are **below the x-axis** will give a **negative answer**, so you might need to split the integral up into bits. For example, if you wanted to find the area between the graph of $y = x^3$ and the x-axis between $x = -2$ and $x = 2$:

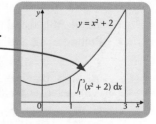

This is the right-hand side of the area you're finding...

$$\int_{-2}^2 x^3\, dx$$

...and this is the left-hand side.

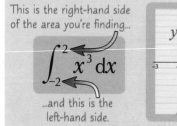

This bit is $\int_0^2 x^3\, dx = 4$. It's **positive** because the area is **above** the x-axis.

This bit is $\int_{-2}^0 x^3\, dx = -4$. It's **negative** because the area is **below** the x-axis.

The value of the integral $\int_{-2}^2 x^3\, dx$ is zero, because the area below the x-axis 'cancels out' the area above. To find the area, you need to work out the two parts **separately** and **add them together**. In this example, the area = 4 + 4 = 8.

Example: The curve $y = (x-2)^2(x+2)$ is shown on the diagram. Find the area bounded by the curve and the x-axis.

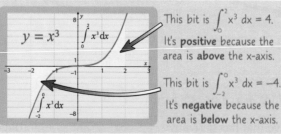

To find the area, you want to integrate $y = (x-2)^2(x+2)$ between -2 and 2.

Expand the brackets: $y = (x^2 - 4x + 4)(x+2) = x^3 - 2x^2 - 4x + 8$

$$A = \int_{-2}^2 y\, dx = \int_{-2}^2 x^3 - 2x^2 - 4x + 8\, dx$$

Integrate each term separately.

$$= \left[\frac{x^4}{4} - \frac{2x^3}{3} - 2x^2 + 8x\right]_{-2}^2$$

$$= \left(\frac{2^4}{4} - \frac{2(2)^3}{3} - 2(2)^2 + 8(2)\right) - \left(\frac{(-2)^4}{4} - \frac{2(-2)^3}{3} - 2(-2)^2 + 8(-2)\right)$$

Stick the limits in.

$$= \frac{20}{3} - -\frac{44}{3}$$

$$= \frac{64}{3}$$

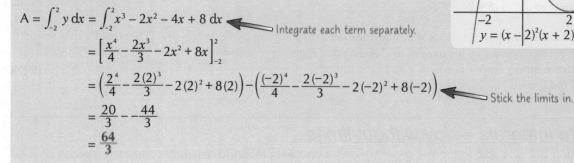

Definite Integrals

Sometimes you have to **Add Two Integrals** together

You could be asked to find "the area enclosed by [a couple of boring old curves] and the *x*-axis".
This might sound pretty hard — until you draw a picture and see what it's all about.
Then it's just a matter of choosing your limits wisely...

Example: Find the area enclosed by the curve $y = x^2$, the line $y = 2 - x$ and the *x*-axis.

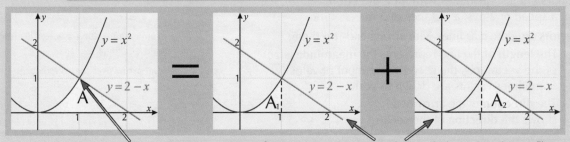

Find out where the graphs meet by **solving** $x^2 = 2 - x$
— they meet at x = 1 (they also meet at x = −2, but this isn't in A).

You have to find area A — but you'll
need to **split** it into two smaller pieces.

It's pretty clear from the picture that you'll have to find the area in two lumps, A_1 and A_2.

The first area you
need to find is A_1:

$$A_1 = \int_0^1 x^2 \, dx$$

$$= \left[\frac{x^3}{3} \right]_0^1 = \left(\frac{1}{3} - 0 \right) = \frac{1}{3}$$

The other area you need is A_2.
A_2 is just a triangle, with base
length 2 − 1 = 1 and height = 1.
So the area of the triangle is:

$$\frac{1}{2} \times b \times h = \frac{1}{2} \times 1 \times 1 = \frac{1}{2}$$

And the area the question
actually asks for is:

$$A = A_1 + A_2$$

$$= \frac{1}{3} + \frac{1}{2} = \frac{5}{6}$$

Practice Questions

Q1 Evaluate the following definite integrals:

a) $\int_0^1 (4x^3 + 3x^2 + 2x + 1) \, dx$

b) $\int_1^2 \left(\frac{8}{x^5} + \frac{3}{\sqrt{x}} \right) dx$

c) $\int_1^6 \frac{3}{x^2} \, dx$.

Q2 a) Evaluate $\int_{-3}^3 (9 - x^2) \, dx$

b) Sketch the area represented by this integral.

Exam Questions

Q1 Find the exact value of $\int_1^4 (2x - 6x^2 + \sqrt{x}) \, dx$. [5 marks]

Q2 The diagram on the right shows a sketch of the curve C, $y = (x - 3)^2(x + 1)$.
Calculate the shaded area between point A, where C intersects
the *x*-axis, and point B, where C touches the *x*-axis. [7 marks]

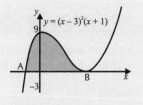

Q3 The curve $y = -(x - 2)^2$ and line $y = \frac{1}{2}x - 6$ are shown on the diagram on the right.

a) Show that the curve and line intersect at the point P (4, −4). [3 marks]

b) Find the shaded area A, bounded by the curve $y = -(x - 2)^2$,
the line $y = \frac{1}{2}x - 6$ and the *x*-axis. [6 marks]

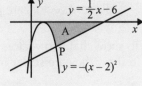

My hobbies? Well, I'm really inte grating. Especially carrots.

*It's still integration — but this time you're putting two numbers into an expression afterwards. So once you've got
the hang of indefinite integration, this definite stuff should easily fall into place. Maths is like that. Though, I admit
it's probably not as much fun as, say, a big banoffee cake. But Maths and cake together? Now we're talking...*

Vectors

You might have seen vectors before at GCSE. If you haven't, no worries, you're in for a treat.
We're going to start with the basics — like what vectors are and how to add them together.

Vectors have **Magnitude** and **Direction** — **Scalars Don't**

1) Vectors have both **size and direction** — e.g. a velocity of 2 m/s
   on a bearing of 050°, or a displacement of 3 m north.
   Scalars are just quantities **without a direction**,
   e.g. a speed of 2 m/s, a distance of 3 m.

2) Vectors are drawn as lines with arrowheads on them.
   - The **length** of the line represents the **magnitude** (size)
     of the vector (e.g. the speed component of velocity).
     Sometimes vectors are drawn **to scale**.
   - The **direction** of the arrowhead
     shows the **direction** of the vector.

There are two ways of writing vectors:
1) Using a lower case, bold letter.

When you're handwriting a vector like this,
you should underline the letter, i.e. a̱.

2) Putting an arrow over the endpoints.

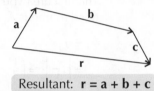

*Two vectors that have
the **same** magnitude
and direction are **equal**.*

Find the **Resultant** by Drawing Vectors **Nose to Tail**

You can add vectors together by drawing the arrows **nose to tail**.
The single vector that goes from the start to the end of the vectors is called the **resultant** vector.

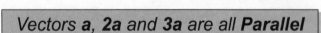

a + b　　　Resultant: **r = a + b**　　　**a + b = b + a**　　　Resultant: **r = a + b + c**

Subtracting a Vector is the Same as Adding a Negative Vector

1) The vector **–a** is in the **opposite direction** to the vector **a**. They're both the **same size**.

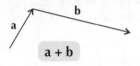

2) So **subtracting a vector** is the same
   as **adding the negative vector**: ➡ $\mathbf{b} - \mathbf{a} = \mathbf{b} + (-\mathbf{a})$

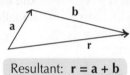

3) You can use the adding and
   subtracting rules to find a vector
   in terms of other vectors.

Example: Find $\overrightarrow{WZ}$ and $\overrightarrow{ZX}$ in terms of **p, q** and **r**.

$\overrightarrow{WZ} = -\mathbf{p} + \mathbf{q} - \mathbf{r}$ 　　 $\overrightarrow{ZX} = \mathbf{r} - \mathbf{q}$

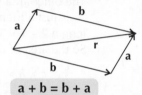

Vectors **a**, **2a** and **3a** are all **Parallel**

You can **multiply** a vector by a **scalar** (just a number, remember)
— the **length changes** but the **direction stays the same**.

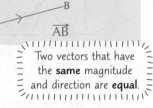

Multiplying a vector by a non-zero scalar always produces a **parallel vector**.

All these vectors are **parallel**:　　$9\mathbf{a} + 15\mathbf{b}$　　$-18\mathbf{a} - 30\mathbf{b}$　　$6\mathbf{a} + 10\mathbf{b}$　◀

This is $\frac{2}{3}(9\mathbf{a} + 15\mathbf{b})$.

This is $-2(9\mathbf{a} + 15\mathbf{b})$.

To show that two vectors are **parallel**, you just need
to show they are **scalar multiples** of each other.

Example: 　$\overrightarrow{CA} = \mathbf{v}$, $\overrightarrow{CB} = \mathbf{u}$. P divides $\overrightarrow{CA}$ in the ratio 1:2, Q divides $\overrightarrow{CB}$
　　　　　in the ratio 1:2. Show that $\overrightarrow{PQ}$ is parallel to $\overrightarrow{AB}$.

$\overrightarrow{AB} = -\mathbf{v} + \mathbf{u}$. P divides $\overrightarrow{CA}$ in the ratio 1:2 so P is one third of the way along $\overrightarrow{CA}$.
This means $\overrightarrow{CP} = \frac{1}{3}\mathbf{v}$, so $\overrightarrow{PC} = -\frac{1}{3}\mathbf{v}$. Similarly, $\overrightarrow{CQ} = \frac{1}{3}\mathbf{u}$.
So, $\overrightarrow{PQ} = -\frac{1}{3}\mathbf{v} + \frac{1}{3}\mathbf{u} = \frac{1}{3}(-\mathbf{v} + \mathbf{u}) = \frac{1}{3}\overrightarrow{AB}$. This shows that $\overrightarrow{PQ}$ is parallel to $\overrightarrow{AB}$.

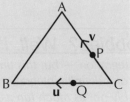

Vectors

Position Vectors Describe Where a Point Lies

You can use a vector to describe the **position of a point**, in relation to the **origin, O**.

The position vector of point A is $\overrightarrow{OA}$. It's usually called vector **a**.
The position vector of point B is $\overrightarrow{OB}$. It's usually called vector **b**.

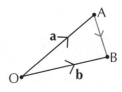

You can write other vectors in terms of position vectors: $\quad \overrightarrow{AB} = -\overrightarrow{OA} + \overrightarrow{OB} = \overrightarrow{OB} - \overrightarrow{OA} = -\mathbf{a} + \mathbf{b} = \mathbf{b} - \mathbf{a}$

Vectors can be described using i and j Units or Column Vectors

1) A **unit vector** is any vector with a **magnitude of 1 unit**.

2) The vectors **i** and **j** are **standard unit vectors**. **i** is in the direction of the **x-axis**, and **j** is in the direction of the **y-axis**. They each have a magnitude of **1 unit**.

3) You use them to say how far **horizontally** and **vertically** you have to go to get from the start of the vector to the end.

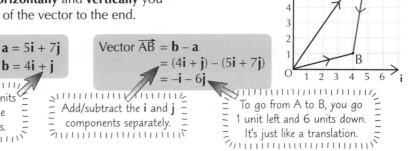

The position vector of point A = **a** = 5**i** + 7**j**
The position vector of point B = **b** = 4**i** + **j**

This tells you that point B lies 4 units to the right and 1 unit above the origin — it's just like coordinates.

Vector $\overrightarrow{AB}$ = **b** – **a**
= (4**i** + **j**) – (5**i** + 7**j**)
= –**i** – 6**j**

*Add/subtract the **i** and **j** components separately.*

To go from A to B, you go 1 unit left and 6 units down. It's just like a translation.

4) Column vectors are a really easy way of writing out vectors.

$$x\mathbf{i} + y\mathbf{j} = \begin{pmatrix} x \\ y \end{pmatrix}$$

5) **Calculating** with them is a breeze. Just add or subtract the **top row**, then add or subtract the **bottom row** separately.

6) When you're **multiplying** a column vector by a **scalar**, you multiply **each number** in the column vector by the scalar.

$$\mathbf{a} = 5\mathbf{i} + 7\mathbf{j} = \begin{pmatrix} 5 \\ 7 \end{pmatrix} \qquad \mathbf{b} = 4\mathbf{i} + \mathbf{j} = \begin{pmatrix} 4 \\ 1 \end{pmatrix}$$

$$\overrightarrow{AB} = \mathbf{b} - \mathbf{a} = \begin{pmatrix} 4 \\ 1 \end{pmatrix} - \begin{pmatrix} 5 \\ 7 \end{pmatrix} = \begin{pmatrix} -1 \\ -6 \end{pmatrix}$$

$$2\mathbf{b} - 3\mathbf{a} = 2\begin{pmatrix} 4 \\ 1 \end{pmatrix} - 3\begin{pmatrix} 5 \\ 7 \end{pmatrix} = \begin{pmatrix} 8 \\ 2 \end{pmatrix} - \begin{pmatrix} 15 \\ 21 \end{pmatrix} = \begin{pmatrix} -7 \\ -19 \end{pmatrix}$$

Practice Questions

Q1 Using the diagram on the right, find these vectors in terms of vectors **a**, **b** and **c**:
   a) $\overrightarrow{AB}$ b) $\overrightarrow{BA}$ c) $\overrightarrow{CB}$ d) $\overrightarrow{AC}$

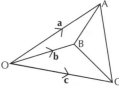

Q2 Give the position vector of point P, which has the coordinates (2, –4). Give your answer in unit vector form.

Q3 Given that vectors **a** and **b** have position vectors $\begin{pmatrix} 3 \\ -4 \end{pmatrix}$ and $\begin{pmatrix} -2 \\ -1 \end{pmatrix}$ respectively, what is $3\mathbf{a} - 2\mathbf{b}$?

Exam Questions

Q1 The points W, X and Y have position vectors $\begin{pmatrix} 1 \\ 3 \end{pmatrix}$, $\begin{pmatrix} -2 \\ 1 \end{pmatrix}$ and $\begin{pmatrix} 5 \\ 4 \end{pmatrix}$ respectively.
Find the position vector of Z such that $\overrightarrow{WX} = \overrightarrow{YZ}$.   [3 marks]

Q2 The points A and B have position vectors –2**i** + 4**j** and 5**i** + **j** respectively.
Point P is on the line AB such that AP : PB = 1 : 3. Determine the position vector of P.   [4 marks]

I've got B and Q units in my kitchen...

If you're asked to show that two vectors are parallel, remember that this is the same as showing they are scalar multiples of each other. So, just show that you can write one as the other multiplied by a scalar and you're laughing.

More Vectors

The magnitude of a vector is its length. The direction of a vector is the angle that the vector makes with the horizontal axis. I know that you're oh so eager to know how to calculate these, so without further ado...

Use **Pythagoras' Theorem** to Find Vector **Magnitudes**

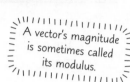

A vector's magnitude is sometimes called its modulus.

1) The **magnitude** of vector **a** is written as $|\mathbf{a}|$, and the magnitude of $\overrightarrow{AB}$ is written as $|\overrightarrow{AB}|$.

2) The **i** and **j** components of a vector form a **right-angled triangle**, so you can use the **Pythagoras formula** to find a vector's magnitude.

3) You might be asked to find a **unit vector** in the direction of a particular vector.

A unit vector in the direction of vector $\mathbf{a} = \dfrac{\mathbf{a}}{|\mathbf{a}|}$

Remember — a unit vector has a magnitude of 1 (see the previous page).

> **Example:** Find the unit vector in the direction of $\mathbf{a} = 5\mathbf{i} + 3\mathbf{j}$.
>
> First find the magnitude of **a**:
>
> $|\mathbf{a}| = \sqrt{5^2 + 3^2} = \sqrt{34} = 5.83...$
>
> So, the unit vector is:
>
> $\dfrac{\mathbf{a}}{|\mathbf{a}|} = \dfrac{\mathbf{a}}{\sqrt{34}} = \dfrac{1}{\sqrt{34}}(5\mathbf{i} + 3\mathbf{j})$

Resolving Means Writing a Vector as **Component Vectors**

1) Splitting a vector up into **i** and **j** vectors means you can work things out with **one component at a time**. When **adding** vectors to get a **resultant vector**, it's easier to **add** the **horizontal** and **vertical** components **separately**.

2) So you **split** the vector into components first — this is called **resolving the vector**.

3) You use a combination of **trig** and **Pythagoras' theorem** to **resolve** a vector into its **component form**.

> **Example:** A ball is travelling at 5 ms⁻¹ at an angle of 30° to the horizontal. Find the horizontal and vertical components of the ball's velocity, **v**.
>
> First, draw a diagram and make a right-angled triangle:
>
> Use trigonometry to find x and y:
>
> $\cos 30° = \dfrac{x}{5} \Rightarrow x = 5 \cos 30°$
>
> $\sin 30° = \dfrac{y}{5} \Rightarrow y = 5 \sin 30°$
>
> So $\mathbf{v} = (5 \cos 30°\mathbf{i} + 5 \sin 30°\mathbf{j}) \text{ ms}^{-1} = \left(\dfrac{5\sqrt{3}}{2}\mathbf{i} + \dfrac{5}{2}\mathbf{j}\right) \text{ ms}^{-1}$

Victor and Hector decided to resolve this the old-fashioned way...

4) The **direction** of a vector is usually measured going **anticlockwise** from the **positive x-axis**. Give the direction in this form unless the question implies otherwise (e.g. if the direction is a bearing).

> **Example:** The acceleration of a body is given by the vector $\mathbf{a} = 6\mathbf{i} - 2\mathbf{j}$ ms⁻². Find the magnitude and direction of the acceleration.
>
> Start with a diagram again. Remember, the y-component "–2" means "down 2".
>
> Using Pythagoras' theorem, you can work out the magnitude of **a**:
>
> $|\mathbf{a}|^2 = 6^2 + (-2)^2 = 40 \Rightarrow |\mathbf{a}| = \sqrt{40} = \mathbf{6.32} \text{ ms}^{-2}$ (3 s.f.)
>
> Use trigonometry to work out the angle:
>
> $\tan \theta = \dfrac{2}{6} \Rightarrow \theta = \tan^{-1}\left(\dfrac{2}{6}\right) = \mathbf{18.4°}$ (1 d.p.)
>
> So the direction of **a** is $360° - 18.4° = \mathbf{341.6°}$ (1 d.p.)
>
> So vector **a** has magnitude **6.32 ms⁻²** (3 s.f.) and direction **341.6°** (1 d.p.).

The angle $\theta = \tan^{-1}\dfrac{y}{x}$ and the direction are often different — drawing a diagram can help you figure out what's what.

In general, a vector with magnitude r and direction θ can be written as $r \cos \theta\, \mathbf{i} + r \sin \theta\, \mathbf{j}$.

The vector $x\mathbf{i} + y\mathbf{j}$ has magnitude $r = \sqrt{x^2 + y^2}$ and makes an angle of $\theta = \tan^{-1}\left(\dfrac{y}{x}\right)$ with the horizontal.

More Vectors

Use a *Vector's Magnitude* to Find the *Distance Between Two Points*

You can calculate the **distance between two points** by finding the **vector** between them, and then using **Pythagoras' Theorem** to calculate its **magnitude**.

> **Example:** The position vectors of points A and B are $4\mathbf{i} - 2\mathbf{j}$ and $2\mathbf{i} + 5\mathbf{j}$ respectively. Calculate the distance between points A and B to 2 decimal places.
>
>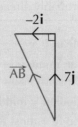
>
> Find the vector $\overrightarrow{AB}$ between the points.
> $\overrightarrow{AB} = 2\mathbf{i} + 5\mathbf{j} - (4\mathbf{i} - 2\mathbf{j}) = (2 - 4)\mathbf{i} + (5 - (-2))\mathbf{j} = -2\mathbf{i} + 7\mathbf{j}$.
> Draw a diagram, and then calculate the magnitude of $\overrightarrow{AB}$ using Pythagoras' theorem.
> $|\overrightarrow{AB}| = \sqrt{(-2)^2 + 7^2} = \sqrt{53}$ so the distance between points A and B is **7.28** (2 d.p.).

Use the *Cosine Rule* to Find the *Angle Between Two Vectors*

The angle between two vectors **a** and **b** can be calculated by constructing a triangle with **a** and **b** as two of its sides. First, calculate the **magnitude** of these vectors, then use the **cosine rule** (see p.36) to find the angle between them.

> **Example:** Find the angle θ between the vectors $\overrightarrow{PQ} = 3\mathbf{i} - \mathbf{j}$ and $\overrightarrow{PR} = -\mathbf{i} + 4\mathbf{j}$.
>
>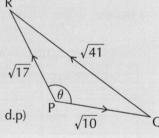
>
> The side lengths of the triangle PQR are: $\overrightarrow{QR} = \overrightarrow{PR} - \overrightarrow{PQ} = -\mathbf{i} + 4\mathbf{j} - (3\mathbf{i} - \mathbf{j}) = -4\mathbf{i} + 5\mathbf{j}$
> $|\overrightarrow{PQ}| = \sqrt{3^2 + (-1)^2} = \sqrt{10}$, $|\overrightarrow{PR}| = \sqrt{(-1)^2 + 4^2} = \sqrt{17}$ and $|\overrightarrow{QR}| = \sqrt{(-4)^2 + 5^2} = \sqrt{41}$
> Use the cosine rule to find angle θ:
> $\cos\theta = \dfrac{(\sqrt{10})^2 + (\sqrt{17})^2 - (\sqrt{41})^2}{2 \times \sqrt{17} \times \sqrt{10}} = \dfrac{-14}{2\sqrt{170}} = \dfrac{-7}{\sqrt{170}}$, so: $\theta = \cos^{-1}\left(\dfrac{-7}{\sqrt{170}}\right) = $ **122.5°** (1 d.p)

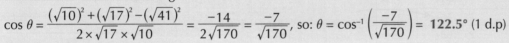

Practice Questions

Q1 Find the unit vector in the direction of $\mathbf{q} = -2\mathbf{i} + 5\mathbf{j}$.

Q2 If A = (1, 2) and B = (3, –1), find: a) $|\overrightarrow{OA}|$ b) $|\overrightarrow{OB}|$ c) $|\overrightarrow{AB}|$

Q3 A vector **s** has a magnitude of 7 and direction 20° above the horizontal. Write **s** in the form $a\mathbf{i} + b\mathbf{j}$.

Q4 The velocity of a ball is modelled with the vector $\mathbf{v} = -\mathbf{i} + 3\mathbf{j}$. Calculate the direction of the vector **v**.

Q5 The position vector of point X is $\begin{pmatrix} 7 \\ -1 \end{pmatrix}$, the position vector of point Y is $\begin{pmatrix} 3 \\ 2 \end{pmatrix}$. Calculate the distance between points X and Y. Hence find the angle between vectors $\overrightarrow{OX}$ and $\overrightarrow{OY}$.

Exam Questions

Q1 The following sketch shows a triangle ABC. M is the midpoint of line BC. Given that $\overrightarrow{AB} = -5\mathbf{i} + 2\mathbf{j}$ and $\overrightarrow{AC} = -2\mathbf{i} + 4\mathbf{j}$, find $|\overrightarrow{AM}|$.

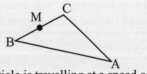

[3 marks]

Q2 a) The movement of a particle is modelled by vector **p**. The particle is travelling at a speed of 7 m/s with direction of 15° above the horizontal. Write **p** in component form. [2 marks]

b) The particle strikes another particle. Its movement is now modelled by vector $\mathbf{q} = 2\sqrt{2}(\mathbf{i} + \mathbf{j})$. Find the amount by which the particle's speed has decreased and state the particle's new direction. [3 marks]

Q3 Points S, T, U and V make a parallelogram, STUV. The position vectors of S, T and V are $\mathbf{i} + \mathbf{j}$, $8\mathbf{i} + \mathbf{j}$ and $-\mathbf{i} + 5\mathbf{j}$ respectively. Find the distance between S and U. Leave your answer in exact surd form. [4 marks]

I don't think you've quite grasped the magnitude of the situation...

The magnitude is just a scalar, which means it doesn't have a direction — i.e. $|\overrightarrow{AB}| = |\overrightarrow{BA}|$. Squaring the numbers gets rid of any minus signs, so it doesn't make any difference which way round you subtract the coordinates. Superb.

Central Tendency and Variation

The mean, median and mode are measures of central tendency or location (roughly speaking, where the centre of the data lies). Then there's the variance and standard deviation, which measure variation and- hey, don't fall asleep...

The **Definitions** are really GCSE stuff

You probably already know these measures of **central tendency**, so learn them now — you'll be needing them loads.

> **Mean** $= \bar{x} = \frac{\Sigma x}{n}$ or $\frac{\Sigma fx}{\Sigma f}$ where each x is a **data value**, f is the **frequency** of each x (the number of times it occurs), and n is the **total number** of data values.
> Σ (sigma) means 'add stuff up' — so Σx means 'add up all the values of x'.
> **Median** = **middle** data value when all the data values are placed **in order of size**.
> **Mode** = **most frequently occurring** data value.

If n is **even**, the **median** is the **average of the middle two values** (the $\frac{n}{2}$th and the $\left(\frac{n}{2}+1\right)$th values).

If n is **odd**, the **median** is the **middle value** (round up $\frac{n}{2}$ to find its position).

Use a **Table** when there are a lot of **Numbers**

Example: The number of letters received one day in 100 houses was recorded. Find the mean, median and mode of the number of letters.

No. of letters	No. of houses
0	11
1	25
2	27
3	21
4	9
5	7

The first thing to do is make a **table** like this one:

No. of letters (x)	No. of houses (f)	fx
0	11 (11)	0
1	25 (36)	25
2	27 (63)	54
3	21	63
4	9	36
5	7	35
Totals	100	213

— Multiply x by f to get this column.

— Put the running total in brackets — it's handy when you're finding the median (but you can stop when you get past halfway).

$\Sigma f = 100$

$\Sigma fx = 213$

The number of letters received by each house is a discrete quantity (e.g. 3 letters). There isn't a continuous set of possible values between getting 3 and 4 letters (e.g. 3.45 letters).

1. Use the totals of the columns to find the mean: **mean** $= \frac{\Sigma fx}{\Sigma f} = \frac{213}{100} = $ **2.13 letters**

2. $\frac{n}{2} = \frac{100}{2} = 50$, so the median is **halfway between** the 50th and 51st data values.
   The **running total** of f shows that the data values in positions 37 to 63 are all 2s.
   This includes positions 50 and 51, so the **median = 2 letters**

3. The **highest frequency** is for 2 letters — so the **mode = 2 letters**

The mean number of letters received increased after this couple moved into the street.

The **Standard Deviation Formulas** look pretty **Tricky**

Standard deviation and **variance** both measure **variation** — i.e. how **spread out** the data is from the mean. The bigger the variance, the more spread out your readings are.

> **Variance** $= \dfrac{\Sigma(x-\bar{x})^2}{n}$ or $\dfrac{\Sigma x^2}{n} - \bar{x}^2$ or $\dfrac{\Sigma fx^2}{\Sigma f} - \bar{x}^2$
>
> **Standard deviation** $= \sqrt{\text{variance}}$

The x-values are the data, $\bar{x}$ is the mean, f is the frequency of each x, and n is the number of data values.

Make sure you're comfortable with these formulas and the versions in the formula booklet (see p.130).

You might see S_{xx} used instead of $\Sigma(x - \bar{x})^2$.

Example: Find the mean and standard deviation of the following numbers: 2, 3, 4, 4, 6, 11, 12

Find the total of the numbers first:

$\Sigma x = 2 + 3 + 4 + 4 + 6 + 11 + 12 = 42$

Then the mean is easy:

mean $= \bar{x} = \frac{\Sigma x}{n} = \frac{42}{7} = 6$

Next find the sum of the squares:

$\Sigma x^2 = 4 + 9 + 16 + 16 + 36 + 121 + 144 = 346$

Use this to find the variance:

Variance $= \frac{\Sigma x^2}{n} - \bar{x}^2 = \frac{346}{7} - 6^2 = 49.428... - 36 = 13.428...$

Take the square root to find the standard deviation:

Standard deviation $= \sqrt{13.428...} = $ **3.66** (3 s.f.)

Central Tendency and Variation

Questions about Standard Deviation can look a bit Weird

They can ask questions about standard deviation in different ways. But you just need to use the same old formulas.

Example: The mean of 10 boys' heights is 180 cm, and the standard deviation is 10 cm.
The mean for 9 girls is 165 cm, and the standard deviation is 8 cm.
Find the mean and standard deviation of the whole group of 19 girls and boys.

Let the boys' heights be x and the girls' heights be y.

Write down the formula for the mean and put the numbers in for the boys: $\bar{x} = \frac{\Sigma x}{n} \Rightarrow 180 = \frac{\Sigma x}{10} \Rightarrow \Sigma x = 1800$

Do the same for the girls: $165 = \frac{\Sigma y}{9} \Rightarrow \Sigma y = 1485$

So the sum of the heights for the boys and the girls $= \Sigma x + \Sigma y = 1800 + 1485 = 3285$

And the **mean height** of the boys and the girls is: $\frac{3285}{19} = $ **172.9 cm** (1 d.p.)

Round the fraction to give your answer. But if you need to use the mean in more calculations, use the fraction (or your calculator's memory) so you don't lose accuracy.

Now for the **variance**.

Write down the formula for the boys first:

$10^2 = \frac{\Sigma x^2}{n} - \bar{x}^2 \Rightarrow 10^2 = \frac{\Sigma x^2}{10} - 180^2 \Rightarrow \Sigma x^2 = 10 \times (100 + 32\,400) = 325\,000$

Do the same for the girls:

$8^2 = \frac{\Sigma y^2}{n} - \bar{y}^2 \Rightarrow 8^2 = \frac{\Sigma y^2}{9} - 165^2 \Rightarrow \Sigma y^2 = 9 \times (64 + 27\,225) = 245\,601$

So the sum of the squares of the heights of the boys and the girls is: $\Sigma x^2 + \Sigma y^2 = 325\,000 + 245\,601 = 570\,601$

Don't use the rounded mean (172.9) — you'll lose accuracy.

The **variance** of all the heights is: $\frac{570\,601}{19} - \left(\frac{3285}{19}\right)^2 = 139.041... \text{ cm}^2$

The **standard deviation** of all the heights is: $\sqrt{139.041...} = $ **11.8 cm** (3 s.f.)

The standard deviation uses the same units as the mean, so the units for the variance must be squared.

Practice Questions

Q1 Calculate the mean, median and mode of the data in the table on the right.

x	0	1	2	3	4
f	5	4	4	2	1

Q2 Find the mean and standard deviation of the following numbers:
11, 12, 14, 17, 21, 23, 27

Q3 The scores from 50 reviews of a product are recorded in the table below.

Score	1	2	3	4	5
Frequency	6	11	22	9	2

Calculate the mean and variance of the data.

For Q3, add rows for fx and fx². Then use the third variance formula given on the previous page.

Q4 a) The mean, $\bar{x}$, of a set of six numbers is 85.5. Find the value of Σx.
b) One more data value is added to the set. The new mean is 84.9. Find the data value that was added.

Exam Question

Q1 In a supermarket, two types of chocolate drops were compared.
The weights, a grams, of 20 chocolate drops of brand A are summarised by: $\Sigma a = 60.3$ g, $\Sigma a^2 = 219$ g²
The mean weight of 30 chocolate drops of brand B was 2.95 g, and the standard deviation was 1 g.
a) Find the mean weight of a brand A chocolate drop. [1 mark]
b) Find the standard deviation of the weight of the brand A chocolate drops. [2 marks]
c) Compare the weights of chocolate drops from brands A and B. [2 marks]
d) Find the standard deviation of the weight of all 50 chocolate drops. [4 marks]

People who enjoy this stuff are standard deviants...

You don't always need to find values like Σx^2 or Σfx — sometimes they're given in exam questions. Your calculator can probably find the mean and standard deviation of a data set too. But you also need to understand the formulas, so make sure you can do these calculations by hand — you could easily get asked to show your working.

Displaying Data

Data can be shown on lots of different charts and graphs. The ones you need to know for this course are shown on the next few pages. You've probably seen a fair few of them before, so they should be bread and butter by now.

Data can be represented Graphically

Bar charts, **dot plots** and **vertical line charts** are all simple ways to show how data is distributed.

15 people were given a blind taste test of four drinks, labelled A, B, C and D, then asked which was their favourite. The number of people who voted for each drink is shown on the diagrams below.

Dot plot:

Each dot represents 1 vote, so 4 people voted for D.

For a large amount of data, drawing dots would be inconvenient, so a bar chart might be more appropriate.

Bar chart:

Vertical line charts are like bar charts, but using lines instead of bars (as you might expect).

Stem and Leaf Diagrams show all the data

Stem and leaf diagrams are another way to represent data — the diagrams show the data values themselves. Each data value is split into a '**stem**' and a '**leaf**'. A complete stem and leaf diagram looks something like this:

This stem and leaf diagram shows the ages of readers of the Daily Pry newspaper.

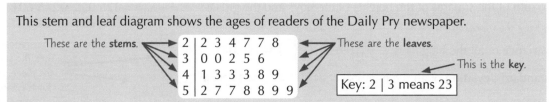

These are the **stems**.

```
2 | 2 3 4 7 7 8
3 | 0 0 2 5 6
4 | 1 3 3 3 8 9
5 | 2 7 7 8 8 9 9
```

These are the **leaves**.

This is the **key**.

Key: 2 | 3 means 23

A stem and leaf diagram always needs a **key** to tell you how to read it. So, in the stem and leaf diagram above, the **first row** represents the values **22, 23, 24, 27, 27,** and **28**, while the **second row** represents the values **30, 30, 32, 35** and **36**. You can read the other two rows in a similar way.

You can show Two Data Sets on a Back-To-Back stem and leaf diagram

Two stem and leaf diagrams can be drawn either side of the same stem — i.e. **back-to-back**. The data on the left hand side of the stem is read '**backwards**' — because the stems are on the right of the leaves.

Example: a) Draw a back-to-back stem and leaf diagram to represent the following data:

Boys' test marks: 50, 20, 18, 38, 34, 19, 8, 44, 15, 32, 9, 19, 41, 26, 22
Girls' test marks: 36, 24, 42, 46, 35, 12, 38, 45, 31, 38, 21, 43, 37, 27, 29, 46

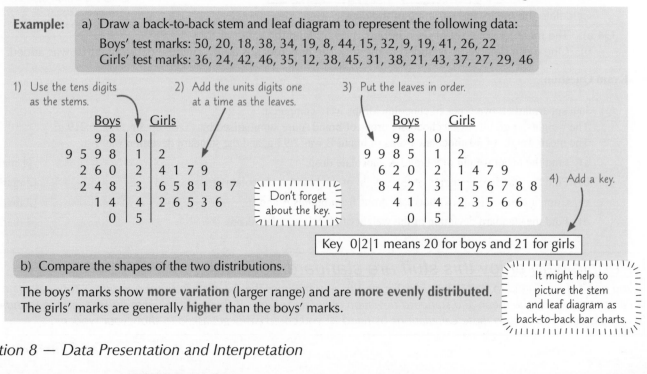

1) Use the tens digits as the stems.

2) Add the units digits one at a time as the leaves.

3) Put the leaves in order.

```
 Boys      Girls            Boys        Girls
  9 8 | 0 |                  9 8 | 0 |
9 5 9 8 | 1 | 2          9 9 8 5 | 1 | 2
  2 6 0 | 2 | 4 1 7 9      6 2 0 | 2 | 1 4 7 9
  2 4 8 | 3 | 6 5 8 1 8 7    8 4 2 | 3 | 1 5 6 7 8 8
    1 4 | 4 | 2 6 5 3 6        4 1 | 4 | 2 3 5 6 6
      0 | 5 |                    0 | 5 |
```

Don't forget about the key.

4) Add a key.

Key 0|2|1 means 20 for boys and 21 for girls

b) Compare the shapes of the two distributions.

The boys' marks show **more variation** (larger range) and are **more evenly distributed**. The girls' marks are generally **higher** than the boys' marks.

It might help to picture the stem and leaf diagram as back-to-back bar charts.

Displaying Data

From a stem and leaf diagram you could be asked to find measures of central tendency (e.g. mean, median, mode).

> **Example:** For the test marks data on the previous page, find:
> a) the mode of the boys' marks,
> b) the median of the boys' marks and the median of the girls' marks. Compare your answers.
>
> a) All the data values for the boys' data appear once except 19, which appears twice — so **mode = 19**.
>
> b) boys' data: there are 15 values, so the median is the 8th value — so **median = 22**.
>
>   girls' data: there are 16 values, so the median is halfway between the 8th and 9th values
>   — so **median** = (36 + 37) ÷ 2 = **36.5**
>
> The median of the girls' data is **higher** than the median of the boys' data,
> which suggests that girls scored higher in the test than boys.

Histograms show Frequency Density

Histograms are glorified bar charts. The main difference is that you plot the **frequency density** rather than the frequency. Frequency density = **frequency ÷ class width**.

The **area** of a bar (**not** its height) represents the **frequency**.

To get histograms right, you have to use the right **upper and lower boundaries** to find each class width (see p.70).

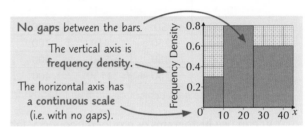

Practice Questions

Q1 a) Draw a vertical line chart for the data below:

Rating (1-5)	1	2	3	4	5
Frequency	2	4	9	5	1

   b) Find the mode of the data.

   c) Comment on the distribution of the data.

Q2 Draw a stem and leaf diagram to represent the data below:
   Class attendance (%): 89, 92, 90, 95, 100, 85, 77, 87, 95, 98

Vinnie was a talented
stem and leaf drawer.

Q3 Find the frequency density in the following cases:
   a) frequency = 25, class width = 10,   b) frequency = 33, class width = 15.

Exam Questions

Q1 The number of runs scored by two cricketers, in 10 matches, are shown below.

Cricketer A: 50, 32, 17, 45, 0, 26, 3, 50, 15, 12
Cricketer B: 27, 22, 33, 34, 38, 44, 41, 17, 20, 31

   a) Draw a back-to-back stem and leaf diagram to represent the data.   [2 marks]
   b) Find the median number of runs scored by both cricketers.   [2 marks]

Q2 The stem and leaf diagram shows the ages at which 30 men and 16 women became grandparents.

<table>
<tr><td align="right">Men</td><td></td><td align="left">Women</td></tr>
<tr><td align="right">8, 3, 3</td><td>4</td><td></td></tr>
<tr><td align="right">8, 7, 7, 7, 5, 3, 2</td><td>5</td><td>5, 6, 7</td></tr>
<tr><td align="right">9, 7, 6, 6, 5, 5, 2, 2, 1, 1, 0</td><td>6</td><td>1, 2, 3, 3, 4, 5, 6, 7, 9</td></tr>
<tr><td align="right">9, 9, 8, 5, 4, 3, 1, 0, 0</td><td>7</td><td>2, 4, 8, 9</td></tr>
</table>

Key: 5 | 6 | 2 means a man who became a grandfather at 65 and a woman who became a grandmother at 62.

   a) Find the median age for the men.   [1 mark]
   b) Compare the distribution of the two data sets.   [2 marks]

Time to make like a stem and leaf diagram and leave...

...but read these last few notices first. You can tell a lot about central tendency and variation from the shape of a distribution. And don't worry if you're a bit unsure on histograms, they're covered in more detail on the next page.

Grouped Data

Sometimes, some helpful person will put a set of data into groups for you. Which isn't always actually very helpful...

To draw a **Histogram** find the **Frequency Density**

Histograms can be drawn for **continuous** data that is **grouped** into 'classes'. As you saw on page 69, you need to plot the **frequency density**, which is found using: frequency density = **frequency ÷ class width**.

Example: Draw a histogram to represent the data in this table, showing the masses of parcels.

Mass (to nearest 100 g)	100-200	300-400	500-700	800-1100
Number of parcels	100	250	600	50

First draw a table showing the **upper and lower class boundaries**, plus the **frequency density**:

Smallest mass of parcel that will go **in that class**.
Biggest mass that will go **in that class**.

Mass of parcel (to nearest 100 g)	Lower class boundary (lcb)	Upper class boundary (ucb)	Class width = ucb − lcb	Frequency	Freq. density = frequency ÷ class width
100-200	50	250	200	100	0.5
300-400	250	450	200	250	1.25
500-700	450	750	300	600	2
800-1100	750	1150	400	50	0.125

Look — no gaps between each ucb and the next lcb.

Now you can draw the histogram:

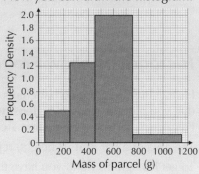

You can use **histograms** or grouped frequency tables to **estimate** the number of readings in a **given range**.

Example: Estimate the number of readings above $x = 20$ on the histogram on the right.

The **area** of the bar is the **total frequency** for that class. You're interested in the **last third** of the class 10–25, and the whole of the class 25–45, so add those two areas:

$$(15 \times 0.8) \div 3 + 20 \times 0.6 = \mathbf{16}$$

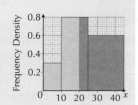

You can also show grouped data on a **frequency polygon**. For each class, plot the **class midpoint** against the **frequency**, then join the points with **straight lines**.

This is a frequency polygon for the parcels data above:

(600, 600)
(350, 250)
(150, 100) (950, 50)

Mass of parcel (g)

For some people, studying histograms is always a classy affair.

If the data's **Grouped** you can **Estimate** the **Mean**

For **grouped data**, you can't find the mean, median or mode **exactly**. You have to estimate them instead.

Example: The data in this table represents the heights of a number of trees. Estimate the mean of these heights.

Height (to nearest m)	0-5	6-10	11-15	16-20
Number of trees	26	17	11	6

Here, you assume that every reading in a class takes the **class midpoint** (which you find by adding the **lower class boundary** to the **upper class boundary** and **dividing by 2**). It's best to make another table...

Height (to nearest m)	Class midpoint (x)	Number of trees (f)	fx
0-5	2.75	26 (26)	71.5
6-10	8	17 (43)	136
11-15	13	11	143
16-20	18	6	108
Totals		60 (= Σf)	458.5 (= Σfx)

Lower class boundary = 0
Upper class boundary = 5.5
So the mid-class value
= (0 + 5.5) ÷ 2 = 2.75

Estimated mean = $\dfrac{458.5}{60}$
= **7.64 m** (3 s.f.)

I've added running totals here — you don't need them for this question, but trust me, they'll come in handy over the next couple of pages...

With grouped data you can't find the mode — only the **modal class**. If all the classes are the **same width**, this is the class with the **highest frequency**. If the classes have different widths, it's the class with the **highest frequency density**. In this example, the modal class is **0-5 m**.

Grouped Data

To **Estimate** the **Median** of Grouped Data, use **Linear Interpolation**

Linear interpolation works by assuming the readings in each class are **evenly spread**.
Here's how you use it to estimate the **median**:

1) Find $n \div 2$ (the position of the median), and work out which class the median falls in.
2) For the class the median is in, the estimated median is:

lcb of class + width of class × $\dfrac{\text{position of median} - \text{number of frequencies before class}}{\text{number of readings in class}}$

You can just use n ÷ 2 here for any n — don't worry about the rules on p.66 in this case.

> **Example:** Using the data from the previous example, estimate the median height of the trees.
>
> $n \div 2 = 60 \div 2 = 30$, so the 'running total' tells you the median must be in the '**6-10**' class.
> For the class 6-10, the lcb is 5.5 and the ucb is 10.5 so the width of the class is $10.5 - 5.5 = 5$.
>
> position of median = n ÷ 2   26 values before the class 6–10
> So **estimated median** $= 5.5 + 5 \times \dfrac{30-26}{17} = 5.5 + 5 \times \dfrac{4}{17} = \mathbf{6.68\ m}$ (3 s.f.)
>
> *This fraction is the proportion of the way through the class that you'd expect to find the median.*

You can estimate the **Standard Deviation** too

Like for the mean, you can estimate the **variance** and **standard deviation** by assuming every
reading takes the value of the **class midpoint** and using the **frequencies** to estimate Σfx and Σfx^2.

> **Example:** Estimate the standard deviation of the heights of the trees in the table on the previous page.
>
> You need to add two more columns to the table you had for the mean, for x^2 and fx^2:
>
> | Height (to nearest m) | x^2 | fx^2 |
> |---|---|---|
> | 0-5 | 7.5625 | 196.625 |
> | 6-10 | 64 | 1088 |
> | 11-15 | 169 | 1859 |
> | 16-20 | 324 | 1944 |
> | | | 5087.625 (= Σfx^2) |
>
> Now you've got the totals in the table, you can calculate estimates for the variance and the standard deviation:
>
> variance $\approx \dfrac{\Sigma fx^2}{\Sigma f} - \overline{x}^2 = \dfrac{5087.625}{60} - (7.64...)^2$
>
> $= 26.39...\ m^2$
>
> so **standard deviation** $\approx \sqrt{26.39...}$
>
> $= \mathbf{5.14\ m}$ (3 s.f.)
>
> *Use the unrounded values for the estimated mean and variance here.*

Practice Questions

Q1 The table on the right shows the lengths in minutes (to the nearest minute) of twenty phone calls. Draw a histogram of the data.

Call length (mins)	0-2	3-5	6-8	9-15
Number of calls	10	6	3	1

Q2 The speeds of 60 cars travelling in a 40 mph speed limit area were measured to the nearest mph. The data is summarised in the table. Calculate estimates of the mean and median, and state the modal class.

Speed (mph)	30-34	35-39	40-44	45-50
Frequency	12	37	9	2

Exam Questions

Q1 The histogram on the right shows the nose-to-tail lengths of 50 lions in a nature reserve. Find the number of lions measuring over 220 cm. [3 marks]

Q2 The profits of 100 businesses are given in this table.

Profit (£p million)	$4.5 \leq p < 5.0$	$5.0 \leq p < 5.5$	$5.5 \leq p < 6.0$	$6.0 \leq p < 6.5$	$6.5 \leq p < 8.0$
No. of businesses	21	26	24	19	10

a) Represent the data in a histogram. [3 marks]
b) Estimate the mean and standard deviation of this data. [5 marks]
c) Use linear interpolation to estimate the median profit. [3 marks]

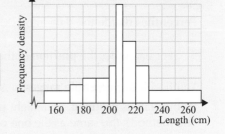

My pop group 'Data Days' topped the charts and won 8 histogrammys...

A class with lower class boundary = 50 g and upper class boundary = 250 g can be written in different ways.
You might see: "100-200 to nearest 100 g", or "50 ≤ mass < 250", or "50-" followed by "250-" for the next class, etc.
They all mean the same — make sure you know how to spot the lcb and ucb for each version.

Interquartile Range and Outliers

All you standard deviation lovers out there will be happy to hear there are even more measures of variation to learn.

The **Range** is a Measure of **Variation**...

The **range** is about the simplest measure of variation you could imagine: | **Range** = highest value – lowest value |

But the range is heavily affected by **extreme values**, so it isn't really the most useful way to measure variation.

Quartiles divide the data into **Four**

You've seen how the **median** divides a data set into **two halves**. Well, the **quartiles** divide the data into **four quarters** — with 25% of the data less than the **lower quartile**, and 75% of the data less than the **upper quartile**. There are various ways you can find the **quartiles**, but if you use the method below, you'll be fine.

① To find the lower quartile (Q_1), work out $\frac{n}{4}$.

(i) If $\frac{n}{4}$ is a **whole number**, the lower quartile is the **average of this term and the one above**.

(ii) If $\frac{n}{4}$ is **not a whole number**, round the number **up** to find the position of the lower quartile.

② To find the upper quartile (Q_3), work out $\frac{3n}{4}$.

(i) If $\frac{3n}{4}$ is a **whole number**, the upper quartile is the **average of this term and the one above**.

(ii) If $\frac{3n}{4}$ is **not a whole number**, round the number **up** to find the position of the upper quartile.

Example: Find the median and quartiles of the following data:
2, 5, 3, 11, 6, 8, 3, 8, 1, 6, 2, 23, 9, 11, 18, 19, 22, 7

The median is also known as Q_2.

First put the list **in order**: 1, 2, 2, 3, 3, 5, 6, 6, 7, 8, 8, 9, 11, 11, 18, 19, 22, 23

You need to find Q_1, Q_2 and Q_3, so work out $\frac{n}{4} = \frac{18}{4}$, $\frac{n}{2} = \frac{18}{2}$, and $\frac{3n}{4} = \frac{54}{4}$.

1) $\frac{n}{4}$ is **not** a whole number (= 4.5), so round up and take the 5th term: $\quad Q_1 = 3$

2) $\frac{n}{2}$ **is** a whole number (= 9), so find the average of the 9th and 10th terms: $\quad Q_2 = \frac{7+8}{2} = \textbf{7.5}$

3) $\frac{3n}{4}$ is **not** a whole number (= 13.5), so round up and take the 14th term: $\quad Q_3 = \textbf{11}$

The **Interquartile Range** is another measure of **Variation**

| **Interquartile range (IQR)** = upper quartile (Q_3) – lower quartile (Q_1) |

The IQR shows the range of the 'middle 50%' of the data.

Example: Find the interquartile range of the data in the previous example.

$Q_1 = 3$ and $Q_3 = 11$, so the interquartile range = $Q_3 – Q_1 = 11 – 3 = \textbf{8}$

Next stop:
the Percent Isles.

Percentiles divide the data into **100**

Percentiles divide the data into 100 — the median is the **50th percentile**, Q_1 is the **25th percentile**, etc.

For example, the **position** of the 11th percentile (P_{11}) is $\frac{11}{100} \times$ total frequency.

You find **interpercentile ranges** by **subtracting** two percentiles, e.g. the 20% to 80% interpercentile range = $P_{80} – P_{20}$.

If your data is **grouped**, you might need to use **linear interpolation** to find the quartiles or percentiles. The method's the same as the one on p.71, just swap 'median' for the percentile or quartile you want.

Example: Estimate the 80th percentile for the tree data at the bottom of p.70.

$\Sigma f = 60$, so the position of the 80th percentile is $\frac{80}{100} \times 60 = 48$, so P_{80} is in the '**11-15 m**' class.

Using the linear interpolation formula: $P_{80} = 10.5 + 5 \times \dfrac{48 - 43}{11}$ ←frequency before class
←frequency in class
l.c.b. ⌐ class width
$\Rightarrow P_{80} = \textbf{12.8 m}$ (3 s.f.)

Interquartile Range and Outliers

Outliers fall Outside Fences

An **outlier** is a **freak** piece of data that lies a long way from the rest of the readings. There are various ways to decide if a reading is an outlier — the method to use will depend on what information you're given in the question.

Example: A data value is said to be an outlier if it is more than 1.5 times the IQR above the upper quartile or more than 1.5 times the IQR below the lower quartile. The lower and upper quartiles of a data set are 70 and 100. Decide whether the data values 30 and 210 are outliers.

> This is one of two methods for finding outliers that you should be familiar with. The other one is 'more than 2 standard deviations away from the mean'.

First you need the IQR: $Q_3 - Q_1 = 100 - 70 = 30$

Then it's a piece of cake to find where your **fences** are.

> 25 and 145 are called **fences**. Any reading lying outside the fences is considered an **outlier**.

Lower fence: $Q_1 - (1.5 \times IQR) = 70 - (1.5 \times 30) = 25$ Upper fence: $Q_3 + (1.5 \times IQR) = 100 + (1.5 \times 30) = 145$

30 is **inside** the lower fence, so it is **not** an outlier. 210 is **outside** the upper fence, so it **is** an outlier.

Outliers Affect what Measure of Variation is Best to Use

- Outliers affect whether the **variance** and **standard deviation** are good measures of **variation**.
- Outliers can make the variance (and standard deviation) **much** larger than it would be otherwise — which means these **freak** pieces of data are having more influence than they deserve.
- If a data set contains outliers, then a better measure of variation is the **interquartile range**.

Use Central Tendency and Variation to Compare Distributions

Example: The table below summarises the marks obtained in Maths 'calculator' and 'non-calculator' papers. Comment on the location and variation of the distributions.

	Lower quartile, Q_1	Median, Q_2	Upper quartile, Q_3	Mean	Standard deviation
Calculator Paper	40	58	70	55	21.2
Non-calculator Paper	35	42	56	46.1	17.8

Location: The **mean**, the **median** and the **quartiles** are all higher for the calculator paper. This means that scores were **generally higher** on the calculator paper.

Variation: The **interquartile range** (IQR) for the calculator paper is $Q_3 - Q_1 = 70 - 40 = 30$. The **interquartile range** (IQR) for the non-calculator paper is $Q_3 - Q_1 = 56 - 35 = 21$. So the **IQR** and the **standard deviation** are both **higher** for the calculator paper. So the scores on the calculator paper are **more spread out** than for the non-calculator paper.

Practice Question

Q1 A data value is considered to be an outlier if it's more than 2 times the standard deviation above or below the mean. If the mean and standard deviation of a data set are 72 and 6.7 respectively, decide which of the following data values are outliers: a) 85   b) 95   c) 0

Exam Question

Q1 The table shows the number of hits received by people at a paintball party.

No. of hits	12	13	14	15	16	17	18	19	20	21	22	23	24	25
Frequency	2	4	6	7	6	4	4	2	1	1	0	0	0	1

   a) Find the median and mode number of hits.   [3 marks]

   b) An outlier is a data value which is more than $1.5 \times (Q_3 - Q_1)$ above Q_3 or below Q_1. Is 25 an outlier? Show your working.   [2 marks]

   c) Explain why the median might be considered a more reliable measure of central tendency than the mean for a data set that is thought to contain an outlier.   [1 mark]

I like my data how I like next door's dog — on the right side of the fence...

Measures of location and variation are supposed to capture the essential characteristics of a data set in just one or two numbers. Don't choose an average that's heavily affected by freaky, far-flung outliers — it won't be much good.

Cumulative Frequency Graphs and Boxplots

Cumulative frequency means 'running total'. Cumulative frequency graphs make medians and quartiles easy to find.

Use **Cumulative Frequency Graphs** to estimate the **Median** and **Quartiles**

Example: The ages of 200 students are shown in the table.

Age in completed years	11-12	13-14	15-16	17-18
Number of students	50	65	58	27

Draw a cumulative frequency graph and use it to estimate the median age, the interquartile range of ages, and how many students have already had their 18th birthday.

1) First draw a table showing the **upper class boundaries** and the **cumulative frequency** (CF):

Age in completed years	Upper class boundary (ucb)	Number of students, f	Cumulative frequency (CF)
Under 11	11	0	0
11-12	13	50	50
13-14	15	65	115
15-16	17	58	173
17-18	19	27	200

The **first** reading in a **cumulative frequency** table must be zero — so add this **extra row** to show the number of students with age **less than 11** is 0.

The CF is the number of students with an age **up to** the ucb — it's basically a **running total**.

The **last** number in the CF column should always be the **total number** of readings.

People say they're '18' right up until their 19th birthday — so the **ucb** of class 17-18 is **19**.

Always plot the upper class boundary of each class.

Next draw the **axes** — cumulative frequency **always** goes on the **vertical axis**. Here, age goes on the other axis.

Then plot the **upper class boundaries** against the **cumulative frequencies**, and join the points.

2) To estimate the **median** from a cumulative frequency graph, go to the **median position** on the vertical scale and read off the value from the horizontal axis.

median position $= \frac{1}{2} \times 200 = 100$,

so median ≈ **14.5 years**

> You can only **estimate** the median, since your data values are in **groups**. This is similar to linear interpolation — see page 71.

Then you can estimate the **quartiles** in the same way. Find their positions first:

Q_1 position $= \frac{1}{4} \times 200 = 50$,
so lower quartile, Q_1 ≈ **13 years**

Q_3 position $= \frac{3}{4} \times 200 = 150$,
so upper quartile, Q_3 ≈ **16.2 years**

IQR $= Q_3 - Q_1 = 16.2 - 13 =$ **3.2 years**

> Because the question says estimate, a **range** of answers would be **correct** for the median and IQR — e.g. anything between 14.25 and 14.75 for the median and anything between 3 and 3.5 for the IQR.

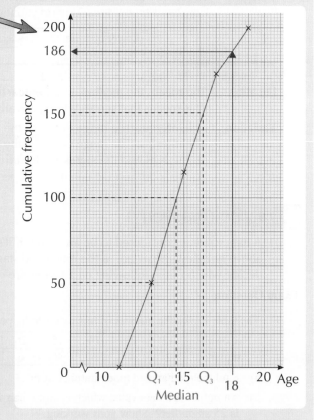

3) To estimate how many students have **not** yet had their 18th birthday, go up from 18 on the **horizontal axis**, and read off the number of students **'younger'** than 18 (= 186).

Then the number of students who are 'older' than 18 is approximately 200 − 186 = **14**.

Cumulative Frequency Graphs and Boxplots

Box Plots are a Visual Summary of a Distribution

Box plots show the median and quartiles in an easy-to-look-at kind of way.
They look like this:

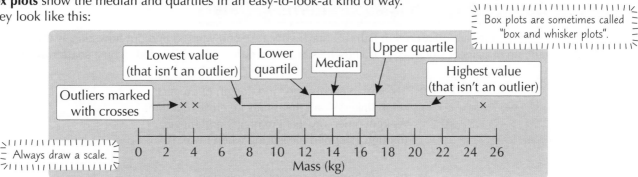

Box plots are sometimes called "box and whisker plots".

Outliers marked with crosses

Lowest value (that isn't an outlier)

Lower quartile

Median

Upper quartile

Highest value (that isn't an outlier)

Always draw a scale.

0 2 4 6 8 10 12 14 16 18 20 22 24 26
Mass (kg)

Use Box Plots to Compare two Distributions

Example: Compare the distributions represented by these two box plots:

Distribution 1:

Distribution 2:

0   20   40   60   80   100
Percentage (%)

Tian Tian was plotting something fiendish. It was a box plot...

Location: The **median** is higher for Distribution 1, showing that the data values are **generally higher** than for Distribution 2.

Variation: The **interquartile range** (IQR) and the **range** for Distribution 1 are higher, showing that the values are **more varied** for Distribution 1 than for Distribution 2.

Practice Questions

Q1 Draw a cumulative frequency diagram of the data given in this table.

Length of tadpole (cm)	0-2	2-4	4-6	6-8
Number of tadpoles	22	12	4	2

Use your diagram to estimate the median and interquartile range.

Q2 Draw a box and whisker diagram for the data below, using the fences $1.5 \times$ IQR above Q_3 or below Q_1 to identify any outliers. Amount of pocket money (in £) received per week by twenty 15-year-olds:
10, 5, 20, 50, 5, 1, 6, 5, 15, 20, 5, 7, 5, 10, 12, 4, 8, 6, 7, 30.

Exam Question

Q1 Two workers iron clothes. Each irons 10 items, and records the time it takes for each, to the nearest minute:

Worker A: 3, 5, 2, 7, 10, 4, 5, 5, 4, 12
Worker B: 3, 4, 8, 6, 7, 8, 9, 10, 11, 9

a) Find the median, the lower quartile and the upper quartile for worker A's times. [2 marks]

b) On graph paper, draw two box plots to show this data, one for each worker.
Use the same scale for both plots and assume there are no outliers. [4 marks]

c) Worker A claims he deserves a pay rise because he works faster than Worker B.
State, giving a reason, whether the data given above supports Worker A's claim. [2 marks]

"It's a cumulative frequency table," she said. It was all starting to add up...

'Cumulative frequency' sounds a bit scarier than 'running total' — but just remember, they're the same thing. And remember to plot the points at the upper class boundary — this makes sense if you remember that a cumulative frequency graph shows how many data values are less than the figure on the x-axis. The rest is more or less easyish.

Correlation

There's a fair bit of fancy stats-speak on these pages. Correlation is all about how closely two quantities are linked and linear regression is just a way to find the line of best fit. Not so scary now, eh...

Draw a **Scatter Diagram** to see **Patterns** in **Data**

1) Sometimes variables are measured in **pairs** — maybe because you want to find out **how closely** they're **linked**. Data made up of pairs of values (x, y) is known as **bivariate data** and can be plotted on a **scatter diagram**.

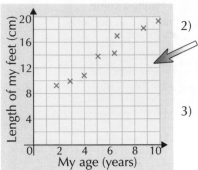

2) The variables 'my age' and 'length of my feet' seem linked — all the points lie **close** to a **line**. As I got older, my feet got bigger and bigger (though I stopped measuring when I was 10).

3) It's a lot harder to see any connection between the variables 'temperature' and 'number of accidents' — the data seems **scattered** pretty much everywhere.

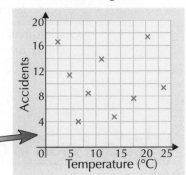

Correlation is a measure of **How Closely** variables are **Linked**

1) If, as one variable gets **bigger**, the other one also gets **bigger**, the scatter diagram might look like the age/length of feet graph above. The line of best fit would have a **positive gradient**. The two variables are **positively correlated** (or there's a positive correlation **between** them).

2) If one variable gets **smaller** as the other one gets **bigger**, then the scatter diagram might look like this one and the line of best fit would have a **negative gradient**. The two variables are **negatively correlated** (or there's a negative correlation **between** them). The circled point is an **outlier** — a point that doesn't fit the pattern of the rest of the data. Outliers can usually be **ignored** when drawing the line of best fit or describing the correlation — they can be **measurement errors** or just '**freak**' observations.

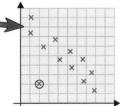

3) If the two variables **aren't** linked at all, you'd expect a **random** scattering of points (like in the temperature/accidents graph above). The variables **aren't correlated** (or there's **no correlation**).

4) Watch out for graphs that show distinct sections of the population like this one — the data will be in **separate clusters**. Here, you can describe both the **overall correlation** and the correlation in **each cluster** — so on this graph, there appears to be **negative correlation** overall, but **no correlation** within each cluster. Different clusters can also be shown on **separate graphs**, with each graph representing a different section of the population.

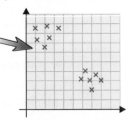

5) Correlation can also be described as '**strong**' or '**weak**'. The **stronger** the correlation is, the closer the points on the scatter diagram are to being in a **straight line**.

BUT you have to be **careful** when writing about two variables that are correlated — changes in one variable might **not cause** changes in the other. They could be linked by a **third factor**, or it could just be **coincidence**. The formal way of saying this is '**correlation** does not imply **causation**'.

Decide which is the **Explanatory Variable** and which is the **Response**

The variable along the **x-axis** is the **explanatory** (or **independent**) variable — it's the variable you can **control**, or the one that is **affecting** the other.

The variable up the **y-axis** is the **response** (or **dependent**) variable — it's the variable you think is **being affected**.

Example: Tasha wants to plot a scatter diagram to show the variables 'load on a lorry' (in tonnes) and 'fuel efficiency' (in km per litre). Identify the response variable and the explanatory variable.

Changing the load on a lorry would lead to a change in the fuel efficiency (e.g. heavier loads would use more fuel). So **fuel efficiency** is the **response** variable and **load on the lorry** is the **explanatory** variable. → *So Tasha should plot load on the x-axis and fuel efficiency on the y-axis.*

Correlation

The **Regression Line** *(line of best fit) is in the form* **y = a + bx**

The **regression line of y on x** (x is the explanatory variable and y is the response variable) is a **straight line** of the form:

$$y = a + bx, \text{ where a} = y\text{-intercept and b} = \text{gradient}$$

You need to be able to **interpret** the values of a and b.

Example: Tasha's data below shows the load on a lorry, x (in tonnes), and the fuel efficiency, y (in km per litre).

x	5.1	5.6	5.9	6.3	6.8	7.4	7.8	8.5	9.1	9.8
y	9.6	9.5	8.6	8.0	7.8	6.8	6.7	6.0	5.4	5.4

The regression line of y on x is calculated to be $y = 14.5 - 0.978x$.
Plot this data on a scatter graph and interpret the values of a and b.

Plot the scatter graph, with load on the x-axis and efficiency on the y-axis.

a = 14.5: with **no load** ($x = 0$) you'd expect the lorry to do 14.5 km per litre of fuel.

b = –0.978: for every **extra** tonne carried, you'd expect the lorry's fuel efficiency to **fall** by 0.978 km per litre.

Use regression lines **With Care**

You can use your regression line to **predict** values of the **response variable**. There are two types of this.

Interpolation — use values of x **within** the data range (e.g. between 5.1 and 9.8 for the lorry example). It's okay to do this — the predicted value should be **reliable**.

Extrapolation — use values of x **outside** the data range (e.g. outside 5.1 and 9.8 for the lorry example). These predictions can be **unreliable**, so you need to be very cautious about them.

Example (continued): Estimate the fuel efficiency when the load is 12 tonnes. Give a reason why your estimate might be unreliable.

Use $x = 12$ in the regression line: $y = 14.5 - 0.978 \times 12 = \mathbf{2.764}$

$x = 12$ is outside the data range (5.1 to 9.8) — this is an **extrapolation** so the estimate may be unreliable.

Professor Snuffles had a fuel efficiency of 1.5 km per doggie biscuit.

Practice Questions

Q1 Describe the correlation shown on the graphs to the right:

a)   b)   c)

Q2 Khalid wants to plot a scatter graph for the variables 'barbecue sales' (thousands) and 'amount of sunshine' (hours). Identify the response variable and the explanatory variable.

Exam Question

Q1 The following times (in seconds) were taken by eight different runners to complete distances of 20 m and 60 m.

Runner	A	B	C	D	E	F	G	H
20-metre time (x)	3.39	3.20	3.09	3.32	3.33	3.27	3.44	3.08
60-metre time (y)	8.78	7.73	8.28	8.25	8.91	8.59	8.90	8.05

a) Plot a scatter diagram to represent the data. [2 marks]

b) Describe the correlation shown on your graph. [1 mark]

c) The equation of the regression line is calculated to be $y = 2.4x + 0.7$. Plot it on your scatter diagram. [1 mark]

d) Use the equation of the regression line to estimate the time it takes to run a distance of 60 m, when the time taken to run 20 m is: (i) 3.15 s, (ii) 3.88 s. Comment on the reliability of your estimates. [2 marks]

What's a statistician's favourite soap — Correlation Street...

Watch out for those outliers — you might need to think about why there's an outlier. Sometimes it can only be down to some sort of error, but in others there could be a realistic reason why a data point might not fit the general trend.

Random Events and Venn Diagrams

Random events happen by chance. Probability is a measure of how likely they are. It can be a chancy business.

A **Random Event** has **Various Outcomes**

1) In a **trial** (or experiment) the things that can happen are called **outcomes**
   (so if I time how long it takes to eat my dinner, 63 seconds is a possible outcome).

2) **Events** are 'groups' of one or more outcomes (so an event might be
   'it takes me less than a minute to eat my dinner every day one week').

3) When all outcomes are **equally likely**, you can work out the **probability** of an event by **counting** the outcomes:

$$P(\text{event}) = \frac{\text{Number of outcomes where event happens}}{\text{Total number of possible outcomes}}$$

Example: I have a bag with 15 balls in — 5 red, 6 blue and 4 green. I pick a ball without looking.
What is the probability the ball is: a) red, b) blue, c) green, d) either red or green?

Any ball is **equally likely** to be picked — there are **15 possible outcomes**.
Of these 15 outcomes, 5 are red, 6 are blue and 4 are green.

And so: a) $P(\text{red ball}) = \frac{5}{15} = \frac{1}{3}$ b) $P(\text{blue ball}) = \frac{6}{15} = \frac{2}{5}$ c) $P(\text{green ball}) = \frac{4}{15}$

You can find the probability of **either** red **or** green in a similar way: d) $P(\text{red or green}) = \frac{5+4}{15} = \frac{9}{15} = \frac{3}{5}$

Venn Diagrams show which **Outcomes** correspond to which **Events**

Say you've got 2 events, **A** and **B**. A **Venn diagram** can show which outcomes satisfy event A,
which satisfy B, which satisfy both, and which satisfy neither.

(i)   All outcomes satisfying event A go in one part of the diagram,
and all outcomes satisfying event B go in another bit.

(ii) If they satisfy both '**A and B**', they go in the dark green middle bit.

(iii) The whole of the green area is '**A or B**'.

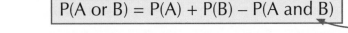

Again, you can work out probabilities of events by counting outcomes and using the formula above.
You can also get a nice formula linking P(A and B) and P(A or B).

$$P(A \text{ or } B) = P(A) + P(B) - P(A \text{ and } B)$$

If you just add up the outcomes in A and the outcomes in B, you end up counting the middle bit twice — that's why you have to subtract it.

Example: If I roll a dice, event A could be 'I get an even number', and
B 'I get a number bigger than 4'. The Venn diagram would be:

$P(A) = \frac{3}{6} = \frac{1}{2}$ $P(B) = \frac{2}{6} = \frac{1}{3}$ Here, I've just counted
outcomes — but I could
$P(A \text{ and } B) = \frac{1}{6}$ $P(A \text{ or } B) = \frac{4}{6} = \frac{2}{3}$ have used the formula.

Example: A survey was carried out to find what pets people like.

The probability they like dogs is 0.6. The probability they like cats is 0.5.
The probability they like gerbils is 0.4. The probability they like dogs and cats is 0.4.
The probability they like cats and gerbils is 0.1, and the probability they like gerbils and dogs is 0.2.
Finally, the probability they like all three kinds of animal is 0.1.

Draw a Venn diagram to show this information, using C for the event 'likes cats',
D for 'likes dogs' and G for 'likes gerbils'.

① Stick in the middle one first
— 'likes all 3 animals' (i.e. C and D and G).

③ Then do the 'likes 1 kind of animal' probabilities,
by making sure the total probability in each
circle adds up to the probability in the question.

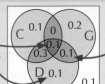

② Then do the 'likes 2 animals' probabilities by taking 0.1
from each given 'likes 2 animals' probability. (If they like
3 animals, they'll also be in the 'likes 2 animals' bits.)

④ Finally, subtract all the probabilities so far from
1 to find 'likes none of these animals'.

Random Events and Venn Diagrams

Example (cont.): Find: a) the probability that someone likes either dogs or cats,
b) the probability that someone likes gerbils but not dogs,
c) the probability that someone who likes dogs **also** likes cats.

a) From the Venn diagram, the probability that someone
likes either dogs or cats is: $0.1 + 0 + 0.1 + 0.3 + 0.1 + 0.1 = \mathbf{0.7}$

b) The probability that someone likes gerbils but not dogs is: $0 + 0.2 = \mathbf{0.2}$

c) For the probability that a dog-lover **also** likes cats,
ignore everything outside the 'dogs' circle.

$$P(\text{dog-lover also like cats}) = \frac{0.3 + 0.1}{0.3 + 0.1 + 0.1 + 0.1} = \frac{2}{3}$$

The **Complement** of 'Event A' is '**Not Event A**'

An event A will either happen or not happen. The event 'A doesn't happen'
is called the **complement** of A (or **A'**). On a Venn diagram, it looks like this: ⟶

A' A

At least one of A and A' has to happen, so... $P(A) + P(A') = 1$ or $P(A') = 1 - P(A)$

Example: Nic keeps his socks loose in a box. He picks out a sock. He calculates that the probability of then
picking out a matching sock is 0.56. What is the probability of him not picking a matching sock?

Call event A 'picks a matching sock'. Then A' is 'doesn't pick a matching sock'.
Now A and A' are **complementary events** (and P(A) = 0.56), so P(A') = 1 − 0.56 = **0.44**

Example: For two events, A and B: P(A') = 0.42, P(A and B') = 0.15, P(B) = 0.55
Use a two-way table to find: a) P(A and B), b) P(A or B').

	A	A'	Total
B	0.43	0.12	**0.55**
B'	**0.15**	0.3	0.45
Total	0.58	**0.42**	1

Start by filling in P(A') = **0.42**, P(A and B') = **0.15** and P(B) = **0.55** in the table,
then use the fact that the probabilities should add up to **1** to find the rest:

a) P(A and B) is the entry in the A column and the B row — this is **0.43**.

b) P(A or B') is the sum of all of the entries in either the A column OR the B'
row – so P(A or B') = 0.43 + 0.15 + 0.3 = **0.88**.
Make sure you don't just add the totals P(A) + P(B') — you'd be counting the 0.15
twice. I've shaded in the bits of the table you want so that you you can see what I mean.

*You can also have two-way tables
showing numbers of outcomes
instead of probabilities. You
probably saw these at GCSE.*

Practice Questions

Q1 Arabella rolls two standard dice and adds the two results together. What is the probability that she scores:
a) a prime number, b) a square number, c) a number that is either a prime number or a square number?

Q2 Half the students in a sixth-form college eat sausages for dinner and 20% eat chips. 10% of those who eat chips
also eat sausages. Show this information in a two-way table, and use it to find the percentage of students who:
a) eat both chips and sausages, b) eat chips but not sausages, c) eat either chips or sausages but not both.

Exam Question

Q1 A soap company asked 120 people about the types of soap (from Brands A, B and C) they bought. Brand A was
bought by 40 people, Brand B by 30 people and Brand C by 25. Both Brands A and B were bought by 8 people,
B and C were bought by 10 people, and A and C by 7 people. All three brands were bought by 3 people.

a) Represent this information in a Venn diagram. [5 marks]

b) (i) If a person is selected at random, find the probability that they buy at least one of the soaps. [2 marks]
(ii) If a person is selected at random, find the probability that they buy at least two of the soaps. [2 marks]

I took some scales with me to the furniture shop — I like to weigh tables...

*I must admit — I kind of like these pages. This stuff isn't too hard, and it's really useful for answering loads of
questions. And one other good thing is that Venn diagrams look, well, nice somehow. But more importantly,
the thing to remember when you're filling one in is that you usually need to 'start from the inside and work out'.*

Mutually Exclusive and Independent Events

Hang on, there was something else to go on this page as well. What was it again... Oh of course — tree diagrams. They blossom from tiny question-acorns into beautiful trees of possibility. How inspiring — not to mention useful...

Tree Diagrams Show Probabilities for Two or More Events

Each 'chunk' of a tree diagram is a **trial**, and each branch of that chunk is a possible **outcome**.
Multiplying probabilities along the branches gives you the probability of a **series** of outcomes.

Example: If Susan plays tennis one day, the probability that she'll play the next day is 0.2. If she doesn't play tennis, the probability that she'll play the next day is 0.6. She plays tennis on Monday. What is the probability she plays tennis on the Wednesday of the same week?

Let T mean 'plays tennis', so
T' means 'doesn't play tennis'.
You're interested in **either** P(T, T) or P(T', T).

P(plays on Wednesday) = P(T, T) + P(T', T)
    = 0.04 + 0.48
    = **0.52**

*To find the probability of one event **or** another happening, you have to **add** the probabilities.*

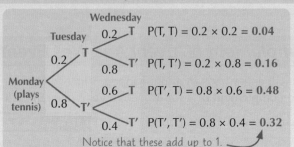

Wednesday
Tuesday 0.2 ⌐T   P(T, T) = 0.2 × 0.2 = **0.04**
    0.2 ⌐T
        0.8 ⌐T'   P(T, T') = 0.2 × 0.8 = **0.16**
Monday
(plays   0.6 ⌐T   P(T', T) = 0.8 × 0.6 = **0.48**
tennis) 0.8 ⌐T'
            0.4 ⌐T'   P(T', T') = 0.8 × 0.4 = **0.32**

Notice that these add up to 1.

Susan was ready for some unlikely outcomes on the tennis court.

Example: A box of biscuits contains 5 chocolate biscuits and 1 lemon biscuit. George takes out 2 biscuits at random, one at a time, and eats them. Find the probability that the second biscuit is chocolate.

Let C mean 'picks a chocolate biscuit' and let L mean 'picks the lemon biscuit'.
The second biscuit being chocolate is shown by 2 'paths' along the branches
— so you can add up the probabilities:

$$P(\text{second biscuit is chocolate}) = \left(\frac{5}{6} \times \frac{4}{5}\right) + \left(\frac{1}{6} \times 1\right) = \frac{2}{3} + \frac{1}{6} = \frac{5}{6}$$

There's a quicker way to do this, as there's only one outcome where the chocolate **isn't** picked last:

$P(\text{second biscuit is **not** chocolate}) = \frac{5}{6} \times \frac{1}{5} = \frac{1}{6}$, so $P(\text{second biscuit is chocolate}) = 1 - \frac{1}{6} = \frac{5}{6}$

It's sometimes easier to find the probability of the **complement** of the event you're interested in.

1st pick 2nd pick

$\frac{4}{5}$ C $\frac{5}{6} \times \frac{4}{5} = \frac{2}{3}$
$\frac{5}{6}$ C
    $\frac{1}{5}$ L $\frac{5}{6} \times \frac{1}{5} = \frac{1}{6}$
$\frac{1}{6}$ L $\frac{1}{1}$ C $\frac{1}{6} \times 1 = \frac{1}{6}$

Here there are no lemon biscuits left, so the tree diagram doesn't branch.

If an object is chosen **with replacement**, the probability of choosing
a particular item is **the same** for each pick. In the example above, if
George puts his first biscuit back instead of eating it, the probability of
picking 2 chocolate biscuits becomes:

$$P(C, C) = \frac{5}{6} \times \frac{5}{6} = \frac{25}{36} > \frac{2}{3}$$

P(C, C) is slightly greater with replacement. This makes sense — there are more chocolate biscuits available for his 2nd pick, so he is more likely to choose one.

Mutually Exclusive Events have No Overlap

If two events **can't both happen** at the same time (i.e. P(A and B) = 0) they're called **mutually exclusive**
(or just '**exclusive**'). If A and B are exclusive, then the probability of A **or** B is: P(A or B) = P(A) + P(B).

More generally,

For *n* exclusive events (i.e. only one of them can happen at a time):
$$P(A_1 \text{ or } A_2 \text{ or ... or } A_n) = P(A_1) + P(A_2) + ... + P(A_n)$$

This is the formula from p.78, with P(A and B) = 0.

Example: Find the probability that a card pulled at random from a standard pack of cards (no jokers) is either a picture card (a Jack, Queen or King) or the 7, 8 or 9 of clubs.

Call **event A** — 'I get a picture card', and **event B** — 'I get the 7, 8 or 9 of clubs'. Then $P(A) = \frac{12}{52}$ and $P(B) = \frac{3}{52}$.
Events A and B are **mutually exclusive** — they can't both happen.
So the probability of either A or B is: $P(A \text{ or } B) = P(A) + P(B) = \frac{12}{52} + \frac{3}{52} = \frac{15}{52}$

Mutually Exclusive and Independent Events

Independent Events have No Effect on each other

If the probability of B happening doesn't depend on whether or not A has happened, then A and B are **independent**.

This means that: | For independent events: **P(A and B) = P(A)P(B)**

> **Example:** V and W are independent events, where P(V) = 0.2 and P(W) = 0.6.
> Find: a) P(V and W), b) P(V or W).

a) Just put the numbers into the formula for independent events: P(V and W) = P(V)P(W) = 0.2 × 0.6 = **0.12**

b) Using the formula on page 78: P(V or W) = P(V) + P(W) − P(V and W) = 0.2 + 0.6 − 0.12 = **0.68**

Sometimes you'll be asked if two events are independent or not. Here's how you work it out...

> **Example:** You are exposed to two infectious diseases — one after the other. The probability you catch the first (A) is 0.25, the probability you catch the second (B) is 0.5, and the probability you catch both of them is 0.2. Are catching the two diseases independent events?

Compare P(A and B) and P(A)P(B) — if they're different, the events **aren't independent**.

$$P(A \text{ and } B) = 0.2 \qquad\qquad P(A)P(B) = 0.25 \times 0.5 = 0.125$$

P(A and B) and P(A)P(B) are different, so they're **not independent**.

Practice Questions

Q1 Zofia has 20 cards numbered 1-20. She picks two cards at random, one at a time, without replacement.
   a) Are the events 'both numbers are prime numbers' and 'the sum of the numbers is less than 10' mutually exclusive? Explain your answer.
   b) Are the events 'the first number is even' and 'the second number is odd' independent? Explain your answer.

Q2 In a school orchestra (made up of pupils in either the upper or lower school), 40% of the musicians are boys. Of the boys, 30% are in the upper school. Of the girls in the orchestra, 50% are in the upper school.
   a) Represent this information on a tree diagram.
   b) Find the probability that a musician chosen at random is in the upper school.

Q3 For lunch, I eat either chicken or beef for my main course, and either chocolate cake or ice cream for dessert. The probability that I eat chicken is $\frac{1}{3}$, and if I do, the probability that I eat ice cream is $\frac{2}{5}$. If I have beef instead, then the probability that I have ice cream is $\frac{3}{4}$. Find the probability that:
   a) I have either chicken or ice cream, but not both,   b) I eat ice cream.

Exam Questions

Q1 Event J and Event K are independent events, where P(J) = 0.7 and P(K) = 0.1.
   a) Find: (i) P(J and K)   [1 mark]
           (ii) P(J or K)   [2 marks]
   b) If L is the event that neither J or K occurs, find P(L and K′).   [2 marks]

Q2 A jar contains 3 red counters and 6 green counters. Three random counters are removed from the jar one at a time. The counters are not replaced after they are drawn.
   a) Draw a tree diagram to show the probabilities of the various outcomes.   [3 marks]
   b) Find the probability that the third counter is green.   [2 marks]
   c) Find the probability that all of the counters are the same colour.   [2 marks]
   d) Find the probability that at least one counter is red.   [2 marks]

All the events that are independent — throw your hands up at me...

Probability questions can be tough. For tricky questions, try drawing a Venn diagram or a tree diagram, even if the question doesn't tell you to — they're really useful for understanding what on earth is going on in a question. And don't forget the definitions of mutually exclusive and independent events — they're key terms you need to know.

Probability Distributions

This is where we handle the probability distribution, so everybody get in line and wait your turn.
No need to push — there's plenty of yummy probability to go around...

Random Variables have Probability Distributions

This first bit isn't particularly interesting. But understanding the difference between X and x (bear with me) might make the later stuff a bit less confusing.

1) X (upper case) is just the **name** of a **random variable**. So X could be 'score on a fair, six-sided dice'.

2) A **random variable** doesn't have a **fixed** value. Like with the dice score — the value on any 'roll' is all down to **chance**.

3) x (lower case) is a **particular value** that X can take. So for one roll of the dice, x could be 1, 2, 3, 4, 5 or 6.

4) **Discrete** random variables only have a **certain number** of possible values. Often these values are whole numbers, but they don't have to be. Usually there are only a few possible values (e.g. the possible scores with one roll of a dice).

5) A **probability distribution** is a **table showing the possible values** of x, and the **probability** for each one.

6) A **probability function** is a formula that generates the probabilities for different values of x.

All the probabilities Add Up To 1

For a discrete random variable X:

$$\sum_{\text{all } x} P(X = x) = 1$$

This says that if you add up the probabilities of all the possible values of X, you get 1.

Example: The random variable X, where X can only take values 1, 2, 3, has probability function $P(X = x) = kx$ for $x = 1, 2, 3$. Find the value of k.

X has three possible values ($x = 1, 2$ and 3), and the probability of each is kx (where you need to find k).

It's easier to understand with a table:

x	1	2	3
$P(X = x)$	$k \times 1 = k$	$k \times 2 = 2k$	$k \times 3 = 3k$

Now just use the formula: $\sum_{\text{all } x} P(X = x) = 1$

Here, this means: $k + 2k + 3k = 6k = 1$, so $k = \dfrac{1}{6}$

> For a discrete random variable where every value of X is equally likely, you get a discrete uniform distribution — e.g. rolling a normal unbiased dice.

The **mode** is the **most likely** value — so it's the value with the **biggest probability**.

Example: The discrete random variable X, where X can only take values 0, 1, 2, 3, 4, has the probability distribution shown below.

x	0	1	2	3	4
$P(X = x)$	0.1	0.2	0.3	0.2	a

Find: a) the value of a,   b) $P(2 \leq X < 4)$,   c) the mode.

a) Use the formula $\sum_{\text{all } x} P(X = x) = 1$ again.

From the table: $0.1 + 0.2 + 0.3 + 0.2 + a = 1$
$0.8 + a = 1$
$a = 0.2$

Careful with the inequality signs — you need to include x = 2 but not x = 4.

b) This is asking for the probability that 'X is greater than or equal to 2, but less than 4'. Easy — just add up the probabilities.

$P(2 \leq X < 4) = P(X = 2) + P(X = 3) = 0.3 + 0.2 = \textbf{0.5}$

c) The mode is the value of x with the biggest probability — so **mode = 2**.

Probability Distributions

Draw a *Diagram* showing *All Possible Outcomes*

Example: An unbiased six-sided dice has faces marked 1, 1, 1, 2, 2, 3.
The dice is rolled twice. Let X be the random variable "sum of the two scores on the dice".
a) Show that $P(X = 4) = \frac{5}{18}$.
b) Find the probability distribution of X.

a) Make a table showing the 36 possible outcomes.

Score on roll 1

+	1	1	1	2	2	3
1	2	2	2	3	3	4
1	2	2	2	3	3	4
1	2	2	2	3	3	4
2	3	3	3	4	4	5
2	3	3	3	4	4	5
3	4	4	4	5	5	6

Score on roll 2

You can see from the table that
10 of these have the outcome $X = 4$,
so $P(X = 4) = \frac{10}{36} = \frac{5}{18}$

b) Use the table to work out the probabilities for the other outcomes and then fill in a table summarising the probability distribution:

$\frac{9}{36}$ of the outcomes are a score of 2

$\frac{12}{36}$ of the outcomes are a score of 3

$\frac{4}{36}$ of the outcomes are a score of 5

$\frac{1}{36}$ of the outcomes are a score of 6

x	2	3	4	5	6
$P(X = x)$	$\frac{1}{4}$	$\frac{1}{3}$	$\frac{5}{18}$	$\frac{1}{9}$	$\frac{1}{36}$

Do complicated questions *Bit By Bit*

Example: A game involves rolling two fair, six-sided dice. If the sum of the scores is greater than 10 then the player wins 50p. If the sum is between 8 and 10 (inclusive) then they win 20p. Otherwise they get nothing. If X is the random variable "amount player wins in pence", find the probability distribution of X.

There are **3 possible values** for X (0, 20 and 50) and you need the **probability** of each.
To work these out, you need the probability of getting various totals on the dice.

1) You need to know $P(8 \leq \text{score} \leq 10)$ — the probability that the score is between 8 and 10 **inclusive** (i.e. including 8 and 10) and $P(11 \leq \text{score} \leq 12)$ — the probability that the score is **greater than** 10. Use a table:

Score on dice 1

+	1	2	3	4	5	6
1	2	3	4	5	6	7
2	3	4	5	6	7	8
3	4	5	6	7	8	9
4	5	6	7	8	9	10
5	6	7	8	9	10	11
6	7	8	9	10	11	12

Score on dice 2

The table: making things easier to understand since 3000 BC (DISCLAIMER: CGP takes no responsibility for the historical accuracy of this 'fact').

2) There are **36 possible outcomes**:

12 of these have a total of **8, 9 or 10** so $P(8 \leq \text{score} \leq 10) = \frac{12}{36} = \frac{1}{3}$

3 of these have a total of **11 or 12** so $P(11 \leq \text{score} \leq 12) = \frac{3}{36} = \frac{1}{12}$

3) Use these to find the probabilities you need:

$P(X = 20p) = P(8 \leq \text{score} \leq 10) = \frac{1}{3}$

$P(X = 50p) = P(11 \leq \text{score} \leq 12) = \frac{1}{12}$

To find $P(X = 0)$ take the total of the two probabilities above from 1 (since $X = 0$ is the only other possibility).

$P(X = 0) = 1 - \left[\frac{12}{36} + \frac{3}{36}\right] = 1 - \frac{15}{36} = \frac{21}{36} = \frac{7}{12}$

4) Now just stick all this info in a table (and check that the probabilities all add up to 1):

x	0	20	50
$P(X = x)$	$\frac{7}{12}$	$\frac{1}{3}$	$\frac{1}{12}$

Check: $\frac{7}{12} + \frac{1}{3} + \frac{1}{12} = \frac{7}{12} + \frac{4}{12} + \frac{1}{12} = 1$ ✓

Probability Distributions

The **Cumulative Distribution Function** is a **Running Total** of probabilities

The **cumulative distribution function** $F(x)$ gives the probability that X will be **less than or equal to** a particular value.

$$F(x_0) = P(X \leq x_0) = \sum_{x \leq x_0} p(x)$$

$p(x) = P(X = x)$

Example: The probability distribution of the discrete random variable H, where H can only take values 0.1, 0.2, 0.3, 0.4, is shown in the table. Draw up a table to show the cumulative distribution of H.

h	0.1	0.2	0.3	0.4
$P(H = h)$	$\frac{1}{4}$	$\frac{1}{4}$	$\frac{1}{3}$	$\frac{1}{6}$

There are 4 values of h, so you have to find the probability that H is **less than or equal to** each of them in turn. It sounds trickier than it actually is — you only have to add up a few probabilities...

$F(0.1) = P(H \leq 0.1)$ — this is the same as $P(H = 0.1)$, since H can't be less than 0.1. So $F(0.1) = \frac{1}{4}$

$F(0.2) = P(H \leq 0.2)$ — this is the probability that $H = 0.1$ or $H = 0.2$.

$F(0.2) = P(H = 0.1) + P(H = 0.2) = \frac{1}{4} + \frac{1}{4} = \frac{1}{2}$

$F(0.3) = P(H \leq 0.3) = P(H \leq 0.2) + P(H = 0.3) = \frac{1}{2} + \frac{1}{3} = \frac{5}{6}$

Here you're just adding one more probability to the previous cumulative probability.

$F(0.4) = P(H \leq 0.4) = P(H \leq 0.3) + P(H = 0.4) = \frac{5}{6} + \frac{1}{6} = 1$

Finally, put these values in a table, and you're done:

h	0.1	0.2	0.3	0.4
$F(h) = P(H \leq h)$	$\frac{1}{4}$	$\frac{1}{2}$	$\frac{5}{6}$	1

$P(X \leq \text{largest value of } x)$ is always 1.

Example: For a discrete random variable X, where X can only take values 1, 2, 3, 4, the cumulative distribution function $F(x) = kx$, for $x = 1, 2, 3$ and 4. Find k, and the probability function.

1) First find k. You know that X has to be 4 or less — so $P(X \leq 4) = 1$.
   Put $x = 4$ into the cumulative distribution function: $F(4) = P(X \leq 4) = 4k = 1$, so $k = \frac{1}{4}$.

2) Now you can work out the probabilities of X being less than or equal to 1, 2, 3 and 4.
   $F(1) = P(X \leq 1) = 1 \times k = \frac{1}{4}$, $F(2) = P(X \leq 2) = 2 \times k = \frac{1}{2}$, $F(3) = P(X \leq 3) = 3 \times k = \frac{3}{4}$, $F(4) = P(X \leq 4) = 1$

3) Then $P(X = 4) = P(X \leq 4) - P(X \leq 3) = 1 - \frac{3}{4} = \frac{1}{4}$, $P(X = 3) = P(X \leq 3) - P(X \leq 2) = \frac{3}{4} - \frac{1}{2} = \frac{1}{4}$,
   Think about it — if it's less than or equal to 4, but it's **not** less than or equal to 3, then it has to be 4.
   $P(X = 2) = P(X \leq 2) - P(X \leq 1) = \frac{1}{2} - \frac{1}{4} = \frac{1}{4}$ and $P(X = 1) = P(X \leq 1) = \frac{1}{4}$
   Because x doesn't take any values less than 1.

4) Finish it all off by making a table. The probability distribution of X is:
   So the probability function is: $P(X = x) = \frac{1}{4}$ for $x = 1, 2, 3, 4$

x	1	2	3	4
$P(X = x)$	$\frac{1}{4}$	$\frac{1}{4}$	$\frac{1}{4}$	$\frac{1}{4}$

This is a uniform distribution (see p.82).

Practice Question

Q1 The random variable X, where X takes values 1, 2, 3, 4, has probability function $P(X = x) = kx$ for $x = 1, 2, 3, 4$.
   a) Find the value of k.
   b) Find $P(X > 2)$
   c) Find $P(1 \leq X \leq 3)$
   d) Draw a table to show:
   (i) the probability distribution,
   (ii) the cumulative distribution.

Exam Question

Q1 The probability function for the discrete random variable X is given by $P(X = x) = \frac{1}{k}x^2$ for $x = 1, 2, 3, 4$.
   Find the value of k and $P(X \leq 2)$. [4 marks]

Fact: the probability of this coming up in the exam is less than or equal to one...

If you've got a probability distribution, you can work out the table for the cumulative distribution function and vice versa. Don't forget, all the stuff so far is for _discrete variables_ — these can only take a certain number of values.

The Binomial Distribution

Welcome to the Binomial Distribution. It's quite a gentle introduction, because this page is basically about counting. If you're thinking some of this looks familiar, you're dead right — you met the binomial expansion back in Section 1.

n different objects can be arranged in *n!* different ways...

There are $n!$ ("*n* **factorial**") ways of arranging *n* **different** objects, where $n! = n \times (n-1) \times (n-2) \times ... \times 3 \times 2 \times 1$.

Example: a) In how many ways can 4 different ornaments be arranged on a shelf?
b) In how many ways can 8 different objects be arranged?

a)   You have **4 choices** for the first ornament, **3 choices** for the second ornament, **2 choices** for the third ornament, and **1 choice** for the last ornament.
So there are $4 \times 3 \times 2 \times 1 = 4! = \mathbf{24}$ arrangements.

b)   There are $8! = \mathbf{40\,320}$ arrangements.

Calculators have a factorial button so you don't need to type all the numbers out.

Of course, not all ornaments deserve to go on the shelf.

...but **Divide by *r!*** if *r* of these objects are the **Same**

If *r* of your *n* objects are **identical**, then the total number of possible arrangements is $(n! \div r!)$.

Example: a) In how many different ways can 5 objects be arranged if 2 of those objects are identical?
b) In how many different ways can 7 objects be arranged if 4 of those objects are identical?

a)   Imagine those 2 identical objects were **different**. Then there would be $5! = 120$ possible arrangements. But because those 2 objects are actually **identical**, you can always **swap them round** without making a different arrangement. So there are really only $120 \div 2 = \mathbf{60}$ different ways to arrange the objects.

b)   There are $\frac{n!}{r!} = \frac{7!}{4!} = \frac{5040}{24} = \mathbf{210}$ different ways to arrange the objects.

Use **Binomial Coefficients** if there are **Only Two Types** of object

See p.28 for more about binomial coefficients.

Binomial Coefficients

$$\binom{n}{r} = {}^nC_r = \frac{n!}{r!(n-r)!}$$

${}^nC_r$ and $\binom{n}{r}$ both mean $\frac{n!}{r!(n-r)!}$

Example: a)   In how many different ways can *n* objects of two types be arranged if *r* are of the first type?
b)   How many ways are there to select 11 players from a squad of 16?
c)   How many ways are there to pick 6 lottery numbers from 59?

a)   If the objects were all **different**, there would be $n!$ ways to arrange them. But *r* of the objects are of the same type and could be **swapped around**, so divide by $r!$. Since there are only **two types**, the other $(n-r)$ could also be **swapped around**, so divide by $(n-r)!$. This means there are $\dfrac{n!}{r!(n-r)!}$ arrangements.

b)   This is basically a 'number of different **arrangements**' problem. Imagine the 16 players are lined up — then you could '**pick**' or '**not pick**' players by giving each of them a sign marked with a tick or a cross. So just find the number of ways to arrange 11 ticks and 5 crosses — this is $\binom{16}{11} = \frac{16!}{11!5!} = \mathbf{4368}$.

c)   Again, numbers are either '**picked**' or '**unpicked**', so there are $\binom{59}{6} = \frac{59!}{6!53!} = \mathbf{45\,057\,474}$ possibilities.

The Binomial Distribution

Use **Binomial Coefficients** to count arrangements of 'successes' and 'failures'

For this bit, you need to use the fact that if $p = $ P(**something happens**), then $1 - p = $ P(**that thing doesn't happen**).

Example: I toss a fair coin 5 times. Find the probability of: a) 0 heads, b) 1 head, c) 2 heads.

First, note that each coin toss is **independent** of the others.
That means you can **multiply** individual probabilities together. P(tails) = P(heads) = 0.5

a) P(0 heads) = P(tails) × P(tails) × P(tails) × P(tails) × P(tails) = 0.5^5 = **0.03125**

These are the $\binom{5}{1} = 5$ ways to arrange 1 head and 4 tails.

b) P(1 head) = [P(heads) × P(tails) × P(tails) × P(tails) × P(tails)] + [P(tails) × P(heads) × P(tails) × P(tails) × P(tails)]
  + [P(tails) × P(tails) × P(heads) × P(tails) × P(tails)] + [P(tails) × P(tails) × P(tails) × P(heads) × P(tails)]
  + [P(tails) × P(tails) × P(tails) × P(tails) × P(heads)]

So P(1 head) = $0.5 \times (0.5)^4 \times \binom{5}{1} = 0.03125 \times \frac{5!}{1!4!}$ = **0.15625**

= P(heads) × [P(tails)]⁴
× ways to arrange 1 head and 4 tails

c) P(2 heads) = $[P(heads)]^2 \times [P(tails)]^3 \times$ ways to arrange 2 heads and 3 tails = $(0.5)^2 \times (0.5)^3 \times \binom{5}{2}$ = **0.3125**

The **Binomial Probability Function** gives P(r successes out of n trials)

The previous example really just shows why this thing-in-a-box must be true.

Binomial Probability Function

$$P(r \text{ successes in } n \text{ trials}) = \binom{n}{r} \times [P(\text{success})]^r \times [P(\text{failure})]^{n-r}$$

This is the probability function for a binomial distribution — see below for more info.

Example: I roll a fair six-sided dice 5 times. Find the probability of rolling:
a) 2 sixes, b) 3 sixes, c) 4 numbers less than 3.

Again, note that each roll of a dice is **independent** of the other rolls.

a) For this part, call "roll a 6" a success, and "roll anything other than a 6" a failure.

Then P(roll 2 sixes) = $\binom{5}{2} \times \left(\frac{1}{6}\right)^2 \times \left(\frac{5}{6}\right)^3 = \frac{5!}{2!3!} \times \frac{1}{36} \times \frac{125}{216}$ = **0.161** (3 d.p.)

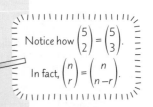

Notice how $\binom{5}{2} = \binom{5}{3}$.

In fact, $\binom{n}{r} = \binom{n}{n-r}$.

b) Again, call "roll a 6" a success, and "roll anything other than a 6" a failure.

Then P(roll 3 sixes) = $\binom{5}{3} \times \left(\frac{1}{6}\right)^3 \times \left(\frac{5}{6}\right)^2 = \frac{5!}{3!2!} \times \frac{1}{216} \times \frac{25}{36}$ = **0.032** (3 d.p.)

c) This time, success means "roll a 1 or a 2", while failure is now "roll a 3, 4, 5 or 6".

Then P(roll 4 numbers less than 3) = $\binom{5}{4} \times \left(\frac{1}{3}\right)^4 \times \frac{2}{3} = \frac{5!}{4!1!} \times \frac{1}{81} \times \frac{2}{3}$ = **0.041** (3 d.p.)

There are **5 Conditions** for a **Binomial Distribution**

Binomial Distribution: B(n, p)

A random variable X follows a binomial distribution if these **5 conditions** are satisfied:

1) There is a **fixed number** (n) of trials.
2) Each trial results in either "**success**" or "**failure**".
3) All the trials are **independent**.
4) The probability of "success" (p) is the **same** in each trial.
5) The variable is the **total number of successes** in the n trials.

Binomial variables are discrete — they only take values 0, 1, 2... n.

n and p are the **parameters** of the binomial distribution.

Then, $P(X = x) = \binom{n}{x} \times p^x \times (1-p)^{n-x}$ for $x = 0, 1, 2,..., n$, and you can write $X \sim B(n, p)$.

If you're asked to comment on the **appropriateness** of a binomial model, you should check whether the variable satisfies **all** of these conditions.

The **expected** number of successes is given by ($n \times p$).

The Binomial Distribution

Use your *Calculator* to find *Binomial Probabilities*

Example: I have an unfair coin. When I toss this coin, the probability of getting heads is 0.35.
Find the probability that it will land on heads fewer than 3 times when I toss it 12 times in total.

If the random variable X represents the number of heads I get in 12 tosses, then $X \sim B(12, 0.35)$.
You need to find $P(X \le 2)$. You **could** work this out 'manually'...

$$P(0 \text{ heads}) + P(1 \text{ head}) + P(2 \text{ heads}) = \left[\binom{12}{0} \times 0.35^0 \times 0.65^{12}\right] + \left[\binom{12}{1} \times 0.35^1 \times 0.65^{11}\right] + \left[\binom{12}{2} \times 0.35^2 \times 0.65^{10}\right]$$

$$= 0.00568... + 0.03675... + 0.10884... = 0.15128... = \mathbf{0.151} \text{ (3 s.f.)}$$

However, it's much quicker to use the **binomial cumulative distribution function** (cdf) on your calculator.
This calculates $P(X \le x)$, for $X \sim B(n, p)$ — just enter the **correct values of** n, p **and** x.
For example, here, $n = 12$ and $p = 0.35$, and you need $P(X \le 2)$ (i.e. $x = 2$).
The calculator tells you that this is **0.15128...**, which is what you worked out above.

Be careful though:

- Some calculators have both a binomial **probability distribution function** (pdf)
  and a binomial **cumulative distribution function** (cdf). You use the **pdf** to find
  e.g. **P(X = 2)** (as on the previous page) and the **cdf** to find e.g. **P(X ≤ 2)** (as above).
- The cdf gives you $P(X \le x)$ — if you want $P(X \ge x)$ (or $P(X < x)$ etc.) you'll have to do
  some fancy probability-wrangling. E.g. $P(X < 7) = P(X \le 6)$, or $P(X > 4) = 1 - P(X \le 4)$.

Countless secrets contained within...

Example: I have a different unfair coin. When I toss this coin, the probability of getting tails is 0.6.
The random variable X represents the number of tails in 12 tosses, so $X \sim B(12, 0.6)$.
If I toss this coin 12 times, find the probability that:
a) it will land on tails more than 8 times,   b) it will land on heads exactly 9 times,
c) it will land on tails more than 3 but fewer than 6 times.

a) You're looking for $P(X > 8)$, which is $1 - P(X \le 8)$ (since '$X > 8$' and '$X \le 8$' are complementary events
   — see p.79). So, from your calculator: $P(X > 8) = 1 - 0.77466... = \mathbf{0.225}$ (3 s.f.)

b) If the coin lands on **heads** 9 times, then it lands on **tails** 3 times. You could use the binomial pdf
   to go straight to the answer, or if your calculator doesn't have one, you can use the cdf instead:
   $P(\text{heads } 9 \text{ times}) = P(X = 3) = P(X \le 3) - P(X \le 2) = 0.01526... - 0.00281... = \mathbf{0.0125}$ (3 s.f.)

c) $P(3 < X < 6) = P(X < 6) - P(X \le 3) = P(X \le 5) - P(X \le 3) = 0.15821... - 0.01526... = \mathbf{0.143}$ (3 s.f.)

Practice Questions

Q1 Find the probability of: a) getting exactly 9 heads when you toss a fair coin 10 times,
                           b) getting at least 9 heads when you toss a fair coin 10 times.

Q2 Find, to 4 decimal places: a) $P(X = 4)$ if $X \sim B(14, 0.27)$ b) $P(Y \le 15)$ if $Y \sim B(20, 0.4)$

Exam Questions

Q1 The random variable X follows the binomial distribution $X \sim B(12, 0.6)$. Find:
   a) $P(X < 8)$ [2 marks]   b) $P(X = 5)$ [1 mark]   c) $P(3 < X \le 7)$ [2 marks]

Q2 Apples are stored in crates of 40. The probability of any apple containing a maggot is 0.15, and is independent of any
   other apple containing a maggot. In a random sample of 40 apples, find the probability that:
   a) fewer than 6 apples contain maggots,   [2 marks]   b) more than 2 apples contain maggots.   [2 marks]
   c) Jin has 3 crates. Find the probability that more than 1 crate contains more than 2 apples with maggots.   [3 marks]
   d) Give one criticism of the assumption that apples contain maggots independently of each other.   [1 mark]

Get your dinner before the party — it's a bi-no-meal function...

Here's a handy trick that might save some time on certain questions: if the number of successes is $X \sim B(n, p)$,
then the number of failures is $Y \sim B(n, 1 - p)$. For example, the number of heads in the blue example is $Y \sim B(12, 0.4)$.

Statistical Sampling

No time for any small talk, I'm afraid. It's straight on with the business of populations and how to find out about them.

A **Population** is a **Group** of people or items

For any statistical investigation, there will be a **group** of people or items that you want to **find out about**. This group is called the **population**.

This could be:

- All the students in a maths class
- All the penguins in Antarctica
- All the chocolate puddings produced by a company in a year

1) Populations are said to be **finite** if it's possible for someone to **count how many** members there are. E.g. all the students in a maths class would be a finite population.

2) If it's **impossible to know exactly how many** members there are, the population is said to be **infinite**.

To **collect information** about your population, you can carry out a **survey**. This means questioning the people or examining the items.

> A population might have a finite number of members in theory, but if it's impossible to count them all in practice, the population is infinite. E.g. all the blades of grass in a field would be an infinite population (even though you could count them all in theory).

A **Census** surveys the **Whole Population**

When you collect information from **every member of a population**, it's called a **census**.

To do this, your population needs to be **finite**. It also helps if it's fairly **small** and **easily accessible** — so that getting information from every member is a straightforward task.

You need to know the **advantages and disadvantages** of doing a census, so here they are:

Census — Advantages	Census — Disadvantages
1) You get **accurate information** about the population, because every member has been surveyed.	1) For large populations, it takes a lot of **time and effort** to carry out.
2) It's a **true representation** of the population — it's **unbiased**.	2) This makes it **expensive** to do.
	3) It can be **difficult** to make sure **all members** are surveyed. If some are missed, bias can creep in.
	4) If the tested items are **used up or damaged** in some way, a census is impractical.

See the next page for more on bias.

Watch out for anything that might make doing a census a silly idea.

A **Sample** is **Part of a Population**

1) If doing a census is impossible or impractical, you can find out about a population by questioning or examining **just a selection** of the people or items. This **selected group** is called a **sample**.

2) Before selecting your sample, you need to identify the **sampling units** — these are the **individual members** of the population. A **full list** of all the **sampling units** is called a **sampling frame**.

3) This list must give a **unique name or number** to each sampling unit, and is used to **represent** the population when selecting a random sample (see the next page).

> **Example:** A company produces 100 chocolate puddings every day, and each pudding is labelled with a unique product number. Every day, a sample of 5 puddings is eaten as part of a quality control test.
>
> a) Why is it necessary for the company to take a sample rather than carry out a census?
>
>   **If they ate all the puddings, there would be none left to sell.**
>
>   *A sampling frame can only be produced when you know exactly who or what makes up the population.*
>
> b) Identify the sampling units.   c) Suggest a sampling frame.
>
>   **The individual puddings**   **A list of all one hundred unique product numbers.**

Statistical Sampling

A *Sample* needs to be *Representative* of its population

Data collected from a **sample** is used to draw conclusions about the **whole population**. So it's vital that the sample is **as much like** the population as possible. A **biased** sample is one which **doesn't fairly represent** the population.

To Avoid Sampling Bias:

1) Select from the **correct population** and make sure **none** of the population is **excluded** — that means drawing up an accurate sampling frame and sticking to it. E.g. if you want to find out the views of residents from a particular street, your sample should only include residents from that street and should be chosen from a full list of the residents.

2) Select your sample at **random** — see below. Non-random sampling methods include things like the sampler just asking their friends (who might all give similar answers), or asking for volunteers (meaning they only get people with strong views on a subject).

3) Make sure all your sample members **respond** — otherwise the results could be biased. E.g. if some of your sampled residents are out when you go to interview them, it's important that you go back and get their views another time.

You need to be able to *Justify Choosing a Sample* over a census

In most situations, it's **more practical** to survey a **sample** rather than carry out a census — make sure you **can explain why**. But remember, the **downside** is that your results **might not be as reliable**, either due to sampling bias, or just the natural variability between samples (see below).

Sampling — Advantages

1) **Quicker** and **cheaper** than a census, and **easier to get hold of** all the required information.

2) It's the only option when surveyed items are **used up or damaged**.

Sampling — Disadvantages

1) **Variability between samples** — each possible sample will give different results, so you could just happen to select one which doesn't accurately reflect the population.
One way to reduce the likelihood of large variability is by using a **large sample size**. The more sampling units that are surveyed, the **more reliable** the information should be.

2) Samples can easily be affected by **sampling bias**.

Different *Sampling Methods* are better in *Different Situations*

If you choose to select a sample, then you need to decide which **method** to use. There are plenty to choose from, and they all have their advantages and disadvantages.

In *Random Sampling*, all members are *Equally Likely* to be selected

In a **simple random sample**, every person or item in the population has an **equal chance** of being selected, and each selection is **independent** of every other selection.

Every single possible sample is equally likely.

To choose a random sample:

* Give a **number** to each **population member**, from a full list of the **population**.
* Generate a list of **random numbers** (using a computer, calculator, dice or random number table).
* **Match** these numbers to the population members to select your sample.

Example: A zoo has 80 raccoons. Describe how the random number table opposite could be used to select a sample of three of them, for a study on tail lengths.

8330	3992	1840
0330	1290	3237
9165	4815	0766

1) First, draw up a **list** of **all 80 raccoons**, giving each one a two-digit number between 01 and 80.

2) Then, find the **first three numbers** between 01 and 80 from the table (**30, 39 and 18**), and select the raccoons with the matching numbers.

Here, the 4-digit numbers were split into two 2-digit numbers. Any numbers greater than 80 were rejected.

Advantage: Every member of the population has an **equal chance** of being selected, so it's **completely unbiased**.

Disadvantage: It can be **inconvenient** if the population is spread over a **large area** — it might be difficult to track down the selected members (e.g. in a nationwide sample).

Section 11 — Statistical Hypothesis Testing

Statistical Sampling

In *Systematic Sampling*, *every **nth Member** is selected*

So you could choose to select every tenth member of the population, for example.

To choose a systematic sample:
- Give a **number** to each population **member**, from a **full list** of the population.
- Calculate a **regular interval** to use by dividing the population size by the sample size.
- Generate a **random** starting point that is less than or equal to the size of the interval. The corresponding member of the population is the **first member** of your sample. Keep **adding** the interval to the starting point to select your sample.

Advantages: It can be used for quality control on a production line — a **machine** can be set up to sample every *n* items. It should also give an **unbiased** sample.

Disadvantage: The regular interval could coincide with a **pattern** — e.g. if every 10th item produced by a machine is faulty and you sample every 10th item, your sample will appear to show that **every item** produced is faulty, or that **no items** are faulty. Either way, your sample will be **biased**.

Opportunity Sampling is also known as *Convenience Sampling*

Opportunity sampling is where the sample is chosen from a section of the population at a particular place and time — whatever is **convenient** for the sampler.

> **Example:** Mel thinks that most people watch her favourite television programme. She asks 20 friends whether they watch the television programme. Give a reason why Mel's sample may be biased.
>
> Mel's friends could be of a **similar age** or the **same gender**, which is **not representative** of the whole population. OR
> *Any sensible comment will do here.*
> Because this is Mel's favourite television programme, she might have **encouraged** her friends to watch it too.

Advantage: Data can be gathered very **quickly** and **easily**.

Disadvantage: It **isn't random** and can be **very biased** — there's no attempt to obtain a **representative** sample.

In *Stratified Sampling*, *the population is divided into **Categories***

If a population is divided into **categories** (e.g. age or gender), you can use a **stratified sample** — this uses the same **proportion** of each category in the sample as there is in the population.

To choose a stratified sample:
- Divide the population into **categories**.
- Calculate the **total** population.
- Calculate the number needed for each category in the sample, using:

$$\text{Size of category in sample} = \frac{\text{size of category in population}}{\text{total size of population}} \times \text{total sample size}$$

- Select the sample for each category at **random**.

Lance, Marek, Brett and Jay were selected to represent the 'Roman soldiers not wearing trousers' category.

> **Example:** A teacher takes a sample of 20 pupils from her school, stratified by year group. The table shows the number of pupils in each year group. Calculate how many pupils from each year group should be in her sample.
>
> | Year Group | No. of pupils |
> |---|---|
> | 7 | 120 |
> | 8 | 80 |
> | 9 | 95 |
> | 10 | 63 |
> | 11 | 42 |
>
> The population is already split into **five categories**, based on **year group**.
> Total population = 120 + 80 + 95 + 63 + 42 = **400**
> Calculate the number needed for each category, rounding to the nearest whole number:
>
> Year 7 = $\frac{120}{400} \times 20 = $ **6**   Year 8 = $\frac{80}{400} \times 20 = $ **4**   Year 9 = $\frac{95}{400} \times 20 = 4.75 \approx$ **5**
>
> Year 10 = $\frac{63}{400} \times 20 = 3.15 \approx$ **3**   Year 11 = $\frac{42}{400} \times 20 = 2.1 \approx$ **2**
>
> *You should check that these add up to the required sample size: 6 + 4 + 5 + 3 + 2 = 20*

Advantages: If the population can be divided up into distinct categories (e.g. age), it's likely to give a **representative sample**. It's useful when results may **vary** depending on category.

Disadvantages: It's not useful when there aren't any **obvious** categories. It can be **expensive** because of the extra detail involved.

Statistical Sampling

Quota Sampling *also divides the population into* Categories

To choose a quota sample:
- Divide the population into **categories**.
- Give each category a **quota** (number of members to sample).
- Collect data until the quotas are met in **all** categories (**without** using random sampling).

The main difference between quota and stratified sampling is that no attempt is made to be random in quota sampling. It's often used in market research.

Advantages: It can be done when there **isn't** a full list of the population. **Every** sample member responds because the interviewer continues to sample until all the quotas are met.

Disadvantage: It can be **easily biased** by the interviewer — e.g. they could **exclude** some of the population.

Clusters *are a bit* Different *to* Categories

To choose a cluster sample:
- Divide the population into **clusters** covering the **whole population**, where **no member** of the population belongs to **multiple clusters**.
- **Randomly** select clusters to use in the sample, based on the required sample size.
- Either use **all** of the members of the selected clusters (a **one-stage** cluster sample), or **randomly sample** within each cluster to form the sample (a **two-stage** cluster sample).

The difference between **clusters** and **categories** is that categories should be groups that you expect to give **different** results to each other (e.g. if you were measuring height, different year groups in a school), while clusters should give **similar** results (e.g. different classes in Year 7).

Advantages: It can be more **practical** than other methods (e.g. quicker or cheaper) in certain situations. You can incorporate **other sampling methods** at either stage, making it quite **adaptable**.

Disadvantages: Because you only sample certain clusters, the results can be less representative of the population as a whole. It's not always possible to separate a population into clusters in a natural way.

Practice Questions

Q1 For each of the following situations, explain whether it would be more sensible to carry out a census or a sample survey:
  a) Ryan has a biased coin. He wants to find the proportion of coin tosses that will result in 'heads'.
  b) Pies are produced in batches of 200. A quality controller wants to check how full the pies are by removing the lids and measuring the depth of the filling.
  c) There are 24 students in Louisa's maths class. She wants to know the average mark for the class in the last maths test.

Q2 Obsidian is carrying out a survey on public transport in his town. He asks 10 people who live on his street for their opinions. What type of sampling is this?

Q3 Explain how you could use systematic sampling to survey people visiting a cinema one Saturday afternoon.

Exam Questions

Q1 One of the history teachers at a school wants to survey a sample of Year 7 pupils in the school.
  a) Identify: (i) the population for the survey, (ii) a suitable sampling frame that she could use. [2 marks]
  b) She uses all of the pupils in her Year 7 class as her sample and gives them a questionnaire, which has questions on a number of different topics. For each of the topics given below, state, with an explanation, whether or not her sample is likely to be biased.
    (i) Pupils' opinions on history lessons at the school. (ii) How far away from the school pupils live. [2 marks]

Q2 A film club has 250 members. 98 of them are retired, 34 are unemployed, 83 work full- or part-time and the rest are students. The secretary wants to survey a sample of 25 members. She uses stratified sampling to select her sample. How many people in each category should she ask? [4 marks]

I need to interview 5.68 people in my class...

Make sure you know the different types of sampling and the advantages and disadvantages of each one.

Hypothesis Tests

There are a lot of technical terms to learn over the next two pages. It might feel a bit hard-going, but don't despair — it's paving the way for a return to some old friends later on (and it'll come in really handy for the exam).

A **Hypothesis** is a **Statement** you want to **Test**

Hypothesis testing is about using **sample data** to **test statements** about **population parameters**. Unfortunately, it comes with a fleet of terms you need to know.

> A parameter is a quantity that describes a characteristic of a population (e.g. mean or variance).

- **Null Hypothesis (H_0)** — a statement about the value of a population parameter. Your data may allow you to **reject** this hypothesis.
- **Alternative Hypothesis (H_1)** — a statement that describes the value of the population parameter if H_0 is rejected.
- **Hypothesis Test** — a statistical test that tests the claim that H_0 makes about the parameter against that made by H_1. It tests whether H_0 should be rejected or not, using evidence from sample data.
- **Test Statistic** — a statistic calculated from sample data which is used to decide whether or not to reject H_0.

1) For any hypothesis test, you need to **write two hypotheses** — a **null hypothesis** and an **alternative hypothesis**.

2) You often choose the **null hypothesis** to be something you actually **think is false**. This is because hypothesis tests can only show that **statements are false** — they **can't** prove that things are **true**. So you're aiming to find **evidence** for what you think is **true**, by **disproving** what you think is **false**.

3) H_0 needs to give a **specific value** to the parameter, since all your calculations will be based on this value. You **assume** this value holds **true** for the test, then see if your data allows you to **reject** it. H_1 is then a statement that describes how you think the **value of the parameter differs** from the value given by H_0.

4) The **test statistic** you choose **depends on the parameter** you're interested in. It should be a **'summary'** of the sample data, and should have a sampling distribution that can be calculated using the parameter value specified by H_0.

> **Example:** A 4-sided spinner has sides labelled A–D. Jemma thinks that the spinner is biased towards side A. She spins it 20 times and counts the number of times, Y, that she gets side A.
>
> a) Write down a suitable null hypothesis to test Jemma's theory.
> b) Write down a suitable alternative hypothesis.
> c) Describe the test statistic Jemma should use.

a) If you assume the spinner is unbiased, each side has a probability of 0.25 of being spun.
Let p = the probability of spinning side A.
Then: $H_0: p = 0.25$ ◄——— *By assuming the spinner is unbiased, the parameter, p, can be given the specific value 0.25. Jemma is then interested in disproving this hypothesis.*

b) If the spinner is biased towards side A, then the probability will be greater than 0.25. So: $H_1: p > 0.25$ ◄—— *This is what Jemma actually thinks.*

c) The test statistic is Y, the number of times she gets side A. ◄—— *Assuming H_0 is true, the sampling distribution of Y is B(20, 0.25) — see p.86.*

Hypothesis Tests can be **One-Tailed** or **Two-Tailed**

> The 'tailed' business is to do with the critical region used by the test — see the next page.

For $H_0: \theta = a$, where θ is a parameter and a is a number:

1) The test is **one-tailed** if H_1 **is specific** about the value of θ compared to a, i.e. $H_1: \theta > a$, or $H_1: \theta < a$.

2) The test is **two-tailed** if H_1 specifies only that θ **doesn't equal** a, i.e. $H_1: \theta \neq a$.

Whether you use a one-tailed or a two-tailed test depends on how you define H_1. And that depends on **what you want to find out about the parameter** and any **suspicions** you might have about it.

> E.g. in the example above, Jemma suspects that the probability of getting side A is **greater than 0.25**. This is what she wants to test, so it is sensible to define $H_1: p > 0.25$.
>
> If she wants to test for **bias**, but is **unsure** if it's towards or against side A, she could define $H_1: p \neq 0.25$.

A very important thing to remember is that the results of a hypothesis test are either '**reject H_0**', or '**do not reject H_0**' — which means you haven't found enough evidence to **disprove** H_0, and **not** that you've proved it.

Hypothesis Tests

If your Data is *Significant*, Reject H_0

1) You would **reject H_0** if the **observed value** of the test statistic is **unlikely** under the null hypothesis.

2) The **significance level** of a test (α) determines **how unlikely** the value needs to be before H_0 is rejected. It also determines the **strength** of the **evidence** that the test has provided — the lower the value of α, the stronger the evidence you have for saying H_0 is false. You'll usually be told what level to use — e.g. 1% ($\alpha = 0.01$), 5% ($\alpha = 0.05$), or 10% ($\alpha = 0.1$). For a **two-tailed** test, you want a level of $\frac{\alpha}{2}$ for **each tail**.

3) To decide whether your result is **significant**:
   - Define the **sampling distribution** of the **test statistic** under the **null hypothesis**.
   - Calculate the **probability** of getting a value that's **at least as extreme** as the **observed value** from this distribution — this is known as the *p*-value.
   - If the *p*-value is **less than or equal to** α (or $\frac{\alpha}{2}$ for a two-tailed test), **reject H_0** in favour of H_1.

   Example: Javed wants to test at the 5% level whether or not a coin is biased towards tails. He tosses the coin 10 times and records the number of tails, X. He gets 9 tails.
   a) Define suitable hypotheses for p, the probability of getting tails.
   b) State the condition under which Javed would reject H_0.

   P(at least as extreme as 9) means 9 or more (this is the p-value).

   Significance level

   a) **H_0: $p = 0.5$ and H_1: $p > 0.5$.**   b) Under H_0, $X \sim B(10, 0.5)$. **If $P(X \geq 9) \leq 0.05$, Javed would reject H_0.**

The *Critical Region* is the *Set of Significant Values*

1) The **critical region** (CR) is the **set of all values of the test statistic** that would cause you to **reject** H_0. The first value that's **inside** the CR is called the **critical value**, so results as extreme (or more) as this are **significant**.

2) **One-tailed tests** have a **single** CR, containing the highest or lowest values. For **two-tailed tests**, the region is **split into two** — half at the lower end and half at the upper end. Each half has a probability of $\frac{\alpha}{2}$.

3) To **test whether your result is significant**, find the critical region and if it **contains the observed value**, reject H_0.

   Example (continued):   c) Find the critical region for the test, at the 5% level.

   This is a **one-tailed** test with H_1: $p > 0.5$, so you're only interested in the **upper end** of the distribution.
   Use the **binomial cdf** on your calculator (see p.87) to find the value of x such that $P(X \geq x) \leq 0.05$ (the significance level). As calculators usually give probabilities for $P(X \leq x)$ you need to use $P(X \geq x) = 1 - P(X < x)$.

   $P(X \geq 8) = 1 - P(X < 8) = 1 - P(X \leq 7) = 1 - 0.9453... = \mathbf{0.0546...} > 0.05$
   $P(X \geq 9) = 1 - P(X < 9) = 1 - P(X \leq 8) = 1 - 0.9892... = \mathbf{0.0107...} < 0.05$

   The **acceptance region** is where you **don't** reject H_0 — i.e. $X \leq 8$.

   So the critical region is $X \geq 9$ ◄ So values of 9 or 10 would cause you to reject H_0: $p = 0.5$.

The **actual significance level** of a test is the probability of **incorrectly rejecting H_0** — i.e. the probability of getting extreme data by chance when H_0 is true. This is often **different** from the level of significance originally asked for in the question. Here, the actual significance level is $P(X \geq 9) = 0.0107$, which is much lower than 0.05.

Practice Question

Q1 In 2012, a survey found that 68% of residents in a town used the local library. In 2016, the proportion was found to be 53%. A hypothesis test was carried out, using H_0: $p = 0.68$ and H_1: $p < 0.68$, and the null hypothesis was rejected. Does this result support the claim that the percentage of local residents using the library fell by 15%?

Exam Question

Q1 One year ago, 43% of customers rated a restaurant as 'Excellent'. Since then, a new chef has been employed, and the manager believes that the approval rating will have gone up. He decides to carry out a hypothesis test to test his belief. Define the null and alternative hypotheses the manager should use.   [1 mark]

I repeat, X has entered the critical region — we have a significant situation...

Don't mix up the p-value with the binomial probability p. I know, I know, it would have been nice if they'd used a different letter, but that's life. Remember to always divide α by 2 whenever you're doing a two-tailed test.

Hypothesis Tests and Binomial Distributions

Remember that binomial distribution you saw in the last section? Well, it's back — with a vengeance. It's time to pick your best 'hypothesis testing' foot and put it firmly forward, because this stuff ain't no gentle walk in the park...

Use a **Hypothesis Test** to **Find Out** about the **Population Parameter p**

Okay, so you know how hypothesis tests work — now it's time to put it into action. Fortunately, you've got all the tools you need to carry out a hypothesis test for anything that's modelled by a **binomial distribution**.

Hypothesis tests for the binomial parameter p all follow the **same general method** — this is what you do:

1) Define the **population parameter** in **context**
— for a binomial distribution it's always p, a **probability** of success, or **proportion** of a population.

2) Write down the **null** hypothesis (H_0) — $H_0: p = a$ for some constant a.

3) Write down the **alternative** hypothesis (H_1)
— H_1 will either be $H_1: p < a$ or $H_1: p > a$ (one-tailed test) or $H_1: p \neq a$ (two-tailed test).

4) State the **test statistic**, X — always just the number of '**successes**' in the sample.

5) Write down the **sampling distribution** of the test statistic under H_0 — $X \sim B(n, p)$ where n is the sample size.

6) State the **significance level,** α — you'll usually be given this.

7) Test for **significance** or find the **critical region** (see previous page).

8) Write your **conclusion** — state whether or not you have **sufficient evidence** to reject H_0.

Example: In a past census of employees, 20% were in favour of a change to working hours. After making changes to staff contracts, the manager now believes that the proportion of staff wanting a change in their working hours has decreased. The manager carries out a random sample of 30 employees, and 2 are in favour of a change in hours.

Stating your hypotheses clearly, test the manager's claim at the 5% level of significance.

1) Let p = **proportion of employees in favour of change to hours**.

2) Assume there's been **no change** in the proportion: $H_0: p = 0.2$ ← *You assume there's been no change in the value of the parameter, so you can give it a value of 0.2. The alternative hypothesis states what the manager actually thinks.*

3) The manager's interested in whether the proportion has **decreased**, so: $H_1: p < 0.2$

4) Let X = the number of employees in the sample who are in favour of change.

5) Under H_0, $X \sim B(30, 0.2)$. ← *The sampling distribution of the test statistic uses the value $p = 0.2$.*

6) The **significance level** is 5%, so $\alpha = 0.05$.

7) Find the p-**value** — the probability of a value for your **test statistic at least as extreme** as the **observed value**. This is a **one-tailed test** and you're interested in the lower end of the distribution. So you want to find the probability of X taking a value less than or equal to 2.
Using the binomial cdf on your calculator:
$P(X \leq 2) = 0.0441...$, and since $0.0441... < 0.05$, the result is **significant**.

8) Now write your **conclusion: There is evidence at the 5% level of significance to reject H_0 and to support the manager's claim that the proportion in favour of change has decreased.**

Always say "there is evidence to reject H_0", or "there is insufficient evidence to reject H_0", never just "accept H_0" or "reject H_1".

To find a **critical region**, your test would look the same except for step 7...

7) Find the **critical region** for a test at this level of significance. This is a **one-tailed test** and you're interested in the lower end of the distribution. The critical region is the biggest possible set of 'low' values of X with a total probability of ≤ 0.05.
Using the binomial cdf on your calculator:
Try $X \leq 2$: $P(X \leq 2) = 0.0441... < 0.05$. Now try $X \leq 3$: $P(X \leq 3) = 0.1227... > 0.05$.
So **CR is $X \leq 2$**. These results fall in the CR, so the result is **significant**.

Marjorie and Edwin were ready to enter the critical region.

Hypothesis Tests and Binomial Distributions

You might be asked to find a *Critical Region* or *Actual Significance Level*

Example: Records show that the proportion of trees in a wood that suffer from a particular leaf disease is 15%. Chloe thinks that recent weather conditions might have affected this proportion. She examines a random sample of 20 of the trees.

a) Using a 10% level of significance, find the critical region for a two-tailed test of Chloe's theory. The probability of rejection in each tail should be less than 0.05.

b) Find the actual significance level of a test based on your critical region from part a).

Chloe finds that 8 of the sampled trees have the leaf disease.

c) Comment on this finding in relation to your answer to part a) and Chloe's theory.

a) Let p = proportion of trees with the leaf disease.

$H_0: p = 0.15$ $H_1: p \neq 0.15$

Let X = number of sampled trees with the disease. Under H_0, $X \sim B(20, 0.15)$.

$\alpha = 0.1$, and since the test is **two-tailed**, the probability of X falling in each tail should be 0.05, at most.

This is a two-tailed test, so you're interested in both ends of the sampling distribution.
The lower tail is the biggest possible set of 'low' values of X with a total probability of ≤ 0.05.
The upper tail is the biggest possible set of 'high' values of X with a total probability of ≤ 0.05.

Using a calculator: Lower tail: Upper tail:
$P(X \leq 0) = 0.0387... < 0.05$ $P(X \geq 6) = 1 - P(X \leq 5) = 1 - 0.9326... = 0.0673... > 0.05$
$P(X \leq 1) = 0.1755... > 0.05$ $P(X \geq 7) = 1 - P(X \leq 6) = 1 - 0.9780... = 0.0219... < 0.05$

So **CR is $X = 0$ or $X \geq 7$**.

b) The **actual significance level** is: $P(X = 0) + P(X \geq 7) = 0.0387... + 0.0219... = \mathbf{0.0607}$ or **6.07%** (3 s.f.)

c) The observed value of 8 is in the critical region. **So there is evidence at the 10% level of significance to reject H_0 and to support Chloe's theory that there has been a change in the proportion of affected trees.**

Practice Questions

Q1 Carry out the following tests of the binomial parameter p.
Let X represent the number of successes in a random sample of size 20:

a) Test $H_0: p = 0.2$ against $H_1: p \neq 0.2$, at the 5% significance level, using $x = 1$.

b) Test $H_0: p = 0.4$ against $H_1: p > 0.4$, at the 1% significance level, using $x = 15$.

Q2 Find the critical region for the following test where $X \sim B(10, p)$:
Test $H_0: p = 0.3$ against $H_1: p < 0.3$, at the 5% significance level.

Exam Question

Q1 Over a long period of time, the chef at an Italian restaurant has found that there is a probability of 0.2 that a customer ordering a dessert on a weekday evening will order tiramisu. He thinks that the proportion of customers ordering desserts on Saturday evenings who order tiramisu is greater than 0.2.

a) State the name of the probability distribution that would be used in a hypothesis test for the value of p, the proportion of Saturday evening dessert eaters ordering tiramisu.   [1 mark]

A random sample of 20 customers who ordered a dessert on a Saturday evening was taken. 7 of these customers ordered tiramisu.

b) (i) Stating your hypotheses clearly, test the chef's theory at the 5% level of significance.   [6 marks]

(ii) Find the minimum number of tiramisu orders needed for the result to be significant.   [1 mark]

My hypothesis is — this is very likely to come up in the exam...

Remember, to make sure that you're not using the binomial pdf by accident (if your calculator has one). Of course, you can use the pdf if you need to find the probability of a single value, as long as you're doing it for the right reasons.

Constant Acceleration Equations

Welcome to the technicolour world of kinematics. Fashions may change, but there will always be questions that involve objects travelling in a straight line. It's just a case of picking the right equations to solve the problem.

There are **Five Constant Acceleration Equations**

These are also called "**suvat**" questions because of the five variables involved:

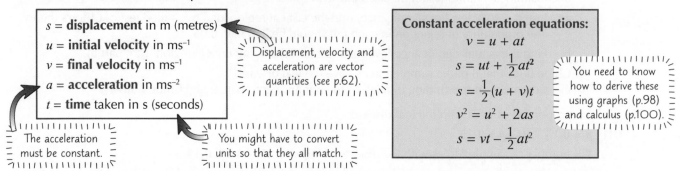

s = **displacement** in m (metres)

u = **initial velocity** in ms⁻¹

v = **final velocity** in ms⁻¹

a = **acceleration** in ms⁻²

t = **time** taken in s (seconds)

Displacement, velocity and acceleration are vector quantities (see p.62).

The acceleration must be constant.

You might have to convert units so that they all match.

Constant acceleration equations:
$$v = u + at$$
$$s = ut + \frac{1}{2}at^2$$
$$s = \frac{1}{2}(u + v)t$$
$$v^2 = u^2 + 2as$$
$$s = vt - \frac{1}{2}at^2$$

You need to know how to derive these using graphs (p.98) and calculus (p.100).

These equations are in the formula booklet, but you still need to be comfortable using them. Questions might give you **three variables** — your job is to **choose** the equation that will find you an unknown **fourth variable**.

Constant acceleration questions often have the following **modelling assumptions** (see p.108 for more on modelling):

1) **The object is a particle** — its dimensions can be ignored and no other forces (e.g. air resistance) act on it.

2) **Acceleration is constant** — so you can use the suvat equations.

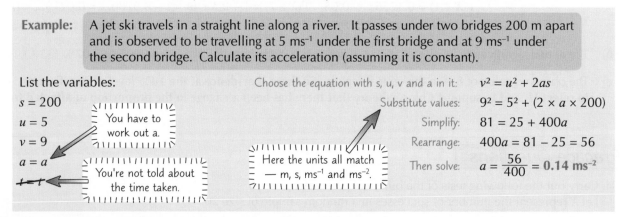

Example: A jet ski travels in a straight line along a river. It passes under two bridges 200 m apart and is observed to be travelling at 5 ms⁻¹ under the first bridge and at 9 ms⁻¹ under the second bridge. Calculate its acceleration (assuming it is constant).

List the variables:

$s = 200$

$u = 5$

$v = 9$

$a = a$

$t = t$

You have to work out a.

You're not told about the time taken.

Choose the equation with s, u, v and a in it: $v^2 = u^2 + 2as$

Here the units all match — m, s, ms⁻¹ and ms⁻².

Substitute values: $9^2 = 5^2 + (2 \times a \times 200)$

Simplify: $81 = 25 + 400a$

Rearrange: $400a = 81 - 25 = 56$

Then solve: $a = \dfrac{56}{400} = \mathbf{0.14 \ ms^{-2}}$

*Motion under Gravity just means taking **a = g***

Assume that $g = 9.8$ ms⁻² unless the exam paper says otherwise. If you don't, you risk losing a mark for accuracy.

Don't be put off by questions involving objects **moving freely under gravity** — they're just telling you the **acceleration is g**.

If the question gives a mass or weight, then it's a **forces** question — see Section 13.

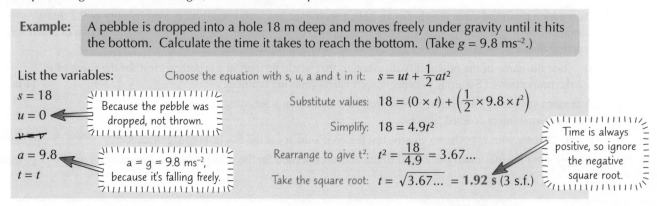

Example: A pebble is dropped into a hole 18 m deep and moves freely under gravity until it hits the bottom. Calculate the time it takes to reach the bottom. (Take $g = 9.8$ ms⁻².)

List the variables:

$s = 18$

$u = 0$

$v = v$

$a = 9.8$

$t = t$

Because the pebble was dropped, not thrown.

a = g = 9.8 ms⁻², because it's falling freely.

Choose the equation with s, u, a and t in it: $s = ut + \frac{1}{2}at^2$

Substitute values: $18 = (0 \times t) + \left(\frac{1}{2} \times 9.8 \times t^2\right)$

Simplify: $18 = 4.9t^2$

Rearrange to give t²: $t^2 = \dfrac{18}{4.9} = 3.67...$

Take the square root: $t = \sqrt{3.67...} = \mathbf{1.92 \ s}$ (3 s.f.)

Time is always positive, so ignore the negative square root.

When an object is projected vertically **upwards**, it helps to choose **up** as the **positive direction**. Gravity always acts **downwards**, so you'd need to use $a = -g$.

At the object's **maximum height**, $v = 0$ — its vertical velocity is momentarily zero before it starts falling again.

Constant Acceleration Equations

Sometimes there's **More Than One Object Moving** at the **Same Time**

For these questions, t is often the same (or connected as in this example) because time ticks along at the same rate for both objects. The distance travelled might also be connected.

> **Example:** Car A travels along a straight road at a constant velocity of 30 ms^{-1}, passing point R at time $t = 0$. Exactly 2 seconds later, a second car, B, travelling at 25 ms^{-1}, moves in the same direction from point R. Car B accelerates at a constant 2 ms^{-2}. Show that, when the two cars are level, $t^2 - 9t - 46 = 0$.

For each car, there are different "*suvat*" variables, so write separate lists and separate equations.

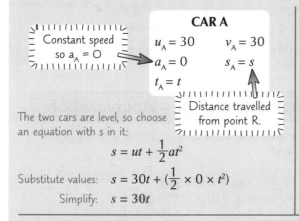

Constant speed so $a_A = 0$

CAR A

$u_A = 30$ $v_A = 30$
$a_A = 0$ $s_A = s$
$t_A = t$

Distance travelled from point R.

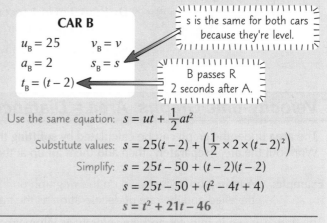

CAR B

$u_B = 25$ $v_B = v$
$a_B = 2$ $s_B = s$
$t_B = (t - 2)$

s is the same for both cars because they're level.

B passes R 2 seconds after A.

The two cars are level, so choose an equation with s in it:

$$s = ut + \frac{1}{2}at^2$$

Substitute values: $s = 30t + (\frac{1}{2} \times 0 \times t^2)$

Simplify: $s = 30t$

Use the same equation: $s = ut + \frac{1}{2}at^2$

Substitute values: $s = 25(t - 2) + \left(\frac{1}{2} \times 2 \times (t - 2)^2\right)$

Simplify: $s = 25t - 50 + (t - 2)(t - 2)$

$s = 25t - 50 + (t^2 - 4t + 4)$

$s = t^2 + 21t - 46$

The distance travelled by both cars is equal, so put the equations for s equal to each other and rearrange:

$30t = t^2 + 21t - 46$
$t^2 - 9t - 46 = 0$, as required

Practice Questions

Take $g = 9.8$ ms^{-2} in each of these questions.

Q1 A motorcyclist accelerates uniformly from 3 ms^{-1} to 9 ms^{-1} in 2 seconds.
What is the distance travelled by the motorcyclist during this acceleration?

Q2 A stone is projected vertically upwards at 7 ms^{-1} from the ground.
How long does it take to reach its maximum height?

Q3 A ball is projected vertically upwards at 3 ms^{-1} from a point 1.5 m above the ground.
How fast will the ball be travelling when it hits the ground?

"Model me as a falling particlllllllleeee..."

Exam Questions

Q1 A window cleaner of a block of flats accidentally drops his sandwich, which falls freely to the ground.
The speed of the sandwich as it passes a high floor is u ms^{-1}.
After a further 1.2 seconds the sandwich is moving at a speed of 17 ms^{-1} past a lower floor.

a) Find the value of u.   [3 marks]
b) The vertical distance between the consecutive floors of the building is h m.
It takes the sandwich another 2.1 seconds to fall the remaining 14 floors to the ground. Find h.   [4 marks]

Q2 A rocket is projected vertically upwards from a point 8 m above the ground at a speed of u ms^{-1}
and travels freely under gravity. The rocket hits the ground at 20 ms^{-1}. Find:

a) the value of u,   [3 marks]
b) how long it takes to hit the ground.   [3 marks]

Newton was one of the first people to realise that gravity sucks...

Make sure you: 1) make a list of the suvat variables EVERY time you get one of these questions,
2) look out for "hidden" values — e.g. "initially at rest..." means $u = 0$,
3) choose and solve the equation that goes with the variables you've got.

Motion Graphs

You can use displacement-time (x/t), and velocity-time (v/t) graphs to represent all sorts of motion.

Displacement-time Graphs: Height = Distance and Gradient = Velocity

The **steeper** the line, the **greater** the velocity. A **horizontal** line has a **zero gradient**, so the object **isn't moving**.

Example: A rabbit's journey is shown on this x/t graph. Describe the motion.

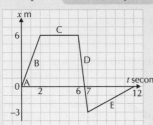

A: Starts from rest (when $t = 0$, $x = 0$).

B: Travels 6 m in 2 seconds at a velocity of $6 \div 2 = 3$ ms^{-1}.

C: Rests for 4 seconds ($v = 0$).

D: Runs 9 m in 1 second at a velocity of $-9 \div 1 = -9$ ms^{-1} in the opposite direction, passing the starting point.

E: Returns to start, travelling 3 m in 5 seconds at a velocity of $3 \div 5 = 0.6$ ms^{-1}.

Velocity is a vector quantity, so the direction needs to be included.

Velocity-time Graphs: Area = Distance and Gradient = Acceleration

The **area** under the graph can be calculated by **splitting** the area into rectangles, triangles or trapeziums. Work out the areas **separately**, then **add** them all up at the end.

Example: A train journey is shown on the v/t graph on the right. Find the distance travelled and the rate of deceleration as the train comes to a stop.

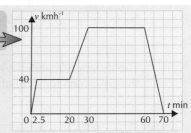

The time is given in minutes and the velocity as kilometres per hour, so divide the time in minutes by 60 to get the time in hours.

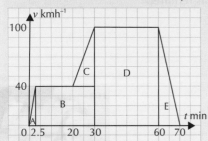

Area of A: $(2.5 \div 60 \times 40) \div 2 = 0.833...$

Area of B: $27.5 \div 60 \times 40 = 18.33...$

Area of C: $(10 \div 60 \times 60) \div 2 = 5$

Area of D: $30 \div 60 \times 100 = 50$

Area of E: $(10 \div 60 \times 100) \div 2 = 8.33...$

Total area = 82.5 so distance is **82.5 km**

You might get a speed-time graph instead of a velocity-time graph — they're pretty much the same, except speeds are always positive, whereas velocities can be negative.

Gradient at the end of the journey: -100 kmh$^{-1} \div (10 \div 60)$ hours $= -600$ kmh^{-2}. So the train decelerates at **600 kmh^{-2}**.

Derive the suvat equations with a Velocity-time Graph

You met the **suvat equations** on p.96 — now it's time to see where they come from. Using a **velocity-time graph** you can derive the equations $v = u + at$ and $s = \frac{1}{2}(u + v)t$, then **use** these to derive the other equations.

Example: The graph shows a particle accelerating uniformly from initial velocity u to final velocity v in t s.

a) Use the graph to derive the equations: (i) $v = u + at$ (ii) $s = \frac{1}{2}(u + v)t$

b) Hence, show that $s = ut + \frac{1}{2}at^2$

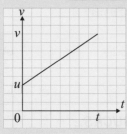

a) (i) It's a v/t graph, so the **gradient** represents the **acceleration**, a. The graph is a **straight line**, crossing the y-axis at u, so using '$y = mx + c$', the equation of the line is $v = u + at$.

  (ii) The **area** under a v/t graph represents the **displacement**, s. Here the area is a trapezium, so just use the formula for area of a trapezium: $s = \frac{1}{2}(u + v)t$

b) Substitute $v = u + at$ into $s = \frac{1}{2}(u + v)t$:

$s = \frac{1}{2}(u + u + at)t = \frac{1}{2}(2u + at)t \Rightarrow s = ut + \frac{1}{2}at^2$

You can derive the other suvat equations in a similar way, or by using calculus — see p.100.

Motion Graphs

Graphs can be used to **Solve Complicated Problems**

Some more complicated problems might involve working out information **not shown directly on the graph**.

Example: A jogger and a cyclist set off at the same time. The jogger runs with a constant velocity. The cyclist accelerates from rest, reaching a velocity of 5 ms⁻¹ after 6 s, and then continues at this velocity. The cyclist overtakes the jogger after 15 s. Use the graph below to find the velocity, u, of the jogger.

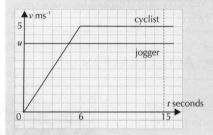

After 15 s, the distance each has travelled is the same, so you can work out the area under the two graphs to get the distances:

Jogger: distance = area = $15u$

Cyclist: distance = area = $\left(\frac{1}{2} \times 6 \times 5\right) + (9 \times 5) = 60$

So $15u = 60 \Rightarrow u = 4$ ms⁻¹

Practice Questions

Q1 Part of an athlete's training drill is shown on the x/t graph to the right.

a) Describe the athlete's motion during the drill.

b) State the velocity of the athlete at $t = 4$.

c) Find the distance travelled by the athlete during the drill.

Q2 A runner starts from rest and accelerates at 0.5 ms⁻² for 5 seconds. She maintains a constant velocity for 20 seconds then decelerates to a stop at 0.25 ms⁻². Find the total distance the runner travelled.

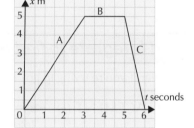

Q3 Using $v = u + at$, and $s = \frac{1}{2}(u + v)t$, show that:

a) $s = vt - \frac{1}{2}at^2$

b) $v^2 = u^2 + 2as$

Exam Questions

Q1 A train journey from station A to station B is shown on the graph on the right. The total distance between stations A and B is 2.1 km.

a) Find the value of V. [3 marks]

b) Calculate the distance travelled by the train while decelerating. [2 marks]

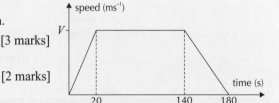

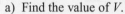

Q2 The velocity-time graph of a moving carriage on a roller coaster ride is shown on the left, where v ms⁻¹ is the velocity of the carriage.

a) Calculate the acceleration of the carriage at $t = 12$ s. [2 marks]

b) Sean says that the carriage travels further in the first 30 seconds of its journey than the second 30 seconds. Is Sean's statement correct? Provide evidence to support your answer. [4 marks]

c) After T seconds, the carriage has travelled 700 m. Find the value of T. [3 marks]

Random tongue-twister #1 — I wish to wash my Irish wristwatch...

If a picture is worth a thousand words then a graph is worth... um... a thousand and one. Make sure you know the features of each type of graph and know what the gradient and the area under the graph tells you.

Using Calculus for Kinematics

The suvat equations you saw on page 96 are just grand when you've got constant acceleration.
But when the acceleration varies with time, you need a few new tricks up your sleeve...

Differentiate to find Velocity and Acceleration from Displacement...

If you've got a particle moving in a **straight line** with acceleration that **varies with time**, you need to use **calculus** to find equations to describe the motion — look back at Sections 7 and 8 for a reminder about calculus.

1) To find an equation for **velocity**, **differentiate** the equation for **displacement** with respect to time.

2) To find an equation for **acceleration**, **differentiate** the equation for **velocity** with respect to time or differentiate the equation for displacement with respect to time **twice**.

$$\text{DISPLACEMENT } (s) \xrightarrow{\text{Differentiate}} \text{VELOCITY } (v) \xrightarrow{\text{Differentiate}} \text{ACCELERATION } (a)$$

Displacement is sometimes written as x instead of s.

Example: A particle moves in a straight line. At time t seconds, the velocity of the particle is v ms^{-1}, where $v = 7t + 5t^2$. Find an expression for the acceleration of the particle at time t.

Velocity is given as a function of time, so differentiate to find the acceleration:

$$v = 7t + 5t^2$$
$$a = \frac{dv}{dt} = (7 + 10t) \text{ ms}^{-2}$$

$$\frac{d}{dx}x^n = nx^{n-1}$$

Tour de Kinematiques
— Velo City, France.

...and Integrate to find Velocity and Displacement from Acceleration

It's similar if you're trying to go "back the other way", except you **integrate** with respect to t rather than differentiate:

$$\text{DISPLACEMENT } (s) \xleftarrow{\text{Integrate}} \text{VELOCITY } (v) \xleftarrow{\text{Integrate}} \text{ACCELERATION } (a)$$

Example: A particle P sets off from O and moves in a straight line. At time t seconds, its velocity is v ms^{-1}, where $v = 12 - t^2$. At $t = 0$, displacement $s = 0$. Find the time taken for P to return to O.

Velocity is given as a function of t, so integrate to find the displacement:

$$s = \int v \, dt = 12t - \frac{t^3}{3} + C$$

$$\int x^n \, dx = \frac{x^{n+1}}{n+1} + C$$

Use the information given in the question to find the value of the constant:

$$0 = 12(0) - \frac{0^3}{3} + C \Rightarrow C = 0 \Rightarrow s = 12t - \frac{t^3}{3}$$

P is at O when s = O, so solve the equation for t:

$$12t - \frac{t^3}{3} = 0 \Rightarrow t(36 - t^2) = 0 \Rightarrow t = 0, 6, \text{ or } -6$$

−6 can't be an answer, as you can't have a negative time.

Time taken for P to return to O is **6 seconds**.

Derive the suvat Equations with Calculus

You've derived the suvat equations with a v/t graph (p.98) — now it's time to use calculus.

Example: Use calculus to derive $v = u + at$ and $s = ut + \frac{1}{2}at^2$.

Acceleration is the rate of change of velocity v with time t:
$$a = \frac{dv}{dt} \Rightarrow v = \int a \, dt$$

Velocity is the rate of change of displacement s with time t:
$$v = \frac{ds}{dt} \Rightarrow s = \int v \, dt$$

Carry out the integration (remember that **a** is a **constant**):
$$v = \int a \, dt = at + C$$

Substitute v = u + at and integrate:
$$s = \int (u + at) \, dt = ut + \frac{1}{2}at^2 + C$$

Use the initial conditions v = u when t = O to find C:
$$u = a(0) + C$$
$$\Rightarrow C = u$$
$$\text{So } v = u + at$$

Use the initial conditions s = O when t = O to find C:
$$0 = u(0) + \frac{1}{2}a(0)^2 + C \Rightarrow C = 0$$
$$\text{So } s = ut + \frac{1}{2}at^2$$

Using Calculus for Kinematics

Differentiate to find *Maximum* / *Minimum* values

Stationary points are when the gradient is zero (see page 53) — you need to differentiate to find them.
To decide whether a stationary point is a **maximum** or a **minimum**, differentiate again.

Example: A particle sets off from the origin at $t = 0$ and moves in a straight line.
At time t seconds, the velocity of the particle is v ms^{-1}, where $v = 9t - 2t^2$.
Find the maximum velocity of the particle.

Differentiate v and put it equal to O
to find any stationary points:

$$v = 9t - 2t^2$$

$$\frac{dv}{dt} = 9 - 4t$$

$$\frac{dv}{dt} = 0 \text{ when } t = \frac{9}{4} = 2.25 \text{ s}$$

If $\frac{d^2y}{dx^2} < 0$, then it's a maximum.

If $\frac{d^2y}{dx^2} > 0$, then it's a minimum.

Differentiate v again to decide whether
this is a maximum or minimum:

$$\frac{d^2v}{dt^2} = -4, \text{ so } t = 2.25 \text{ s is a } \textbf{maximum}.$$

Substitute t = 2.25 s into the expression for v:

$$v = 9(2.25) - 2(2.25^2) = 10.125 \text{ ms}^{-1}$$
So the maximum velocity is **10.125 ms^{-1}**.

Practice Questions

Q1 A particle moves along a straight line from the origin with velocity $v = 8t^2 - 2t$.
    a) Find the acceleration of the particle at time t.
    b) Find the displacement of the particle at time t.

Q2 A particle sets off from the origin at $t = 0$ s. Its displacement, in metres, at time t is $s = 6 \sin\left(\frac{1}{3}t\right)$.
    Find an expression for the acceleration of the particle at time t.

Q3 A particle is at rest at the origin at $t = 0$ s. It moves in a straight line with acceleration a ms^{-2},
    where $a = e^{\frac{1}{4}t}$. Find the displacement of the particle at time $t = 8$ s.

Exam Questions

Q1 A model train sets off from a station at time $t = 0$ s. It travels in a straight line, then returns to the station.
    At time t seconds, the distance, in metres, of the train from the station is $s = \frac{1}{100}(10t + 9t^2 - t^3)$, where $0 \leq t \leq 10$.
    a) Sketch the graph of s against t and hence explain the restriction $0 \leq t \leq 10$ s.   [3 marks]
    b) Find the maximum distance of the train from the station.   [5 marks]

Q2 A particle sets off from the origin O at $t = 0$ s and moves in a straight line.
    At time t seconds, the velocity of the particle is v ms^{-1}, where

$$v = \begin{cases} 9t - 3t^2 & 0 \leq t \leq 2 \text{ s} \\ \dfrac{24}{t^2} & t > 2 \text{ s} \end{cases}$$

    a) Find the maximum speed of the particle in the interval $0 \leq t \leq 2$ s.   [4 marks]
    b) Find the displacement of the particle from O at
        (i) $t = 2$ s   [3 marks]
        (ii) $t = 6$ s   [4 marks]

Calculus in kinematics — it's deriving me crazy...

This is one of those times when calculus is useful (told you so). The stuff you saw in Sections 5 and 6 can be applied to mechanics questions, so make sure you've really got calculus nailed. Then you've just got to remember that DISPLACEMENT differentiates to VELOCITY differentiates to ACCELERATION (and integrate to go the other way).

Forces and Modelling

Force questions and modelling go hand in hand, but you need to understand all the mechanics lingo.
For starters, 'modelling' in maths doesn't have anything to do with plastic aeroplane kits... or catwalks.

Types of forces

Weight (*W*)

Due to the particle's mass, *m* and the force of gravity, *g*: $W = mg$. Weight always acts **downwards**.

$W = mg$

The Normal Reaction (*R* or *N*)

The reaction from a surface. Reaction always acts **perpendicular (90°) to the surface**.

R
W

Tension (*T*)

T

Force in a taut rope, wire or string.

W

Friction (*F*)

A resistance force due to the **roughness** between a body and a surface.
Always acts **against** motion, or likely motion.

Cake (*C*)
A force to be reckoned with.
Always acts towards my mouth,
and opposes likely hunger.

Thrust or Compression

Force in a rod (e.g. the pole of an open umbrella).

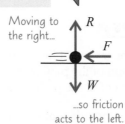
Moving to
the right...
R
F
W
...so friction
acts to the left.

Air resistance and drag
forces also resist motion.

Talk the Talk

Mechanics questions use a lot of words that you already know, but here they're used
to mean something very **precise**. Learn these definitions so you don't get caught out:

Particle	the body is a point so its dimensions don't matter	**Rigid**	the body does not bend
Light	the body has no mass	**Thin**	the body has no thickness
Static	not moving	**Equilibrium**	no resultant force
Rough	the surface will oppose motion with friction / drag	**Plane**	a flat surface
Beam or Rod	a long particle (e.g. a carpenter's plank)	**Inextensible**	the body can't be stretched
Uniform	the mass is evenly spread out throughout the body	**Smooth**	the surface doesn't have friction / drag opposing motion
Non-uniform	the mass is unevenly spread out		

You need to know the S.I. Units...

S.I. units are a system of units that are designed to be consistent all around the world.
The three main **base units** that you'll come across are:

| Length: **metre (m)** | Time: **second (s)** | Mass: **kilogram (kg)** |

Other units, such as newtons, are called **derived** S.I. units because they're **combinations** of the base units.

All quantities can be measured in units derived from the base S.I. units, which can usually be found using
their formula. For example, the formula for speed is distance ÷ time. Distance is a length measured in metres,
and time is measured in seconds, so the S.I. unit of speed is metres ÷ second, written m/s or ms^{-1}.

Watch out for non-S.I. units that sneak into questions here and there — you can measure length in inches and feet,
but these are **imperial** units, not S.I. units. Certain units, like **miles per hour**, are **derived non-S.I.** units.

Forces and Modelling

You'll have to make lots of **assumptions** when tackling **modelling** problems.

> **Example:** Model the following situations by drawing a force diagram and listing any assumptions made.

1 The book on a table

A book is put flat on a table. One end of the table is slowly lifted and the angle to the horizontal is measured when the book starts to slide.

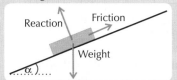

Assumptions:
The book is a **particle**, so its dimensions don't matter.
The table is **rigid**, and its surface is a **rough plane**.
There's **no** wind or other **external forces** involved.

> Modelling is a **cycle** — use the model to **solve** the problem, **compare** it to real life, **evaluate** your results, then **improve** the model and **start again**.

2 The balance

A pencil is placed on a table and a ruler is put across the pencil. A 1p coin and a 10p coin are placed on the ruler either side of the pencil, so that the ruler balances on the pencil.

Assumptions:
The coins are **particles**.
The ruler is **rigid**.
The support acts at a **single point**.

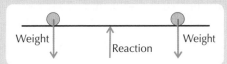

3 The sledge

A sledge is being steadily pulled by a small child on horizontal snow.

Assumptions:
Friction is **too big** to be ignored (i.e. it's not ice).
The string is **horizontal** (it's a small child).
The sledge is a **particle** (so its size doesn't matter).

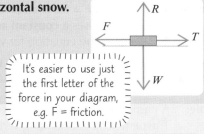

> It's easier to use just the first letter of the force in your diagram, e.g. F = friction.

4 The mass on a string

A ball is held by two strings, A and B, at angles α and β to the vertical.

Assumptions:
The ball is modelled as a **particle** (its dimensions don't matter).
The strings are **light** (their mass can be ignored).
The strings are **inextensible** (they can't stretch).

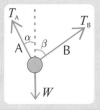

Practice Questions

Q1 The density of an object is given by its mass, divided by its volume.
Give the S.I. units of mass and volume and hence find the S.I. unit of density.

Q2 A ball is dropped onto a cushion from above. Draw a model, stating any assumptions made,
showing the ball: a) as it is released, b) after it has landed.

Exam Question

Q1 A car is modelled as a particle travelling at a constant speed along a smooth horizontal surface.
Explain two ways in which this model could be adjusted to be more realistic. [2 marks]

I can't get up yet — I'm modelling myself as a static particle in a rough bed...

Make sure you're completely familiar with the different forces and all the jargon that gets bandied about in mechanics.
Keep your models as simple as possible — that will make answering the questions as simple as possible too.

Newton's Laws

*That clever chap Isaac Newton established 3 laws involving motion. You need to know **all** of them.*

Newton's Laws of Motion

Newton's First Law	Newton's Second Law	Newton's Third Law
A body will **stay at rest** or **maintain a constant velocity** — unless an extra force acts to **change** that motion.	$$F_{net} = ma$$ F_{net} (the **overall resultant force**) is equal to the mass multiplied by the acceleration. F_{net} and a act in the same direction.	For **two bodies** in contact with each other, the force each applies to the other is **equal in magnitude** but **opposite in direction**.

$F_{net} = ma$ is sometimes just written as F = ma, but it means the same thing.

Calculating the **Resultant Force** is an **Essential Skill**

Using the first and second laws almost always involves finding the **resultant force**, usually called F_{net}.
If the resultant force on an object is **zero** then the object is **in equilibrium** (or **at rest**). Calculating the resultant force on an object is just like finding the **resultant vector**, which you saw on p.62-63.

Example: An object is held in equilibrium by the forces $(3\mathbf{i} - 2\mathbf{j})$ N, $(-4\mathbf{i} - 4\mathbf{j})$ N and $\mathbf{F}$.
Find the magnitude of the force $\mathbf{F}$ to 3 significant figures.

The object is in equilibrium, so the resultant force is zero — so both the **i** and **j** components sum to 0:
$$3 - 4 + F_i = 0 \Rightarrow F_i = 1 \qquad -2 - 4 + F_j = 0 \Rightarrow F_j = 6 \qquad \text{So } F = \mathbf{i} + 6\mathbf{j} \text{ N}$$
Now find the magnitude (see p.64): $|F| = \sqrt{1^2 + 6^2} = \sqrt{37} = \mathbf{6.08}$ N (3 s.f.)

Weight is given by **Mass × Acceleration Due To Gravity**

A common use of the formula $F = ma$ is calculating the **weight** of an object. An object's weight is a **force** caused by **gravity**. Gravity causes a **constant** acceleration of approximately 9.8 ms^{-2}, denoted $\mathbf{g}$.
Putting this into $F = ma$ gives the equation for weight (W): $\quad\longrightarrow\quad$ $$W = mg$$

Remember that weight is a **force** (measured in **newtons**) while mass is measured in **kg** — you might have to **convert units** before using the formula.

g can actually vary a little from 9.8 depending on where you are, but you can always assume it's constant.

Example: A particle of mass 12 kg is acted on by a constant upwards force F.
The particle is accelerating vertically downwards at a rate of 7 ms^{-2}.
Find: a) W, the weight of the particle,   b) the magnitude of the force F.

a) Using the formula for weight:
$$W = mg$$
$$= 12 \times 9.8 = \mathbf{117.6 \text{ N}}$$

b) Resolving vertically ($\downarrow$):
$$F_{net} = ma \Rightarrow 117.6 - F = 12 \times 7$$
$$F = 117.6 - 84 = \mathbf{33.6 \text{ N}}$$

$F\uparrow$ 7 ms^{-2} $\downarrow$ W

Resolve Forces in Perpendicular Directions

You might also have to use the constant acceleration equations — you know, the ones from page 96.

Example: A horizontal force of 5 N acts on a mass of 4 kg travelling along a smooth horizontal plane.
a) Find the acceleration of the mass and the normal reaction from the plane. Take $g = 9.8$ ms^{-2}.

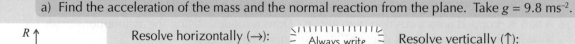

$R\uparrow$ a → → 5 N $\downarrow 4g$

Resolve horizontally ($\rightarrow$):
$$F_{net} = ma$$
$$5 = 4a$$
$$a = \mathbf{1.25 \text{ ms}^{-2}} \text{ in the direction of the horizontal force}$$

Always write $F_{net} = ma$ first.

Resolve vertically ($\uparrow$):
$$F_{net} = ma, \text{ so}$$
$$R - 4g = 4 \times 0$$
$$R = 4g = \mathbf{39.2 \text{ N}}$$

b) Find the velocity of the particle 6 seconds after it moves off from rest.

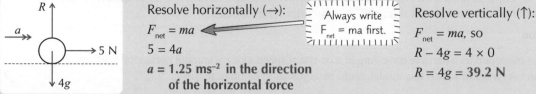

You know that: $u = 0$, $v = v$, $a = 1.25$, $t = 6$ Using $v = u + at$: $v = 0 + 1.25 \times 6 = \mathbf{7.5 \text{ ms}^{-1}}$
It started at rest.   From part a).

Newton's Laws

You can apply *F = ma* to *i* and *j* Vectors too

Example: a) A particle of mass *m* kg is acted upon by two forces, (6**i** – **j**) N and (2**i** + 4**j**) N, resulting in an acceleration of magnitude 9 ms^{-2}. Find the value of *m*.

Resultant force, F_{net} = (6**i** – **j**) + (2**i** + 4**j**) = (8**i** + 3**j**) N

Magnitude of F_{net} = $|F_{net}|$ = $\sqrt{8^2 + 3^2}$ = $\sqrt{73}$ = 8.544... N

F_{net} = *ma*, so 8.544... = 9*m*

hence *m* = **0.949 kg** (3 s.f.)

b) The force of (2**i** + 4**j**) N is removed. Calculate the magnitude of the new acceleration.

Magnitude = $\sqrt{6^2 + (-1)^2}$ = $\sqrt{37}$ = 6.082... N

$a = \frac{F}{m} = \frac{6.082...}{0.949...}$ = **6.41 ms^{-2}** (3 s.f.)

You can put **i** and **j** or column vectors straight into *F = ma* (or ***F = ma***).
F and ***a*** will both be in vector form, but mass is always scalar.

Example: The resultant force on a particle of mass 2 kg is given by the column vector $\begin{pmatrix} 14 \\ -6 \end{pmatrix}$ N. Calculate its velocity vector, 4 seconds after it begins moving from rest.

Using F_{net} = *ma* with vectors: $\begin{pmatrix} 14 \\ -6 \end{pmatrix} = 2a \Rightarrow a = \begin{pmatrix} 7 \\ -3 \end{pmatrix}$ ms^{-2} — Divide each component by 2.

Now, list the variables you know: $u = \begin{pmatrix} 0 \\ 0 \end{pmatrix}$, $v = v$, $a = \begin{pmatrix} 7 \\ -3 \end{pmatrix}$, $t = 4$ — It starts at rest, so each component of **u** is 0.

Use *v = u + at*: $v = \begin{pmatrix} 0 \\ 0 \end{pmatrix} + \begin{pmatrix} 7 \\ -3 \end{pmatrix} \times 4 = \begin{pmatrix} 28 \\ -12 \end{pmatrix}$ ms^{-1}

Practice Questions

Q1 A horizontal force of 2 N acts on a 1.5 kg particle initially at rest on a smooth horizontal plane. Find the speed of the particle 3 seconds later.

Q2 A particle of mass 6 g is acted on by a constant force ***F***. The particle reaches a velocity of $\begin{pmatrix} 200 \\ 125 \end{pmatrix}$ ms^{-1} 5 seconds after beginning to accelerate from rest. Find the magnitude and direction of ***F***.

Q3 Two forces act on a particle of mass 8 kg which is initially at rest on a smooth horizontal plane. The two forces are (24**i** + 18**j**) N and (6**i** + 22**j**) N (with **i** and **j** being perpendicular unit vectors in the plane). Find the magnitude and direction of the particle's resulting acceleration and the magnitude of its displacement after 3 seconds.

Exam Questions

Q1 Two forces, (*x***i** + *y***j**) N and (5**i** + **j**) N, act on a particle P of mass 2.5 kg. The resultant of the two forces is (8**i** – 3**j**) N.

Find: a) the values of *x* and *y*, [2 marks]

b) the magnitude and direction of the acceleration of P, [5 marks]

c) the particle's velocity vector, 5 seconds after it accelerates from rest. [2 marks]

Q2 A skydiver with mass 60 kg falls vertically from rest, experiencing a constant air resistance force, *R*, as they fall. After 7 seconds, they have fallen 200 m.

a) Find the magnitude of the air resistance on the skydiver to 3 significant figures. [6 marks]

b) State any assumptions that you have made in part a). [2 marks]

Interesting Newton fact: Isaac Newton had a dog called Diamond...

Also, did you know that Isaac Newton and Stephen Hawking both held the same position at Cambridge University? Don't ask me how I know such things, just bask in my amazing knowledge of all things trivial.

Connected Particles

Like Laurel goes with Hardy and Ben goes with Jerry, some particles are destined to be together...

Connected Particles act like One Mass

Particles connected together have the **same speeds** and **accelerations** as each other, unless the connection **fails**. If it does, the force connecting them (usually **tension** or **thrust**) will disappear.

Example: A person of mass 70 kg is standing in a lift of mass 500 kg attached to a vertical inextensible, light cable. Given that the lift is accelerating vertically upwards at a rate of 0.6 ms^{-2}, find:
a) T, the tension in the cable,   b) the force exerted by the person on the floor of the lift.

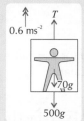

You're not given g, so take g = 9.8 ms^{-2}.

a) Resolving vertically ($\uparrow$) for the **whole system**:

$F_{net} = ma$
$T - 570g = 570 \times 0.6$
$T = (570 \times 0.6) + (570 \times 9.8)$
$\quad = 5928$ N

b) Resolving vertically ($\uparrow$) for the **person** in the lift:

$F_{net} = ma$
$R - 70g = 70 \times 0.6$
$R = 42 + 70g$
$\quad = 728$ N

You could resolve all the forces on the lift, but it's easier to find the reaction force R on the person from the lift (which has equal magnitude, by Newton's third law).

Example: A 30 tonne locomotive engine is pulling a single 10 tonne carriage as shown. They are accelerating at 0.3 ms^{-2} due to the force P generated by the engine. It's assumed that there are no forces resistant to motion. Find P and the tension in the coupling.

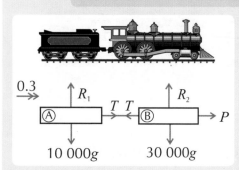

For carriage (A): $F_{net} = ma$
$\quad\quad\quad\quad\quad\quad T = 10\,000 \times 0.3$
$\quad\quad\quad\quad\quad\quad T = 3000$ N

For engine (B): $F_{net} = ma$
$\quad\quad\quad\quad\quad P - T = 30\,000 \times 0.3$
$\quad\quad\quad\quad\quad P - 3000 = 9000$
$\quad\quad\quad\quad\quad\quad\quad P = 12\,000$ N

You can often resolve forces on each object to get a pair of simultaneous equations that you can solve. They're really easy here though since there's only one force on A.

Pulleys (and 'Pegs') are always Smooth

Out in the real world, things are complicated and scary. In AS Maths, though, you can always assume that there's no **friction** on a **pulley** or a **peg**, and the **tension** in a **string** will be the **same** either side of it. What a relief.

Example: Masses of 3 kg and 5 kg are connected by an inextensible string and hang vertically either side of a smooth pulley. They are released from rest. Find their acceleration and the time it takes for each to move 40 cm. State any assumptions made in your model. Take $g = 9.8$ ms^{-2}.

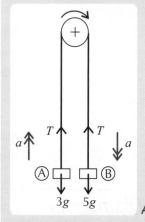

For A: $F_{net} = ma$
Resolving upwards: $T - 3g = 3a$ ①

For B: $F_{net} = ma$
Resolving downwards: $5g - T = 5a$
$\quad\quad\quad\quad\quad\quad\quad T = 5g - 5a$ ②

Sub ② into ①: $(5g - 5a) - 3g = 3a$
$\quad\quad\quad\quad\quad a = 2.45$ ms^{-2}

List variables: $s = 0.4$ m, $u = 0$, $a = 2.45$ ms^{-2}, $t = t$

Use an equation with s, u, a and t in it: $s = ut + \frac{1}{2}at^2$

$0.4 = (0 \times t) + \left(\frac{1}{2} \times 2.45 \times t^2\right)$ So $t = \sqrt{\frac{0.8}{2.45}} = 0.571$ s (3 s.f.)

Assumptions: The 3 kg mass does not hit the pulley; there's no air resistance; the string is 'light' so the tension is the same for both A and B, and it doesn't break; the string is inextensible so the acceleration is the same for both masses.

Connected Particles

Use F = ma in the **Direction Each Particle Moves**

Example: A mass of 3 kg is placed on a smooth horizontal table. A light inextensible string connects it over a smooth peg to a 5 kg mass which hangs vertically as shown. Find the tension in the string if the system is released from rest. Take $g = 9.8$ ms^{-2}.

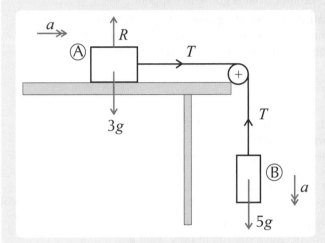

For A:
Resolve horizontally: $F_{net} = ma$
$$T = 3a$$
$$a = \frac{T}{3} \quad \text{①}$$

For B:
Resolve vertically: $F_{net} = ma$
$$5g - T = 5a \quad \text{②}$$

Sub ① into ②: $\quad 5g - T = 5 \times \frac{T}{3}$
$$\text{So } \frac{8}{3}T = 5g$$
$$T = 18.4 \text{ N (3 s.f.)}$$

Practice Questions

Q1 A person of mass 60 kg is standing in a lift of mass 600 kg connected to a light, inextensible vertical wire. The force exerted on them by the lift while it is moving is 640 N. Find the acceleration of the lift and the tension in the wire.

Q2 Two particles are connected by a light inextensible string, and hang in a vertical plane either side of a smooth pulley. When released from rest the particles accelerate at 1.2 ms^{-2}. If the heavier mass is 4 kg, find the weight of the other.

The state of these wires is certainly resulting in a **lot** of tension (don't try this at home).

Exam Questions

Q1 A car of mass 1500 kg is pulling a caravan of mass 500 kg. They experience resistance forces totalling 1000 N and 200 N respectively. The forward force generated by the car's engine is 2500 N. The coupling between the two does not break.

a) Find the acceleration of the car and caravan. [2 marks]

b) Find the tension in the coupling. [2 marks]

Q2 Two particles A and B are connected by a light inextensible string which passes over a smooth fixed pulley as shown. A has a mass of 7 kg and B has a mass of 3 kg. The particles are released from rest with the string taut, and A falls freely until it strikes the ground travelling at a speed of 5.9 ms^{-1}. A does not rebound after hitting the floor.

a) Find the time taken for A to hit the ground. [4 marks]

b) How far will B have travelled when A hits the ground? [2 marks]

c) Find the time (in s) from when A hits the ground until the string becomes taut again. [4 marks]

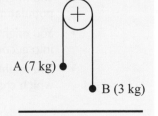

Connected particles — together forever... *isn't it beautiful?*

It makes things a lot easier when you know that connected particles act like one mass, and that you won't have to deal with rough pulleys. Those examiners occasionally do try to make your life easier, honestly (if only a little bit).

Modelling and Problem Solving

Modelling and problem solving are two of the three overarching themes of the AS-level Maths course (the third being proof, which is covered in Section 1). This means that they could come up in exam questions on any topic.

A *Mathematical Model* simplifies a *Real-life Situation*

A **mathematical model** is a mathematical description of a real-life situation. Modelling involves **simplifying** the situation so that you can understand its behaviour and predict what is going to happen.

Modelling in maths generally boils down to using an **equation** or a **set of equations** to predict what will happen in real life. You'll meet it in **all** areas of this course including population growth in **algebra** (see pages 48-49), moving objects in **mechanics** (see Section 12) and probability distributions in **statistics** (see Section 10).

Models *use* Assumptions

Models are always **simplifications** of the real-life situation. When you construct a model, you have to make **assumptions**. In other words, you **ignore** or **simplify** some factors that might affect the real-life outcome, in order to keep the maths simpler. For example:

- A population growth model might ignore the fact that the population will eventually run out of **food**, because that won't happen in the **time period** you're modelling.
- A model for the speed of a moving object might ignore **air resistance**, because that would make the maths much **more complicated**, or because you might only want a **general result** for objects of all shapes and sizes.
- Probability distributions based on past data often assume the **conditions** in future trials will be the **same** as when the past data was recorded.

There are lots of special terms to describe the assumptions you might make in mechanics — there's a list of them on page 102.

> **Example:** Leon owns a gooseberry farm. This week, he had 5 workers picking fruit, and they picked a total of 1000 punnets of gooseberries. Leon wants to hire more workers for next week. He predicts that next week, if the number of workers on his farm is w, the farm will produce p punnets of gooseberries, where $p = 200w$.
> Suggest three assumptions Leon has made in his model.

This is a model because it is a prediction of how many punnets will be produced — the actual number could be higher or lower. The model predicts that the average number of punnets produced per worker each week will be the same. For example:

- There will be enough gooseberries to fill 200 punnets per worker, however many workers he employs.
- The weather is good enough to allow each worker to work the same number of hours each week.
- Any new workers he employs will work at the same speed, on average.

There are lots more possible answers here.

You might have to *Criticise* or *Refine* a model

An important part of the modelling process is **refining** a model. This usually happens after the model has been **tested** by comparing it with real-world outcomes, or if you find out some **extra information** that affects the model. Refining a model usually means changing some of the **assumptions**. For example:

- You might adjust a population growth model if you found that **larger populations** were more susceptible to **disease**, so grew more slowly.
- You might decide to refine a model for the speed of an object to take into account the **friction** from the surface the object is travelling over.
- You might adjust a probability distribution if you collect **more data** which changes the **relative frequency** of the outcomes.

You could be asked to criticise or evaluate a model — e.g. you might need to assess if any assumptions are unrealistic.

> **Example: (cont.)** Leon discovers that the weather forecast for next week is bad, and his workers are only likely to be able to pick gooseberries for half the number of hours they did this week. How should the model be refined?

If the workers can only pick for half the time, they'll probably pick half as many gooseberries.
The refined model would be $p = 200w \div 2 \implies p = 100w$.

Modelling and Problem Solving

Problem Solving questions are more Challenging

Some maths questions can be straightforward to answer — you're told what maths you need to use, then you use it to get a solution. 'Problem solving' questions are those tricky ones where you have to work out for yourself exactly what maths you need to do.

Problem solving questions include:
- questions that don't have 'scaffolding' (i.e. they're not broken down into parts a), b), c) etc.),
- questions where the information is disguised (e.g. a 'wordy' context, or a diagram),
- questions that need more than one area of maths,
- questions that test if you actually understand the maths as well as being able to use it.

The Problem Solving Cycle can be Useful for maths questions

When it's not obvious what you're supposed to do with a question, you can use the problem solving cycle. This breaks the problem up into the following steps:

1. Specify the problem
The first thing to do is work out what the question is actually asking. The question might be phrased in an unusual way or it might be written in a 'wordy' context, where you need to turn the words into maths.

2. Collect information
Write down what you know. All the information you need to answer the question will either be given in the question somewhere (possibly on a diagram), or it'll require facts that you should already know.

3. Process and represent information
When you know what you're trying to find out, and what you already know, you can do the calculation to answer the question.

4. Interpret results
Don't forget to give your answer in terms of the original context. The result of your calculation won't necessarily be the final answer.

5. Repeat (if necessary)

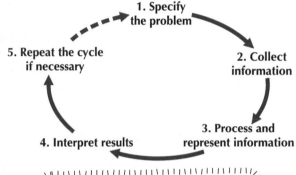

When you're doing an exam question, it's unlikely that you'll need to repeat the problem solving cycle once you've calculated the answer — just be aware that it's part of the general problem solving process.

You could also be asked to evaluate the accuracy or limitations of your solutions.

Example: Armand cuts out a semicircle from a rectangular sheet of cardboard measuring 20 cm by 40 cm and throws the rest away. The cardboard he throws away has an area of 398.08 cm². How long is the straight side of the semicircle?

1) What are you trying to find? *The length of the straight side of a semicircle is the diameter of the circle, which is twice the radius.*

2) What do you know? *The total area of the sheet of cardboard is 20 cm × 40 cm.*
398.08 cm² *was thrown away, so the rest is the area of the semicircle. The area of a semicircle* $= \frac{1}{2} \times$ *area of a circle* $= \frac{1}{2}\pi r^2$.

3) Do the maths. Area of semicircle $= (20 \times 40) - 398.08 = 800 - 398.08 = 401.92$ cm²
So: $401.92 = \frac{1}{2}\pi r^2$
$\Rightarrow r^2 = 401.92 \times 2 \div \pi = 803.84 \div \pi \Rightarrow r = \sqrt{803.84 \div \pi}$ cm
$\Rightarrow d = 2r = 2 \times \sqrt{803.84 \div \pi} = 31.99... = 32.0$ cm (3 s.f.)

4) Give the answer in the context of the question. The length of the straight side of the semicircle is **32.0 cm** (3 s.f.).

99% of modelling jobs require AS-level maths...

You can apply the problem solving cycle to all sorts: 1. Need to pass AS-level Maths exams. 2. Buy CGP revision guide. 3. Knuckle down and get revising. 4. Do some questions and check your answers.* 5. Get the kettle on and repeat.

*cheeky plug for our fabulous Exam Practice Workbooks

Do Well in Your Exams

Exam Structure and Technique

Good exam technique can make a big difference to your mark, so make sure you read this stuff carefully.

Get familiar with the **Exam Structure**

Pure maths is covered in Sections 1-7, statistics in Sections 8-11 and mechanics in Sections 12-13.

For **AS-level Mathematics**, you'll be sitting **two papers**.
Each paper has the **same** examination time, number of marks and weight.

Paper 1 (Pure Mathematics and Mechanics) **1 hour 30 mins**　　**80** marks	**50%** of your AS-level	Covers material from **Sections 1-7 and 12-13** of this book.
Paper 2 (Pure Mathematics and Statistics) **1 hour 30 mins**　　**80** marks	**50%** of your AS-level	Covers material from **Sections 1-11** of this book.

Each paper is split into **Section A: Pure Mathematics** and **Section B: Mechanics/Statistics**.
There may be some questions in Section B that need a bit of pure maths.
On **both** papers, **Section A** is worth approximately **two-thirds** of the marks
and **Section B** is worth approximately **one-third**.

Some formulas are given in the **Formula Booklet**

In the exam, you'll be given a **formula booklet** that lists some of the formulas you might need.
The relevant ones for AS-level are shown on page 130.
You don't need to learn these formulas but you do need to know **how to use** them.

Manage Your Time sensibly

1) The **number of marks** tells you roughly **how long** to spend on a question — you've got just over a minute per mark in the exam. If you get stuck on a question for too long, it may be best to **move on** so you don't run out of time for the others.

2) You don't have to work through the paper **in order** — you could leave questions on topics you find harder until last.

Be **Careful** with **Calculations**

You should always show your **calculations** for all questions — you may get some marks for your **method** even if you get the answer wrong. But you should bear the following in mind:

1) You should give your final answer to a sensible number of **decimal places** or **significant figures** that is **appropriate** to the context, unless the **question** specifies otherwise. In Mechanics, for example, if some of the quantities in the question are given to 3 s.f. and others are given to 2 s.f. then your final answer should be given to 2 s.f. (the **lowest degree of accuracy** in the question). Writing out the unrounded answer, then your rounded answer shows that you know your stuff.

2) Don't **round** your answer until the **very end**. A lot of calculations in AS-level Maths are quite **long**, and if you round too early you could introduce errors to your final answer. When using a **calculator** you can **store** full decimals, which you can then use in further calculations.

3) For some questions, you can use your calculator to **check** your answer. Just make sure you've included **all** the working out first, so you don't lose any marks.

4) Your calculator must have an **iterative function** (usually an ANS key), and must be able to compute **summary statistics** and **probabilities** from **statistical distributions** (see page 87 for more information).

5) **Calculators** that manipulate algebra, do symbolic differentiation and integration or have retrievable formulas stored in them are **banned** from the exam. If you're not sure whether your calculator is allowed, **check** with your teacher or exam board.

Exam Structure and Technique

Make Sure You *Read the Question*

1) It sounds obvious, but it's really important you read each question **carefully**, and give an answer that matches what you've been asked.

2) Look at **how many marks** a question is worth before answering. It'll tell you roughly **how much information** you need to include.

3) Look for **key words** in the question — often the first word in the question. These give you an idea of the **kind of answer** you should write. Some of the commonly used key words are given in the table below:

Key words	Meaning in the exam
Find / Calculate / Determine	These are general terms that could be used for pretty much **anything**. You should always **give working** to show how you found the answer.
Solve	When given an **equation**, solving means finding the **value(s)** of the **variable** (e.g. x or a).
Give / State / Write down	No working is required — often for an **assumption**, **reason** or **example**.
Explain	You must give **reasons**, not just a description — these **can** include **calculations** as part of your explanation.
Show that	You're given a **result** that you have to show is true. Because you're given the answer, you should include **every step** of your working.
Prove	Use a **logical argument** to show the statement or equation you're asked to prove is true.
Plot	**Accurately** mark points on a graph. You might also need to join the points with a line or a curve, or draw a line of best fit.
Sketch	Draw a diagram showing the **main features** of the graph. This doesn't have to be drawn to **scale**, but will need to include some of the following: correct **shape**, *x*- and *y*- **intercepts**, **asymptotes**, and **turning points**.
Verify	You're given a numerical **solution** to a problem, and you have to **show** that it really is a solution — usually by **substituting** it into an equation from earlier in the question.
Hence	Use the **previous statement** or **question** part to answer the next bit of the question. '**Hence or otherwise**' means there's another way to answer the question — so if you can't quite see what they want you to do with the 'hence' bit, you can solve it another way and still get all the marks (but be aware that the other way might take longer).
Exact	If a question asks for an **exact value**, don't round. This usually means giving an answer in terms of something like e, ln, or π, a **square** (or other) **root**, or a **fraction** you can't write as a terminating decimal.

Get *Familiar* with the *Large Data Set*

Throughout the AS Maths course you'll be working with the **large data set**. This is a group of **tables** containing information about **purchased quantities of foods and drinks** in different regions of the UK. The large data set will only be used in Paper 2 for AS-Level Maths.

Questions in this paper might:

1) assume that you're familiar with the **terminology**, **contexts**, and some of the **broad trends** of the data (e.g. London is generally different to the other regions),

2) use **summary statistics** based on the large data set (this might reduce the time needed for some calculations),

3) include **statistical diagrams** based on the large data set,

4) be based on a **sample** from the large data set.

Going through 14 years of shopping receipts was no easy task...

The last gag in the book is always a disappointment Tent...

Revising exam technique doesn't sound the most exciting thing in the world (monkey tennis?), but it will actually make a big difference to your mark. In fact, exam technique is a skill that you can master — next time you do an exercise, try to apply the stuff you've seen on these pages to the questions. It's also worth spending some time working with the large data set — you'll be glad that you did when you're facing the large data set questions in the exam.

Answers

Section 1 — Algebra and Functions

Page 3 — Proof
Practice Questions

1 a) {2} b) {1, 2, 4, 7, 14, 28} c) {–1, 1}
2 a) E.g. $x = 1$, $y = -2$. Any answer where $\frac{x}{y} < 1$ holds and $x > y$ is correct.

b) E.g. $x = 0$, $y = 1$. Any x and y that satisfy $y = 1 - x$ also correct.

Exam Questions

1 Expand and simplify the brackets:
$n^2 + 12n + 36 - (n^2 + 2n + 1) = 10n + 35$ *[1 mark]*
$= 5(2n + 7)$ *[1 mark]*
If n is an integer, $(2n + 7)$ is also an integer, and any number that can be written as 5 × an integer is divisible by 5.
So $(n + 6)^2 - (n + 1)^2$ is divisible by 5. *[1 mark]*

2 Prove by exhaustion. For any integer n, the difference between a number and its square is: $n^2 - n = n(n - 1)$
If n is even, $(n - 1)$ is odd and an even number times an odd number is even, so $n(n - 1)$ is even.
If n is odd, $(n - 1)$ is even and an odd number times an even number is even, so $n(n - 1)$ is even.
So, since n must either be even or odd, the difference between a number and its square is even for any integer n.
[3 marks available — 1 for considering cases where n is odd and even separately, 1 for correct working to show $n^2 - n$ is even in both cases and 1 for a correct conclusion]

3 Expand the brackets: $x^2 + x - 2 > 2x - 2 \Rightarrow x^2 - x > 0$ *[1 mark]*
When $x = 1$, $1^2 - 1 = 0$, so $x = 1$ is a counter-example. *[1 mark]*
Therefore the statement is false. *[1 mark]*
The counter-example could be any value of x in the range $0 \le x \le 1$.

Page 5 — Laws of Indices and Surds
Practice Questions

1 a) x^8 b) a^{15} c) x^6 d) a^8 e) $x^4 y^3 z$ f) $\frac{b^2 c^5}{a}$
2 a) 4 b) 2 c) 8 d) 1 e) $\frac{1}{7}$
3 a) $2\sqrt{7}$ b) $\frac{\sqrt{5}}{6}$ c) $3\sqrt{2}$ d) $\frac{3}{4}$
4 $136 + 24\sqrt{21}$
5 $3 - \sqrt{7}$

Exam Questions

1 a) $(5\sqrt{3})^2 = (5^2)(\sqrt{3})^2 = 25 \times 3 = 75$ *[1 mark]*
b) $(5 + \sqrt{6})(2 - \sqrt{6}) = 10 - 5\sqrt{6} + 2\sqrt{6} - 6$ *[1 mark]*
$= 4 - 3\sqrt{6}$ *[1 mark]*

2 $10000\sqrt{10} = 10^4 \cdot 10^{\frac{1}{2}}$ *[1 mark]* $= 10^{4 + \frac{1}{2}}$
$= 10^{\frac{9}{2}}$, so $k = \frac{9}{2}$ *[1 mark]*

3 Multiply top and bottom by $3 + \sqrt{5}$ to rationalise the denominator:
$\frac{5 + \sqrt{5}}{3 - \sqrt{5}} = \frac{(5 + \sqrt{5})(3 + \sqrt{5})}{(3 - \sqrt{5})(3 + \sqrt{5})}$ *[1 mark]*
$= \frac{15 + 5\sqrt{5} + 3\sqrt{5} + 5}{9 - 5}$ *[1 mark]*
$= \frac{20 + 8\sqrt{5}}{4}$ *[1 mark]* $= 5 + 2\sqrt{5}$ *[1 mark]*

Page 8 — Polynomials
Practice Questions

1 a) $x^2 - y^2$ b) $x^2 + 2xy + y^2$
c) $25y^2 + 210xy$ d) $3x^2 + 10xy + 3y^2 + 13x + 23y + 14$
2 $(\sqrt{x} + \sqrt{2})(\sqrt{x} - \sqrt{2}) = \sqrt{x}\sqrt{x} - \sqrt{2}\sqrt{x} + \sqrt{2}\sqrt{x} - \sqrt{2}\sqrt{2}$
$= \sqrt{x^2} - \sqrt{2^2} = x - \sqrt{4} = x - 2$, as required
3 a) $xy(2x + a + 2y)$ b) $a^2 x(1 + b^2 x)$
c) $8(2y + xy + 7x)$ d) $(x - 2)(x - 3)$

4 a) $(x + 7)(x - 1)$ b) $(x + 2)(x - 6)$
c) $(3x + 8)(3x - 8)$ d) $(4x + 5)(x - 4)$
5 a) $\frac{2x + 5}{3}$ b) $\frac{4}{x - 3}$ c) $\frac{2(x - 3)}{x + 1}$

Exam Questions

1 $\frac{2x^2 - 9x - 35}{x^2 - 49} = \frac{(2x + 5)(x - 7)}{(x + 7)(x - 7)} = \frac{2x + 5}{x + 7}$
[3 marks available — 1 for factorising numerator, 1 for factorising denominator and 1 for correct final answer]

2 $2x^4 - 32x^2 = 2x^2(x^2 - 16)$ *[1 mark]* $= 2x^2(x + 4)(x - 4)$ *[1 mark]*

3 a) The common denominator is $x^2(2x + 1)$
$\frac{x}{2x + 1} + \frac{3}{x^2} + \frac{1}{x} = \frac{x \cdot x^2}{x^2(2x + 1)} + \frac{3(2x + 1)}{x^2(2x + 1)} + \frac{x(2x + 1)}{x^2(2x + 1)}$
$= \frac{x^3 + 6x + 3 + 2x^2 + x}{x^2(2x + 1)} = \frac{x^3 + 2x^2 + 7x + 3}{x^2(2x + 1)}$
[3 marks available — 1 for method of putting all fractions over a common denominator, 1 for correct numerator and 1 for correct denominator in final answer]

b) The common denominator is $(x + 1)(x - 1)$
$\frac{2}{x^2 - 1} - \frac{3x}{x - 1} + \frac{x}{x + 1}$
$= \frac{2}{(x + 1)(x - 1)} - \frac{3x(x + 1)}{(x + 1)(x - 1)} + \frac{x(x - 1)}{(x + 1)(x - 1)}$
$= \frac{2 - 3x^2 - 3x + x^2 - x}{(x + 1)(x - 1)} = \frac{2 - 2x^2 - 4x}{(x + 1)(x - 1)} = \frac{2(1 - 2x - x^2)}{(x + 1)(x - 1)}$
[3 marks available — 1 for method of putting all fractions over a common denominator, 1 for correct numerator and 1 for correct denominator in final answer]

Page 11 — Algebraic Division
Practice Questions

1 a) 106 b) 106 c) 41 d) 41
2 a) Factor b) Not a factor c) Not a factor d) Factor
3 $(x^3 + 2x^2 - x + 19) \div (x + 4) = x^2 - 2x + 7$ remainder -9
4 a) $f(x) = (x + 2)(3x^2 - 10x + 15) - 36$
b) $f(x) = (x + 2)(x^2 - 3) + 10$
c) $f(x) = (x + 2)(2x^2 - 4x + 14) - 31$
5 $2x^3 + 8x^2 + 7x + 8 = (2x^2 + 2x + 1)(x + 3) + 5$
So $2x^3 + 8x^2 + 7x + 8 \div (x + 3) = 2x^2 + 2x + 1$ remainder 5

Exam Questions

1 a) (i) Remainder $= f(1) = 2(1)^3 - 5(1)^2 - 4(1) + 3 = -4$ *[1 mark]*
(ii) Remainder $= f\left(-\frac{1}{2}\right) = 2\left(-\frac{1}{8}\right) - 5\left(\frac{1}{4}\right) - 4\left(-\frac{1}{2}\right) + 3$
$= \frac{7}{2}$ *[1 mark]*

b) If $f(-1) = 0$ then $(x + 1)$ is a factor.
$f(-1) = 2(-1)^3 - 5(-1)^2 - 4(-1) + 3$ *[1 mark]*
$= -2 - 5 + 4 + 3 = 0$, so $(x + 1)$ is a factor of $f(x)$. *[1 mark]*

c) $(x + 1)$ is a factor, so divide $2x^3 - 5x^2 - 4x + 3$ by $x + 1$:
$2x^3 - 5x^2 - 4x + 3 - \underline{2x^2}(x + 1) = 2x^3 - 5x^2 - 4x + 3 - 2x^3 - 2x^2$
$= -7x^2 - 4x + 3$
$-7x^2 - 4x + 3 - (\underline{-7x})(x + 1) = -7x^2 - 4x + 3 + 7x^2 + 7x = 3x + 3$
Finally $3x + 3 - \underline{3}(x + 1) = 0$
so $2x^3 - 5x^2 - 4x + 3 = (2x^2 - 7x + 3)(x + 1)$ *[1 mark for dividing by x + 1, 1 mark for correct quadratic factor]*
Factorising the quadratic gives:
$2x^3 - 5x^2 - 4x + 3 = (2x - 1)(x - 3)(x + 1)$ *[1 mark]*
You might've used a different method to divide by (x + 1).

2 a) $f(p) = (4p^2 + 3p + 1)(p - p) + 5 = 0 + 5 = 5$ *[1 mark]*
b) $f(-1) = -1$
$f(-1) = (4(-1)^2 + 3(-1) + 1)((-1) - p) + 5 = (4 - 3 + 1)(-1 - p) + 5$
$= 2(-1 - p) + 5 = 3 - 2p$ *[1 mark]*
So $3 - 2p = -1 \Rightarrow p = 2$ *[1 mark]*
c) $f(1) = (4 + 3 + 1)(1 - 2) + 5 = -3$ *[1 mark]*

Answers

3   First put $x = -6$ into both sides of the identity
$x^3 + 15x^2 + 43x - 30 \equiv (Ax^2 + Bx + C)(x + 6) + D$:
$(-6)^3 + 15(-6)^2 + 43(-6) - 30 = D \Rightarrow 36 = D$
Now set $x = 0$ to get $-30 = 6C + D$, so $C = -11$
Equating the coefficients of x^3 gives $1 = A$.
Equating the coefficients of x^2 gives $15 = 6A + B \Rightarrow B = 9$
So $x^3 + 15x^2 + 43x - 30 = (x^2 + 9x - 11)(x + 6) + 36$
[3 marks available — 1 each for correct values of C and D, and 1 for correct values of A and B]
You could also do this question by algebraic long division.

Page 13 — Solving Quadratic Equations
Practice Questions
1 a) $x = 3$ or -4 b) $x = 2$ or -1
  c) $x = \pm\frac{1}{2}$ d) $x = 7$ or $-\frac{2}{3}$
2    $x = 4$ or $-\frac{7}{3}$
3 a) $x = 1$ or 5 b) $x = \frac{7 + \sqrt{13}}{6}$ or $\frac{7 - \sqrt{13}}{6}$
  c) $x = \frac{3 + \sqrt{13}}{2}$ or $\frac{3 - \sqrt{13}}{2}$ d) $x = -2 + \sqrt{10}$ or $x = -2 - \sqrt{10}$
4    $x = \frac{9}{4}$ or -4

Exam Questions
1 a) $3x^2 + 2x - 2 = 3\left(x^2 + \frac{2}{3}x\right) - 2 = 3\left(x + \frac{1}{3}\right)^2 + d$ *[1 mark]*
   $3\left(x + \frac{1}{3}\right)^2 + d = 3x^2 + 2x - 2 \Rightarrow 3x^2 + 2x + \frac{1}{3} + d = 3x^2 + 2x - 2$
   $\Rightarrow d = -2 - \frac{1}{3} = -\frac{7}{3}$ *[1 mark]*
   So $3x^2 + 2x - 2 = 3\left(x + \frac{1}{3}\right)^2 - \frac{7}{3}$ *[1 mark]*
  b) $3\left(x + \frac{1}{3}\right)^2 - \frac{7}{3} = 0 \Rightarrow \left(x + \frac{1}{3}\right)^2 = \frac{7}{9} \Rightarrow x = \frac{-1 \pm \sqrt{7}}{3}$
   So $x = 0.55$ or -1.22 (to 2 d.p.) *[1 mark]*
2    $6x^2 = 1 - 3x \Rightarrow 6x^2 + 3x - 1 = 0 \Rightarrow 6\left(x^2 + \frac{1}{2}x\right) - 1 = 0$ *[1 mark]*
   $6\left(x^2 + \frac{1}{2}x\right) - 1 = 6\left(x + \frac{1}{4}\right)^2 + d \Rightarrow 6\left(x + \frac{1}{4}\right)^2 + d = 6x^2 + 3x - 1$
   $\Rightarrow 6x^2 + 3x + \frac{3}{8} + d = 6x^2 + 3x - 1$
   $\Rightarrow d = -1 - \frac{3}{8} = -\frac{11}{8}$ *[1 mark]*
   So $6\left(x + \frac{1}{4}\right)^2 - \frac{11}{8} = 0$. *[1 mark]* Now solve this to find x:
   $6\left(x + \frac{1}{4}\right)^2 = \frac{11}{8} \Rightarrow \left(x + \frac{1}{4}\right)^2 = \frac{11}{48} \Rightarrow x = -\frac{1}{4} \pm \sqrt{\frac{11}{48}} = -\frac{1}{4} \pm \frac{\sqrt{33}}{12}$
   So the exact solutions are $x = -\frac{1}{4} + \frac{\sqrt{33}}{12}$ or $-\frac{1}{4} - \frac{\sqrt{33}}{12}$ *[1 mark]*

Page 15 — Quadratic Functions and Graphs
Practice Questions
1 a)
b)
c)
d)

2   Completing the square gives: $f(x) = 2(x - 3)^2 + 5$
   The smallest $2(x - 3)^2$ can be is zero, so the minimum of $f(x)$ is 5.
   The graph never crosses the x-axis, so $f(x) = 0$ has no real roots.

Exam Questions
1 a) E.g. If $7 + 2\sqrt{6}$ is a root of $f(x) = 0$, then $f(7 + 2\sqrt{6}) = 0$
   $\Rightarrow (7 + 2\sqrt{6})^2 - 14(7 + 2\sqrt{6}) + k = 0$ *[1 mark]*
   $\Rightarrow 49 + 28\sqrt{6} + 24 - 98 - 28\sqrt{6} + k = 0$ *[1 mark]*
   $\Rightarrow -25 + k = 0 \Rightarrow k = 25$ *[1 mark]*
   So $f(7 - 2\sqrt{6}) = (7 - 2\sqrt{6})^2 - 14(7 - 2\sqrt{6}) + 25$
   $= 49 - 28\sqrt{6} + 24 - 98 + 28\sqrt{6} + 25 = 0$ *[1 mark]*
   so $7 - 2\sqrt{6}$ is the other root of $f(x)$.
   You'd still get the marks if you used a different method here.
  b)

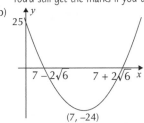

[3 marks available — 1 for u-shaped curve, 1 for correct x- and y-intercepts and 1 for correct coordinates of minimum point]
2 a) The completed square is: $(x - 6)^2 + d = x^2 - 12x + 36 + d$ *[1 mark]*
   Equating coefficients gives $15 = 36 + d$,
   so $d = 15 - 36 = -21$. *[1 mark]*
   The final expression is $(x - 6)^2 - 21$.
  b) The minimum occurs when the expression in brackets is equal to 0, so the minimum is -21. *[1 mark]*
   The expression in brackets is equal to 0, when $x = 6$. *[1 mark]*

Page 17 — The Quadratic Formula
Practice Questions
1 a) i) discriminant = 0, 1 repeated real root   ii) $x = -\frac{7}{2}$
  b) i) discriminant = -3, no real roots
  c) i) discriminant = 0, 1 repeated real root   ii) $x = \frac{\sqrt{2}}{3}$
  d) i) discriminant = 121, 2 real roots,   ii) $x = \frac{1}{2}$ or -5
2    $k > 4$ or $k < -4$

Exam Questions
1   For equal roots, $b^2 - 4ac = 0$. $a = 1$, $b = 2k$ and $c = 4k$, so:
   $b^2 - 4ac = (2k)^2 - (4 \times 1 \times 4k)$ *[1 mark]*
   $= 4k^2 - 16k = 4k(k - 4) = 0$ *[1 mark]*
   so $k = 4$ (as k is non-zero) *[1 mark]*
2 a) For distinct real roots, $b^2 - 4ac > 0$ *[1 mark]*
   $a = p + 1$, $b = p + 1$ and $c = 1$
   so $b^2 - 4ac = (p + 1)^2 - 4(p + 1)(1) > 0$ *[1 mark]*
   $\Rightarrow p^2 + 2p + 1 - 4p - 4 > 0 \Rightarrow p^2 - 2p - 3 > 0$ *[1 mark]*
  b) The graph of $y = p^2 - 2p - 3$ crosses the horizontal axis when
   $p^2 - 2p - 3 = (p + 1)(p - 3) = 0$ *[1 mark]*
   So it crosses at $p = -1$ and $p = 3$
   The quadratic is u-shaped (since the coefficient of p^2 is positive)
   so $p^2 - 2p - 3 > 0$ outside of these values: *[1 mark]*
   $p < -1$ or $p > 3$ *[1 mark]*

Page 19 — Simultaneous Equations
Practice Questions
1 a) $x = -3$, $y = -4$ b) $x = -\frac{1}{6}$, $y = -\frac{5}{12}$
2 a) $\left(\frac{1}{4}, -\frac{13}{4}\right)$ b) $(4, 5)$ c) $(-5, -2)$

3 a) The line and the curve meet at the points $(2, -6)$ and $(7, 4)$.
  b) The line is a tangent to the parabola at the point $(2, 26)$.
  c) There are no solutions, so the line and the curve never meet.

Answers

Exam Questions

1 First, take the linear equation and rearrange it to get x on its own:
$x = 6 - y$. *[1 mark]* Now substitute this into the quadratic:
$(6 - y)^2 + 2y^2 = 36$ *[1 mark]*
$\Rightarrow 36 - 12y + y^2 + 2y^2 = 36 \Rightarrow 3y^2 - 12y = 0$
$\Rightarrow y^2 - 4y = 0 \Rightarrow y(y - 4) = 0$ *[1 mark]*
so $y = 0$ and $y = 4$ *[1 mark]*
Put the y-values back into the equation for x to find the x-values.
When $y = 0$, $x = 6 - y = 6 - 0 = 6$
When $y = 4$, $x = 6 - y = 6 - 4 = 2$
So the coordinates are (6, 0) and (2, 4) *[1 mark for each answer]*

2 a)
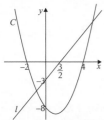

[4 marks available — 1 for u-shaped curve, 1 for correct curve x- and y-intercepts, 1 for correct line x- and y-intercepts, and 1 for line and curve crossing at two points]

b) At points of intersection, $2x - 3 = (x + 2)(x - 4)$ *[1 mark]*
$2x - 3 = x^2 - 2x - 8 \Rightarrow 0 = x^2 - 4x - 5$ *[1 mark]*

c) $x^2 - 4x - 5 = 0 \Rightarrow (x - 5)(x + 1) = 0$ so $x = 5$, $x = -1$ *[1 mark]*
When $x = 5$, $y = (2 \times 5) - 3 = 7$ and when $x = -1$,
$y = (2 \times -1) - 3 = -5$, so the points of intersection are
(5, 7) and (−1, −5). *[1 mark for both points correct]*

Page 21 — Inequalities

Practice Questions

1 a) $x > \dfrac{5}{2}$ b) $x > -4$ c) $x \le -3$

2 a) $x > -\dfrac{38}{5}$ b) $y \le \dfrac{7}{8}$ c) $y \le -\dfrac{3}{4}$

3 a) $-\dfrac{1}{3} \le x \le 2$ b) $x < -2$ or $x > \dfrac{3}{2}$
c) $x \le -3$ or $x \ge -2$

4 a) $\{x: x \le -3\} \cup \{x: x \ge 1\}$ b) $\{x: x < -\dfrac{1}{2}\} \cup \{x: x > 1\}$
c) $\{x: -3 < x < 2\}$ or $\{x: x > -3\} \cap \{x: x < 2\}$

5
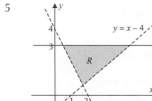

Exam Questions

1 a) $3x + 2 \le x + 6 \Rightarrow 2x \le 4 \Rightarrow x \le 2$ *[1 mark]*
b) $20 - x - x^2 > 0 \Rightarrow (4 - x)(5 + x) > 0$
The graph crosses the x-axis at $x = 4$ and $x = -5$. *[1 mark]*.
The coefficient of x^2 is negative so the graph is n-shaped.
So $20 - x - x^2 > 0$ when $-5 < x < 4$. *[1 mark]*
c) x satisfies both $x \le 2$ and $-5 < x < 4$ when $-5 < x \le 2$. *[1 mark]*

2 a) $3 \le 2p + 5 \le 15$
Subtract 5 from each part to give: $-2 \le 2p \le 10$
Now divide each part by 2 to give: $-1 \le p \le 5$
[1 mark for −1 ≤ p and 1 mark for p ≤ 5]
For inequalities with three parts you add, subtract, multiply or divide each part by the same thing, as with regular two part inequalities.
b) $q^2 - 9 > 0 \Rightarrow (q + 3)(q - 3) > 0$
The function is 0 at $q = -3$ and $q = 3$. *[1 mark]*
The coefficient of q^2 is positive so the graph is u-shaped.
So $q^2 - 9 > 0$ when $q < -3$ or $q > 3$. *[1 mark]*

3 $y = 2x^2 - x - 3 = (2x - 3)(x + 1)$ is a u-shaped quadratic that
crosses the x-axis at -1 and $\dfrac{3}{2}$.
$y = 1 - \dfrac{1}{2}x$ is a straight line that crosses the x-axis at 2.
Test the origin in the inequalities:
$y = 2x^2 - x - 3 \Rightarrow 0 > -3$, which is true, so the region includes the area above the quadratic.
$y = 1 - \dfrac{1}{2}x \Rightarrow 0 \ge 1$, which is false, so the region includes the area above the straight line.
The region bounded by these areas is shown by R.

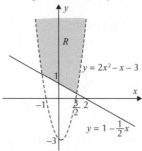

[4 marks available — 1 for quadratic graph drawn with correct shape and as dotted line, 1 for correct intercepts on quadratic, 1 for correct straight line drawn as solid line and 1 for correct region shaded]

Page 23 — Cubics

Practice Questions

1 a)
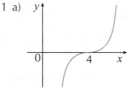   b)
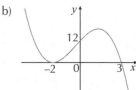

c)
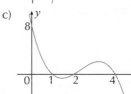   d)
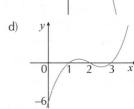

2 a) $f(1) = 1^3 - 1^2 - 2(1) + 2 = 0$, so $(x - 1)$ is a factor.
$f(x) = (x - 1)(x^2 - 2)$
b) $g(-4) = (-4)^3 + 3(-4)^2 - 10(-4) - 24 = 0$, so $(x + 4)$ is a factor.
$g(x) = (x + 4)(x + 2)(x - 3)$
c) $h\left(\dfrac{1}{2}\right) = 2\left(\dfrac{1}{2}\right)^3 + 3\left(\dfrac{1}{2}\right)^2 - 8\left(\dfrac{1}{2}\right) + 3 = 0$, so $(2x - 1)$ is a factor.
$h(x) = (2x - 1)(x - 1)(x + 3)$
d) $k\left(\dfrac{2}{3}\right) = 3\left(\dfrac{2}{3}\right)^3 + 10\left(\dfrac{2}{3}\right)^2 + 10\left(\dfrac{2}{3}\right) - 12 = 0$, so $(3x - 2)$ is a factor.
$k(x) = (3x - 2)(x^2 + 4x + 6)$

3 $f(x) = (x + 5)(x - 1)(x - 7)$

Exam Questions

1
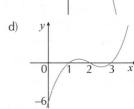

[3 marks available — 1 for correct shape, 1 for crossing x-axis at $x = -\dfrac{1}{2}$ and touching the x-axis at $x = 2$ and 1 for correct y-axis intercept at y = 4]

Answers

2 a) $f\left(-\frac{1}{2}\right) = 6\left(-\frac{1}{2}\right)^3 + 37\left(-\frac{1}{2}\right)^2 + 5\left(-\frac{1}{2}\right) - 6$

$= -\frac{6}{8} + \frac{37}{4} - \frac{5}{2} - 6 = 0$ *[1 mark]*

So, by the factor theorem, $(2x - 1)$ is a factor of f(x). *[1 mark]*

b) $f(x) = (2x + 1)(3x^2 + 17x - 6)$ *[1 mark]*

$= (2x + 1)(3x - 1)(x + 6)$ *[1 mark]*

c)

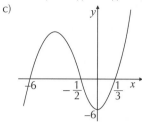

*[3 marks available — 1 for correct shape,
1 for correct y-intercept and 1 for correct x-intercepts]*

3   $f(1) = 7(1)^3 - 26(1)^2 + 13(1) + 6 = 0$, so $(x - 1)$ is a factor *[1 mark]*

$f(x) = (x - 1)(7x^2 - 19x - 6)$ *[1 mark]*

$f(x) = (x - 1)(7x + 2)(x - 3)$ *[1 mark]*

So $f(x) = 0$ when $x = 1$, $x = -\frac{2}{7}$ or $x = 3$ *[1 mark]*

Page 26 — Graphs of Functions

Practice Questions

1   a) **C**   b) **D**   c) **B**   d) **A**

2   a)

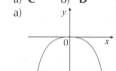

b)

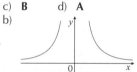

c)

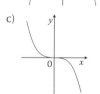

d)

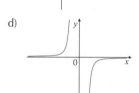

3

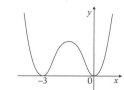

4   a)

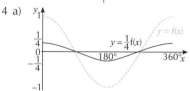

b)

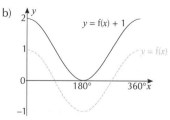

c)

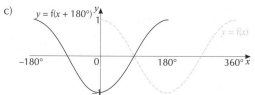

Exam Questions

1   For $f(x) = (1 - x)(x + 4)^3$, the coefficient of x^4 is negative,
so the graph is negative for large positive and negative values of x.
Putting in $x = 0$ gives the y-intercept as $(1 - 0)(0 + 4)^3 = 64$.
The x-intercepts are at $x = 1$ and $x = -4$. The root at $x = -4$ is a
repeated 'triple root' so the curve crosses the x-axis here.

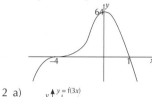

*[4 marks — 1 mark for each
intercept, 1 mark for correct shape]*

2   a)

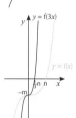

*[2 marks available — 1 mark for crossing x-axis
at $x = \frac{1}{3}n$, 1 mark for crossing y-axis at $y = -m$]*

b)

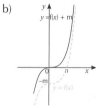

*[2 marks available — 1 mark for translating
upwards by m, 1 mark for crossing through
the origin]*

c)

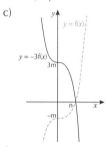

*[2 marks available — 1 mark for reflecting
in y-axis and 1 mark for crossing y-axis
at $y = 3m$]*

d)

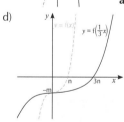

*[2 marks available — 1 mark for
crossing x-axis at $x = 3n$, 1 mark
for crossing y-axis at $y = -m$]*

Page 27 — Proportion

Practice Questions

1   $k = 4$

2   $k = 15$

Exam Question

1   a) $A \propto \frac{1}{t}$, so $A = \frac{k}{t}$

So if $A = 2.6$ when $t = 5.5$: $2.6 = \frac{k}{5.5} \Rightarrow k = 14.3$ *[1 mark]*

b)

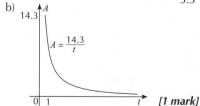

[1 mark]

The graph has an asymptote at $A = 0$. *[1 mark]*

There's only one asymptote — the relation is only defined for $t \geq 1$,
so the vertical asymptote isn't needed.

Answers

c) E.g. When t is close to zero, the value of A would be very large. This would suggest that the area of the island was almost infinite immediately after the storm, which is unrealistic. *[1 mark for a valid reason why the model is inappropriate for small t]*

Page 29 — Binomial Expansions

Practice Questions

1   1 5 10 10 5 1
2    $1 + 12x + 66x^2 + 220x^3$
3    $1 - 32x + 480x^2 - 4480x^3$
4    $32 + 240x + 720x^2 + 1080x^3$

Exam Questions

1   First five terms of $(4 + 3x)^6$ are:
$4^6 + \binom{6}{1}4^5(3x) + \binom{6}{2}4^4(3x)^2 + \binom{6}{3}4^3(3x)^3 + \binom{6}{4}4^2(3x)^4$
$= 4096 + (6 \times 1024 \times 3)x + (15 \times 256 \times 9)x^2 + (20 \times 64 \times 27)x^3$
$\qquad\qquad\qquad\qquad\qquad\qquad + (15 \times 16 \times 81)x^4$
$= 4096 + 18\,432x + 34\,560x^2 + 34\,560x^3 + 19\,440x^4$
[1 mark for each correct term]

2   The x^3 term in $(1 + px)^7$ is $\binom{7}{3}(px)^3$ *[1 mark]*
$35p^3x^3 = 280x^3 \Rightarrow 35p^3 = 280$ *[1 mark]*
$\qquad\qquad \Rightarrow p^3 = 8 \Rightarrow p = 2$ *[1 mark]*

Section 2 — Coordinate Geometry

Page 33 — Geometry of Lines and Circles

Practice Questions

1 a) i) $y + 1 = 3(x - 2)$ ii) $y = 3x - 7$ iii) $3x - y - 7 = 0$
  b) i) $y + \frac{1}{3} = \frac{1}{5}x$ ii) $y = \frac{1}{5}x - \frac{1}{3}$ iii) $3x - 15y - 5 = 0$

2    $y = \frac{3}{2}x - 4$

3    $y = -\frac{1}{2}x + 4$

4    $y = \frac{3}{2}x + \frac{15}{2}$

5    $(x - 3)^2 + (y + 1)^2 = 49$

6 a) 3, (0, 0)   b) 2, (2, –4)   c) 5, (–3, 4)

Exam Questions

1 a) i) $3y = 15 - 4x \Rightarrow y = -\frac{4}{3}x + 5$
      so the gradient of the line PQ is $m = -\frac{4}{3}$. *[1 mark]*
   ii) Find the coordinates of P and Q:
      P: $0 + 3p = 15 \Rightarrow p = 5 \Rightarrow$ P has coordinates (0, 5)
      Q: $4q + -9 = 15 \Rightarrow q = 6 \Rightarrow$ Q has coordinates (6, –3)
      [1 mark for both correct]
      Then use the formula:
      Length $= \sqrt{(6-0)^2 + ((-3)-5)^2} = \sqrt{6^2 + (-8)^2} = \sqrt{36 + 64}$
      $= \sqrt{100} = 10$ *[1 mark]*
  b) Gradient of the line $= -1 \div -\frac{4}{3} = \frac{3}{4}$, *[1 mark]* so $y = \frac{3}{4}x + c$
     Use the midpoint formula to find the coordinates of R:
     Midpoint $= \left(\frac{0+6}{2}, \frac{5+(-3)}{2}\right) = \left(\frac{6}{2}, \frac{2}{2}\right) = (3, 1)$ *[1 mark]*
     Now use the x- and y-values of R to find c:
     $1 = \frac{3}{4}(3) + c \Rightarrow 1 = \frac{9}{4} + c \Rightarrow c = -\frac{5}{4} \Rightarrow y = \frac{3}{4}x - \frac{5}{4}$ *[1 mark]*

2 a) Using the formula $y - y_1 = m(x - x_1)$, with the coordinates of point S for the x- and y-values and $m = -2$,
     $y - (-3) = -2(x - 7)$ *[1 mark]*
     $y + 3 = -2x + 14 \Rightarrow y = -2x + 11$ *[1 mark]*
  b) Putting $x = 5$ into $y = -2x + 11$ gives $y = 1$,
     so T does lie on the line. *[1 mark]*

3 a) Use the midpoint formula to find the coordinates of L:
     Midpoint $= \left(\frac{5+(-1)}{2}, \frac{8+4}{2}\right) = \left(\frac{4}{2}, \frac{12}{2}\right) = (2, 6)$ *[1 mark]*
     Gradient of JK $= \frac{8-4}{5-(-1)} = \frac{4}{6} = \frac{2}{3}$ *[1 mark]*
     so gradient of $l_1 = -1 \div \frac{2}{3} = -\frac{3}{2}$ *[1 mark]*
     Now, putting this gradient and the x- and y-coordinates of L into the formula $y - y_1 = m(x - x_1)$ gives:
     $y - 6 = -\frac{3}{2}(x - 2) \Rightarrow y = -\frac{3}{2}x + 3 + 6 \Rightarrow y = -\frac{3}{2}x + 9$ *[1 mark]*
     $\qquad\qquad\qquad \Rightarrow 3x + 2y - 18 = 0$ *[1 mark]*
  b) Putting $x = 0$ into $y = -\frac{3}{2}x + 9$ gives $y = 9$, *[1 mark]*
     so M = (0, 9). *[1 mark]*
  c) Putting $y = 0$ into $3x + 2y - 18 = 0$ gives $x = 6$, *[1 mark]*
     so N = (6, 0). *[1 mark]*

4 a) Rearrange equation and complete the square:
     $x^2 - 2x + y^2 - 10y + 21 = 0$ *[1 mark]*
     $(x - 1)^2 - 1 + (y - 5)^2 - 25 + 21 = 0$ *[1 mark]*
     $(x - 1)^2 + (y - 5)^2 = 5$ *[1 mark]*
     Compare with $(x - a)^2 + (y - b)^2 = r^2$:
     centre = (1, 5) *[1 mark]* radius $= \sqrt{5} = 2.24$ (3 s.f.) *[1 mark]*
  b) The point (3, 6) and centre (1, 5) both lie on the diameter.
     Gradient of the diameter $= \frac{6-5}{3-1} = 0.5$ *[1 mark]*
     Q $(q, 4)$ also lies on the diameter, so $\frac{4-6}{q-3} = 0.5$ *[1 mark]*
     $-2 = 0.5q - 1.5$, so $q = (-2 + 1.5) \div 0.5 = -1$ *[1 mark]*
  c) Tangent at Q is perpendicular to the diameter at Q,
     so gradient $m = -\frac{1}{0.5} = -2$
     $y - y_1 = m(x - x_1)$, and (–1, 4) is a point on the line, so:
     $y - 4 = -2(x + 1)$
     $y - 4 = -2x - 2 \Rightarrow 2x + y - 2 = 0$ is the equation of the tangent.
     [3 marks available — 1 mark for correct value for gradient, 1 mark for substituting Q in straight-line equation, 1 mark for correct equation of the tangent in the form ax + by + c = 0]

Section 3 — Trigonometry

Page 35 — Trig Functions and Graphs

Practice Questions

1 a) $\frac{\sqrt{3}}{2}$ b) $\frac{1}{\sqrt{2}}$ c) $\sqrt{3}$ d) $\frac{1}{2}$

2 a) 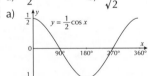   b)

c)

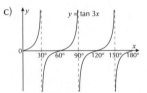

Exam Questions

1   The coordinates of any point on the unit circle are $(\cos\theta, \sin\theta)$,
     so $\cos\theta = 0.914$ and $\sin\theta = -0.407$.
     $\cos\theta = 0.914 \Rightarrow \theta = \cos^{-1}(0.914) = 24°$ (nearest degree)
     or $\sin\theta = -0.407 \Rightarrow \theta = \sin^{-1}(-0.407) = -24°$ (nearest degree)
     [1 mark for either answer]
     So the angle is $360° - 24° = 336°$ *[1 mark]*
     (0.914, –0.407) is in the bottom right quadrant of the unit circle diagram on p.34, so the correct angle is $360° - \theta$ (for cos) or $\theta + 360°$ (for sin).

Answers

2 a)
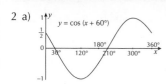
[2 marks — 1 mark for correct shape of cos x graph, 1 mark for shift of 60° to the left]

b) The graph of $y = \cos(x + 60°)$ cuts the x-axis at 30° and 210°, so for $0 \le x \le 360°$, $\cos(x + 60°) = 0$ when $x = 30°$ *[1 mark]* and $x = 210°$. *[1 mark]*

3
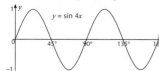
[2 marks — 1 mark for correct shape of sin x graph, 1 mark for 2 repetitions of the sine wave between 0 and 180°]

Page 37 — Trig Formulas and Identities
Practice Questions
1 a) $B = 125°$, $a = 3.66$ m, $c = 3.10$ m, area $= 4.64$ m²
  b) $r = 20.05$ km, $P = 1.49°$, $Q = 168.51°$
2 22.3°, 49.5° and 108.2° (1 d.p.)

Exam Questions
1 $3 \cos x = 2 \sin x$, and $\tan x = \dfrac{\sin x}{\cos x}$,

Divide through by cos x to give: $3\dfrac{\cos x}{\cos x} = 2\dfrac{\sin x}{\cos x}$ *[1 mark]*

$\Rightarrow 3 = 2 \tan x \Rightarrow \tan x = \dfrac{3}{2}$ (= 1.5) *[1 mark]*

2 a) Sketch a diagram to show what's going on:

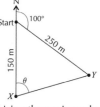

Using the cosine rule: $a^2 = b^2 + c^2 - 2bc \cos A$
If XY is a, then angle $A = 180° - 100° = 80°$.
$XY^2 = 150^2 + 250^2 - (2 \times 150 \times 250 \times \cos 80°)$ *[1 mark]*
    $= 71976.386...$
$XY = \sqrt{71976.386...} = 268.284...$
    $= 268$ m to the nearest m *[1 mark]*
  b) Using the sine rule and the answer to part a):
$\dfrac{a}{\sin A} = \dfrac{b}{\sin B}$, so $\dfrac{250}{\sin \theta} = \dfrac{268.284...}{\sin 80°}$ *[1 mark]*
Rearranging gives:
$\dfrac{\sin \theta}{\sin 80°} = \dfrac{250}{268.284...}$ *[1 mark]* = 0.93 (2 d.p.) *[1 mark]*

Page 39 — Solving Trig Equations
Practice Question
1 a) (i) $\theta = 240°, 300°$ (ii) $\theta = 135°, 315°$ (iii) $\theta = 135°, 225°$
  b) (i) $\theta = -147.0°, -123.0°, -57.0°, -33.0°, 33.0°, 57.0°,$
      $123.0°, 147.0°$
    (ii) $\theta = -17.5°, 127.5°$ (iii) $\theta = 179.8°$

Exam Question
1 a) Solutions are in the range $-45° \le x - 45° \le 360° - 45°$ (= 315°).

$2 \cos(x - 45°) = \sqrt{3} \Rightarrow \cos(x - 45°) = \dfrac{\sqrt{3}}{2}$ *[1 mark]*

Solving this gives $x - 45° = 30°$, which is in the range — so it's a solution. From the symmetry of the cos graph there's another solution at $360° - 30° = 330°$. But this is outside the range for $x - 45°$, so you can ignore it. Using symmetry again, there's also a solution at $-30°$ — and this one is in your range. *[1 mark]*
So solutions for $x - 45°$ are $-30°$ and $30° \Rightarrow x = 15°$ and $x = 75°$ *[1 mark for both correct]*
It's useful to sketch a graph or a CAST diagram here.
Remember that $\cos 30° = \dfrac{\sqrt{3}}{2}$, from the trig values table on p.34.

  b) $\sin 2x = -\dfrac{1}{2}$, so look for solutions in the range $0 \le 2x \le 720°$.
It's easier to see what's going on by drawing a graph for this one:

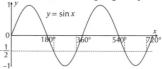

The graph shows there are 4 solutions between 0 and 720°.
Putting $\sin 2x = -\dfrac{1}{2}$ into your calculator gives you the solution $2x = -30°$, but this is outside the range. From the graph, you can see that the solutions within the range occur at $180° + 30°$, $360° - 30°$, $540° + 30°$ and $720° - 30°$, *[1 mark]*
so $2x = 210°, 330°, 570°$ and $690°$. *[1 mark]*
Dividing by 2 gives: $x = 105°, 165°, 285°$ and $345°$
[1 mark for all 4 correct solutions]

Page 41 — Using Trig Identities
Practice Questions
1 $x = 70.5°$ (1 d.p.), 120°, 240°, 289.5° (1 d.p.)
2 $x = -30°$
3 $(\sin y + \cos y)^2 + (\cos y - \sin y)^2 \equiv 2$
4 $\dfrac{\sin^4 x + \sin^2 x \cos^2 x}{\cos^2 x - 1} \equiv \dfrac{\sin^2 x(\sin^2 x + \cos^2 x)}{(1 - \sin^2 x) - 1} \equiv \dfrac{\sin^2 x}{-\sin^2 x} \equiv -1$

Exam Questions
1 a) $\sin^2 x = 1 - \cos^2 x$, so
    $2(1 - \cos x) = 3 \sin^2 x \Rightarrow 2(1 - \cos x) = 3(1 - \cos^2 x)$ *[1 mark]*
    $2 - 2\cos x = 3 - 3\cos^2 x \Rightarrow 3\cos^2 x - 2\cos x - 1 = 0$ *[1 mark]*
  b) From (a), the equation can be written as:
    $3\cos^2 x - 2\cos x - 1 = 0$
    Now this looks suspiciously like a quadratic equation, so factorise:
    $(3\cos x + 1)(\cos x - 1) = 0$ *[1 mark]*
    $\Rightarrow \cos x = -\dfrac{1}{3}$ or $\cos x = 1$ *[1 mark for both]*
    For $\cos x = -\dfrac{1}{3}$, $x = 109.5°$ (1 d.p.), *[1 mark]*
    and a second solution can be found from
    $x = (360° - 109.5°) = 250.5°$. *[1 mark]*
    For $\cos x = 1$, $x = 0°$ *[1 mark]* and $x = 360°$. *[1 mark]*
2 Using $\cos^2 x + \sin^2 x = 1$:
    $3\cos^2 x = \sin^2 x \Rightarrow 3\cos^2 x = 1 - \cos^2 x$ *[1 mark]*
    $\Rightarrow 4\cos^2 x = 1 \Rightarrow \cos^2 x = \dfrac{1}{4} \Rightarrow \cos x = \pm\dfrac{1}{2}$ *[1 mark]*
    For $\cos x = \dfrac{1}{2}$: $x = 60°$ *[1 mark]* and $x = -60°$ *[1 mark]*
    For $\cos x = -\dfrac{1}{2}$: $x = 120°$ *[1 mark]* and $x = -120°$ *[1 mark]*
    You shouldn't divide by cos² x, as it can be zero in the range $-180° \le x \le 180°$ (and dividing by zero is the worst thing imaginable).

Answers

Section 4 — Exponentials and Logarithms

Page 43 — Exponentials and Logs

Practice Questions

1 a) 3 b) −3 c) 2
2 a) $\log 75$ b) $\log 2$ c) 0
3 $\log_b (x + 1)$
4 a) 2.380 (4 s.f.) b) 199500 (4 s.f.) c) 1.088 (4 s.f.)

Exam Questions

1 $\log_7 (y + 3) + \log_7 (2y + 1) = 1$
$\Rightarrow \log_7 ((y + 3)(2y + 1)) = 1$ *[1 mark]*
To remove the $\log_7$, do 7 to the power of each side:
$(y + 3)(2y + 1) = 7^1 = 7$ *[1 mark]*
Multiply out, rearrange, and re-factorise:
$2y^2 + 7y + 3 = 7 \Rightarrow 2y^2 + 7y - 4 = 0$
$\Rightarrow (2y - 1)(y + 4) = 0$ *[1 mark]*
$\Rightarrow y = \frac{1}{2}$ or $y = -4$,
but since $y > 0$, $y = \frac{1}{2}$ is the only solution. *[1 mark]*

2 a) $3^x = 5$, so taking logs of both sides gives $\log 3^x = \log 5$ *[1 mark]*
$\Rightarrow x \log 3 = \log 5$ *[1 mark]*
$\Rightarrow x = \frac{\log 5}{\log 3} = 1.46$ to 2 d.p. *[1 mark]*

b) $3^{2x} = (3^x)^2$ (from the power laws) *[1 mark]*,
so let $y = 3^x$ and $y^2 = 3^{2x}$. This gives a quadratic in y:
$y^2 - 14y = -45 \Rightarrow y^2 - 14y + 45 = 0 \Rightarrow (y - 5)(y - 9) = 0$ *[1 mark]*,
so $y = 5$ or $y = 9 \Rightarrow 3^x = 5$ or $3^x = 9$ *[1 mark for both values of 3^x]*
From a), $3^x = 5 \Rightarrow x = 1.46$ to 2 d.p.
and $3^x = 9 \Rightarrow x = 2$ (since $3^2 = 9$) *[1 mark]*

Page 45 — Using Exponentials and Logs

Practice Questions

1 $x = -0.258$ (3 s.f.)
2 $y = -2$ or $y = 3.77$ (3 s.f.)
3 14.2 years (1 d.p.)

Exam Question

1 a) Make a table of values for t and $\log_{10} p$ (round values to 3 d.p.):

t	1	2	3	4	5
$\log_{10} p$	1	1.114	1.230	1.380	1.544

[1 mark for all values correct]
Plot the graph and draw the line of best fit:

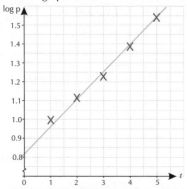

[1 mark for plotting points correctly and drawing a suitable line of best fit]

b) You are given the equation $p = ab^t$. Using the laws of logs, this rearranges to: $\log p = t \log b + \log a$
Comparing this to $y = mx + c$ shows that the gradient of the graph is equal to $\log b$ and the vertical-axis intercept is equal to $\log a$. *[1 mark for both correct]*

Use gradient $= \frac{y_2 - y_1}{x_2 - x_1}$ with points (x_1, y_1) and (x_2, y_2) chosen from your line of best fit to find $\log b$.
e.g. taking the points (3, 1.25) and (4, 1.4) gives
gradient $\frac{1.4 - 1.25}{4 - 3} = 0.15$ *[1 mark]*
So $\log b = 0.15 \Rightarrow b = 1.41$ (2 d.p.) *[1 mark for $0.9 \leq b \leq 1.9$]*
Now read off your vertical-axis intercept to find $\log a$:
$\log a = 0.82 \Rightarrow a = 6.61$ (2 d.p.) *[1 mark for $6.5 \leq a \leq 7.5$]*
Don't worry if your values aren't exactly the same as in this solution. It will depend on the line of best fit you have drawn — everybody's will be slightly different. The examiners have a range of answers which are allowed, so as long as yours are within that range then you'll be fine. Look back at page 45 if you struggled with this question — it is quite tricky.

c) $t = 10 \Rightarrow p = 6.61(1.41)^{10} = 205.30$
So the author's income will be approximately £205 000.
[1 mark for answer between £150 000 and £250 000]

d) E.g. 10 years is a large extrapolation from the data.
[1 mark for a valid reason]
Lots of things could change the author's income in this time — e.g. sales of the book slow down or the author publishes another book.

Page 47 — e^x and $\ln x$

Practice Questions

1 a) C b) A c) D d) B
2 a) $x = 0.8959$ to 4 d.p. b) $x = -0.8830$ to 4 d.p.
c) $x = 0.1223$ to 4 d.p. d) $x = 0.8000$ to 4 d.p.
3 a) $x = \frac{e^{-3} + 28}{8}$ or $\frac{1}{8e^3} + \frac{7}{2}$ b) $x = 0$

Exam Questions

1 a) $6e^x = 3 \Rightarrow e^x = 0.5$ *[1 mark]* $\Rightarrow x = \ln 0.5$ or $-\ln 2$ *[1 mark]*
b) $e^{2x} - 8e^x + 7 = 0$. This looks like a quadratic, so use $y = e^x$.
If $y = e^x$, then $y^2 - 8y + 7 = 0$. This will factorise to give:
$(y - 7)(y - 1) = 0$ *[1 mark]* $\Rightarrow y = 7$ or $y = 1$.
So $e^x = 7$ and $e^x = 1$ *[1 mark for both]*
$\Rightarrow x = \ln 7$ and $x = \ln 1 = 0$ *[1 mark for each correct answer]*
c) $4 \ln x = 3 \Rightarrow \ln x = 0.75$ *[1 mark]* $\Rightarrow x = e^{0.75}$ *[1 mark]*
d) $\ln x + \frac{24}{\ln x} = 10$
You need to get rid of that fraction, so multiply through by $\ln x$:
$(\ln x)^2 + 24 = 10 \ln x \Rightarrow (\ln x)^2 - 10 \ln x + 24 = 0$
This looks like a quadratic, so use $y = \ln x$.
$y^2 - 10y + 24 = 0 \Rightarrow (y - 6)(y - 4) = 0$ *[1 mark]*
$\Rightarrow y = 6$ or $y = 4$ *[1 mark]*
So $\ln x = 6 \Rightarrow x = e^6$, *[1 mark]* or $\ln x = 4 \Rightarrow x = e^4$ *[1 mark]*
2 a) $2e^x + 18e^{-x} = 20$
Multiply through by e^x to remove the e^{-x} (since $e^x \times e^{-x} = 1$).
$2e^{2x} + 18 = 20e^x \Rightarrow 2e^{2x} - 20e^x + 18 = 0 \Rightarrow e^{2x} - 10e^x + 9 = 0$
This now looks like a quadratic equation, so use $y = e^x$ to simplify.
$y^2 - 10y + 9 = 0 \Rightarrow (y - 1)(y - 9) = 0$ *[1 mark]*
$\Rightarrow y = 1$ or $y = 9$ *[1 mark]*.
So $e^x = 1 \Rightarrow x = 0$ *[1 mark]* or $e^x = 9 \Rightarrow x = \ln 9$ *[1 mark]*
b) $2 \ln x - \ln 3 = \ln 12 \Rightarrow 2 \ln x = \ln 12 + \ln 3$
Use the log laws to simplify at this point.
$\Rightarrow \ln x^2 = \ln 36$ *[1 mark]* $\Rightarrow x^2 = 36$ *[1 mark]* $\Rightarrow x = 6$ *[1 mark]*
x must be positive as $\ln (-6)$ does not exist.

Page 49 — Modelling with e^x and $\ln x$

Practice Question

1 a) £7500 b) £1015 (to the nearest £)
c) 13.5 years (to 1 d.p.) d)
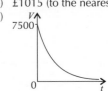

Answers

Exam Questions

1 a) When $t = 0$ (i.e. when the mink were introduced to the habitat)
$M = 74 \times e^0 = 74$, so there were 74 mink originally. *[1 mark]*

b) After 3 years, $M = 74 \times e^{0.6 \times 3}$ *[1 mark]* = 447 mink. *[1 mark]*
You can't round up here as there are only 447 whole mink.

c) For $M = 10\,000$:
$10\,000 = 74e^{0.6t} \Rightarrow e^{0.6t} = 10\,000 \div 74 = 135.1351$
$\Rightarrow 0.6t = \ln 135.1351 = 4.9063$ *[1 mark]*
$\Rightarrow t = 4.9063 \div 0.6 = 8.2$ years
so it would take 9 complete years for the population
to exceed 10 000. *[1 mark]*

d)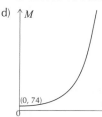
[1 mark for correct shape of graph, and 1 mark for (0, 74) as a point on the graph.]

2 a) B is the value of A when $t = 0$.
From the table, $B = 50$. *[1 mark]*

b) Substitute $t = 5$ and $A = 42$ into $A = 50e^{-kt}$:
$42 = 50e^{-5k} \Rightarrow e^{-5k} = \frac{42}{50} \Rightarrow e^{5k} = \frac{50}{42}$ *[1 mark]*
$\Rightarrow 5k = \ln\left(\frac{50}{42}\right) = 0.17435$
$\Rightarrow k = 0.17435 \div 5 = 0.0349$ to 3 s.f. *[1 mark]*

c) $A = 50e^{-0.0349t}$ [using values from a) and b)],
so when $t = 10$, $A = 50 \times e^{-0.0349 \times 10}$ *[1 mark]*
$= 35$ to the nearest whole number. *[1 mark]*

d) The half-life will be the value of t when A reaches half of the
original value of 50, i.e. when $A = 25$.
$25 = 50e^{-0.0349t} \Rightarrow \frac{25}{50} = e^{-0.0349t} \Rightarrow \frac{50}{25} = e^{0.0349t}$
$\Rightarrow e^{0.0349t} = 2$ *[1 mark]*
$\Rightarrow 0.0349t = \ln 2$ *[1 mark]*
So $t = \ln 2 \div 0.0349 = 20$ days to the nearest day. *[1 mark]*

Section 5 — Differentiation

Page 52 — Differentiation

Practice Questions

1 a) $\frac{dy}{dx} = 2x$ b) $\frac{dy}{dx} = 4x^3 + \frac{1}{2\sqrt{x}}$

c) $\frac{dy}{dx} = -\frac{14}{x^3} + \frac{3}{2\sqrt{x^3}} + 36x^2$

2 $\frac{dy}{dx} = -16$

3 Tangent: $y = 3x - 42$,   Normal: $x + 3y - 34 = 0$

4 $f(x) = 5x \Rightarrow f'(x) = \lim_{h \to 0}\frac{5(x+h) - 5x}{h} = \lim_{h \to 0}\frac{5x + 5h - 5x}{h}$
$= \lim_{h \to 0}\frac{5h}{h} = \lim_{h \to 0}(5) = 5$

Exam Questions

1 Rewrite the expression as $x^{-\frac{1}{2}} + x^{-1}$
Then differentiate to get $\frac{dy}{dx} = -\frac{1}{2}x^{-\frac{3}{2}} - x^{-2}$ *[1 mark]*
Putting $x = 4$ into the derivative gives:
$-\frac{1}{2}4^{-\frac{3}{2}} - 4^{-2} = -\frac{1}{2}(\sqrt{4})^{-3} - \frac{1}{4^2} = -\frac{1}{16} - \frac{1}{16} = -\frac{1}{8}$ *[1 mark]*

2 a) $\frac{dy}{dx} = 3mx^2 - 2x + 8$ *[1 mark]*

b) Rearranging the equation of the line parallel to the normal
gives the equation $y = 3 - 4x$, so it has a gradient of -4. *[1 mark]*
The normal also has gradient -4 because it is parallel
to this line, so the gradient of the curve at P is
$-1 \div$ the gradient of the normal $= -1 \div -4 = \frac{1}{4}$ *[1 mark]*

c) (i) When $x = 5$, the gradient is $3mx^2 - 2x + 8 = \frac{1}{4}$ *[1 mark]*
Now find the value of m:
$m(3 \times 5^2) - (2 \times 5) + 8 = \frac{1}{4}$ *[1 mark]*
$75m - 2 = \frac{1}{4} \Rightarrow 75m = \frac{9}{4} \Rightarrow m = \frac{9}{300} = 0.03$ *[1 mark]*

(ii) When $x = 5$, $y = (0.03 \times 5^3) - (5^2) + (8 \times 5) + 2$ *[1 mark]*
$= 3.75 - 25 + 40 + 2 = 20.75$ *[1 mark]*

3 $y = \frac{x^3}{3} - 2x^2 - 4x + \frac{86}{3} \Rightarrow \frac{dy}{dx} = x^2 - 4x - 4$
When $x = 4$: $y = \frac{64}{3} - 32 - 16 + \frac{86}{3} = 2$ *[1 mark]*
$\frac{dy}{dx} = 16 - 16 - 4 = -4$ *[1 mark]*

$y = \sqrt{x} = x^{\frac{1}{2}} \Rightarrow \frac{dy}{dx} = \frac{1}{2}x^{-\frac{1}{2}} = \frac{1}{2\sqrt{x}}$
When $x = 4$: $y = \sqrt{4} = 2$ *[1 mark]*
$\frac{dy}{dx} = \frac{1}{2\sqrt{4}} = \frac{1}{4}$ *[1 mark]*

For both curves, when $x = 4$, $y = 2$,
so they both pass through the point (4, 2) *[1 mark]*.
If you multiply the two gradients at the point (4, 2) together,
you get $-4 \times \frac{1}{4} = -1$, so the curves are perpendicular *[1 mark]*.

4 $f(x) = x^4 \Rightarrow f'(x) = \lim_{h \to 0}\frac{(x+h)^4 - x^4}{h}$ *[1 mark]*
Using the binomial formula:
$(x+h)^4 = x^4 + 4hx^3 + 6h^2x^2 + 4h^3x + h^4$ *[1 mark]*
So $f'(x) = \lim_{h \to 0}\frac{x^4 + 4hx^3 + 6h^2x^2 + 4h^3x + h^4 - x^4}{h}$ *[1 mark]*
$= \lim_{h \to 0}\frac{4hx^3 + 6h^2x^2 + 4h^3x + h^4}{h}$
$= \lim_{h \to 0}(4x^3 + 6hx^2 + 4h^2x + h^3)$ *[1 mark]*
As $h \to 0$, the last three terms become 0, so $f'(x) = 4x^3$ *[1 mark]*

Page 55 — Stationary Points

Practice Questions

1 $(7, -371)$ and $(-3, 129)$

2 $(1, 4)$ is a minimum, $(-1, -4)$ is a maximum.

3 a) Increasing when $x > 0.5$, decreasing when $x < 0.5$

b) Increasing when $x < 0$, decreasing when $x > 0$

4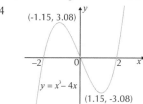

Exam Questions

1 a) $y = 6 + \frac{4x^3 - 15x^2 + 12x}{6} = 6 + \frac{2}{3}x^3 - \frac{5}{2}x^2 + 2x$ *[1 mark]*
$\frac{dy}{dx} = 2x^2 - 5x + 2$ *[1 mark]*

b) Stationary points occur when $2x^2 - 5x + 2 = 0$.
Factorising the equation gives: $(2x - 1)(x - 2) = 0$
So the stationary points are at $x = 2$ and $x = \frac{1}{2}$. *[1 mark]*
When $x = 2$, $y = 6 + \frac{4(2^3) - 15(2^2) + (12 \times 2)}{6} = 5\frac{1}{3}$ *[1 mark]*
When $x = \frac{1}{2}$, $y = 6 + \frac{4\left(\frac{1}{2}\right)^3 - 15\left(\frac{1}{2}\right)^2 + 12\left(\frac{1}{2}\right)}{6} = 6\frac{11}{24}$ *[1 mark]*
So coordinates of the stationary points of the curve are
$\left(2, 5\frac{1}{3}\right)$ and $\left(\frac{1}{2}, 6\frac{11}{24}\right)$.

Answers

c) Differentiate again to find $\frac{d^2y}{dx^2} = 4x - 5$ *[1 mark]*

When $x = 2$, $\frac{d^2y}{dx^2} = 4(2) - 5 = 3$, which is positive,

so $\left(2, 5\frac{1}{3}\right)$ is a minimum *[1 mark]*

When $x = \frac{1}{2}$, $\frac{d^2y}{dx^2} = 4\left(\frac{1}{2}\right) - 5 = -3$, which is negative,

so $\left(\frac{1}{2}, 6\frac{11}{24}\right)$ is a maximum *[1 mark]*

2 a) First, expand the brackets to get $y = 3x^3 - 8x^2 + 3x + 2$ *[1 mark]*

$\Rightarrow \frac{dy}{dx} = 9x^2 - 16x + 3$ *[1 mark]*

$\frac{dy}{dx} = 0$ at the stationary point, so use the quadratic formula:

$x = \frac{16 \pm \sqrt{(-16)^2 - (4 \times 9 \times 3)}}{2 \times 9} = \frac{16 \pm 2\sqrt{37}}{18}$

$\Rightarrow x = 1.56$ and 0.213 (3 s.f.) *[1 mark]*

Substituting these values for x into the original equation for y gives $y = -1.40$ and 2.31 (3 s.f.), so the stationary points have coordinates $(1.56, -1.40)$ and $(0.213, 2.31)$. *[1 mark]*

b) $\frac{d^2y}{dx^2} = 18x - 16$ *[1 mark]*

At $x = 1.56$, $\frac{d^2y}{dx^2} = 12.16... > 0$, so it's a minimum *[1 mark]*

At $x = 0.213$, $\frac{d^2y}{dx^2} = -12.16... < 0$, so it's a maximum *[1 mark]*

c) y is a positive cubic function, with a minimum at $(1.56, -1.40)$ and a maximum at $(0.213, 2.31)$, from parts a) and b).
The curve crosses the y-axis when $x = 0 \Rightarrow y = 2$ *[1 mark]*
The initial equation can be factorised to find where it intersects the x-axis: $y = (x - 1)(3x^2 - 5x - 2) = (x - 1)(3x + 1)(x - 2)$

So $y = 0$ when $x = 1, -\frac{1}{3}$ and 2. *[1 mark]*

The sketch looks like this:　*[1 mark]*

3 a) $f'(x) = 2x^3 - 3 = 0$ at the stationary point. *[1 mark]*
$\Rightarrow 2x^3 = 3 \Rightarrow x = 1.1447... = 1.14$ (3 s.f.) *[1 mark]*

$f(1.1447...) = \frac{1}{2}(1.1447...)^4 - 3(1.1447...) = -2.58$ (3 s.f.) *[1 mark]*
So the coordinates of the stationary point are $(1.14, -2.58)$.

b) $f''(x) = 6x^2$ *[1 mark]*
At the stationary point, $f''(x) = 6(1.1447...)^2 = 7.862... > 0$,
so it is a minimum. *[1 mark]*

c) (i) As the stationary point is a minimum, $f(x)$ is increasing on the right of the stationary point — i.e. when $x > 1.14$ *[1 mark]*

(ii) Similarly, $f(x)$ is decreasing on the left of the stationary point — i.e. when $x < 1.14$ *[1 mark]*

d) The graph intersects the x-axis when $f(x) = 0 \Rightarrow \frac{1}{2}x^4 - 3x = 0$
$\Rightarrow x\left(\frac{1}{2}x^3 - 3\right) = 0 \Rightarrow x = 0$ or $x = \sqrt[3]{6} = 1.82$ (3 s.f.) *[1 mark]*
So the graph looks like this:　*[1 mark]*

Page 57 — Using Differentiation

Practice Questions

1　146 ml/s

2　$m = 53.3$ g (3 s.f.), $h_{max} = 94.8$ m (3 s.f.)

Exam Questions

1 a) Find the value of x that gives the minimum value of y, i.e. the stationary point of curve y, by differentiating and solving $\frac{dy}{dx} = 0$: $\frac{dy}{dx} = \frac{1}{\sqrt{x}} - \frac{27}{x^2}$ *[1 mark]*

$\frac{dy}{dx} = 0 \Rightarrow \frac{1}{\sqrt{x}} - \frac{27}{x^2} = 0 \Rightarrow \frac{1}{\sqrt{x}} = \frac{27}{x^2} \Rightarrow x^{\frac{3}{2}} = 27$ *[1 mark]*

$\Rightarrow x = 9$ *[1 mark]*

So the minimum coal consumption is at 9 mph. *[1 mark]*

b) $\frac{d^2y}{dx^2} = \frac{54}{x^3} - \frac{1}{2\sqrt{x^3}}$ *[1 mark]*
At the stationary point, $x = 9 \Rightarrow \frac{d^2y}{dx^2} = \frac{54}{9^3} - \frac{1}{2\sqrt{9^3}} = 0.055... > 0$
so the stationary point is a minimum. *[1 mark]*

c) $y = 2\sqrt{9} + \frac{27}{9} = 9$ units of coal *[1 mark]*

2 a) Surface area $= 2(d \times x) + 2\left(d \times \frac{x}{2}\right) + \left(x \times \frac{x}{2}\right)$

$= 2dx + dx + \frac{x^2}{2} = 3dx + \frac{x^2}{2}$ *[1 mark]*

Surface area $= 72 \Rightarrow 3dx + \frac{x^2}{2} = 72 \Rightarrow x^2 + 6dx = 144$ *[1 mark]*

$\Rightarrow d = \frac{144 - x^2}{6x}$ *[1 mark]*

Volume = width × height × depth $= \frac{x}{2} \times x \times d$

$V = \frac{x^2}{2} \times \frac{144 - x^2}{6x} = \frac{144x^2 - x^4}{12x} = 12x - \frac{x^3}{12}$ as required *[1 mark]*

b) Differentiate V and then solve $\frac{dV}{dx} = 0$: $\frac{dV}{dx} = 12 - \frac{x^2}{4}$ *[1 mark]*

$12 - \frac{x^2}{4} = 0 \Rightarrow \frac{x^2}{4} = 12 \Rightarrow x^2 = 48$ *[1 mark]*

$\Rightarrow x = \sqrt{48} = 4\sqrt{3}$ *[1 mark]*

c) $\frac{d^2V}{dx^2} = -\frac{x}{2}$ *[1 mark]*
so when $x = 4\sqrt{3}$, $\frac{d^2V}{dx^2} = -2\sqrt{3}$ *[1 mark]*
$\frac{d^2V}{dx^2}$ is negative, so it's a maximum point. *[1 mark]*

$x = 4\sqrt{3}$ at V_{max}, so $V_{max} = (12 \times 4\sqrt{3}) - \frac{(4\sqrt{3})^3}{12}$
$V_{max} = 55.4$ m^3 (3 s.f.) *[1 mark]*

Section 6 — Integration

Page 59 — Integrating $f(x) = x^n$

Practice Questions

1 a) $2x^5 + C$　b) $\frac{3x^2}{2} + \frac{5x^3}{3} + C$　c) $\frac{3x^4}{4} + \frac{2x^3}{3} + C$

2　$y = 3x^2 - 7x + 4$

3　$f(x) = \frac{3x^4}{4} + 2x - \frac{11}{4}$

Exam Questions

1 a) Multiply out the brackets and simplify the terms:
$(5 + 2\sqrt{x})^2 = (5 + 2\sqrt{x})(5 + 2\sqrt{x})$
$= 25 + 10\sqrt{x} + 10\sqrt{x} + 4x = 25 + 20\sqrt{x} + 4x$
So $a = 25$, $b = 20$ and $c = 4$
[3 marks available — 1 mark for each constant]

b) Integrate your answer from a), treating each term separately:
$\int (25 + 20\sqrt{x} + 4x)\ dx = 25x + \left(20x^{\frac{3}{2}} \div \frac{3}{2}\right) + \left(\frac{4x^2}{2}\right) + C$

$= 25x + \frac{40\sqrt{x^3}}{3} + 2x^2 + C$

[3 marks available — 1 mark for each term. Lose 1 mark if C missing or answers not simplified (surds not necessary)]
Don't forget to add C, don't forget to add C, don't forget to add C. Once, twice, thrice I beg of you, because it's very important.

2 a) The tangent at $(1, 2)$ has the same gradient as the curve at that point, so use $f'(x)$ to calculate the gradient: *[1 mark]*
$f'(1) = 1^3 - 2 = -1$ *[1 mark]*
Put this into the straight-line equation $y - y_1 = m(x - x_1)$: *[1 mark]*
$y - 2 = -1(x - 1) \Rightarrow y = -x + 1 + 2 = -x + 3$ *[1 mark]*

b) $f(x) = \int \left(x^3 - \frac{2}{x^2}\right) dx = \int (x^3 - 2x^{-2}) \, dx$ *[1 mark]*

$= \frac{x^4}{4} - 2\frac{x^{-1}}{-1} + C = \frac{x^4}{4} + 2x^{-1} + C = \frac{x^4}{4} + \frac{2}{x} + C$ *[1 mark]*

Now use the coordinates (1, 2) to find the value of C: *[1 mark]*

$2 = \frac{1^4}{4} + \frac{2}{1} + C \Rightarrow 2 - \frac{1}{4} - 2 = C \Rightarrow C = -\frac{1}{4}$

So $f(x) = \frac{x^4}{4} + \frac{2}{x} - \frac{1}{4}$ *[1 mark]*

Page 61 — Definite Integrals

Practice Questions

1 a) 4   b) $-\frac{33}{8} + 6\sqrt{2}$ c) $\frac{5}{2}$

2 a) 36   b)

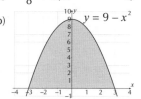

Exam Questions

1 $\int_1^4 (2x - 6x^2 + \sqrt{x}) \, dx = \left[x^2 - 2x^3 + \frac{2\sqrt{x^3}}{3}\right]_1^4$

[3 marks available — 1 for each correct term]

$= \left(4^2 - (2 \times 4^3) + \frac{2\sqrt{4^3}}{3}\right) - \left(1^2 - (2 \times 1^3) + \frac{2\sqrt{1^3}}{3}\right)$ *[1 mark]*

$= -\frac{320}{3} - \left(-\frac{1}{3}\right) = -\frac{319}{3}$ *[1 mark]*

2 The limits are the x-values when $y = 0$, so first solve:

$(x - 3)^2(x + 1) = 0$ *[1 mark]*

$x = 3$ and $x = -1$ *[1 mark for both values correct]*

Hence, to find the area, calculate:

$\int_{-1}^3 (x - 3)^2(x + 1) \, dx = \int_{-1}^3 (x^3 - 5x^2 + 3x + 9) \, dx$ *[1 mark]*

$= \left[\frac{x^4}{4} - \frac{5}{3}x^3 + \frac{3}{2}x^2 + 9x\right]_{-1}^3$

[2 marks — 1 for increasing each power of x by one, 1 for correct integral]

$= \left(\frac{3^4}{4} - \frac{5}{3}3^3 + \frac{3}{2}3^2 + (9 \times 3)\right)$

$\quad - \left(\frac{(-1)^4}{4} - \left(\frac{5}{3} \times (-1)^3\right) + \left(\frac{3}{2} \times (-1)^2\right) + (9 \times (-1))\right)$ *[1 mark]*

$= 15\frac{3}{4} - \left(-5\frac{7}{12}\right) = 21\frac{1}{3}$ *[1 mark]*

3 a) The curve and the line intersect when the equations are equal:

$-(x - 2)^2 = \frac{1}{2}x - 6$ *[1 mark]*

$\Rightarrow -x^2 + 4x - 4 = \frac{1}{2}x - 6 \Rightarrow 2x^2 - 7x - 4 = 0$

$\Rightarrow (2x + 1)(x - 4) = 0 \Rightarrow x = -\frac{1}{2}$ and $x = 4$

Point P has positive x coordinate, so $x = 4$. *[1 mark]*

Put this into one of the equations: $y = -(4 - 2)^2 = -4$. *[1 mark]*

So the coordinates of P are (4, −4).

b) Find where the curve and line intersect the x-axis.

Curve: $0 = -(x - 2)^2 \Rightarrow x - 2 = 0 \Rightarrow x = 2$

Line: $0 = \frac{1}{2}x - 6 \Rightarrow x = 12$

Area A is the sum of the area under the curve between 2 and 4 (A_1) and the area under the line from between 4 and 12 (A_2).

A_1: $\int_2^4 -(x - 2)^2 \, dx$ *[1 mark]* $= \int_2^4 -x^2 + 4x - 4 \, dx$

$= \left[-\frac{x^3}{3} + 2x^2 - 4x\right]_2^4$ *[1 mark]*

$= \left(-\frac{4^3}{3} + 2(4^2) - 4(4)\right) - \left(-\frac{2^3}{3} + 2(2^2) - 4(2)\right)$ *[1 mark]*

$= -\frac{16}{3} - -\frac{8}{3} = -\frac{8}{3}$ *[1 mark]*

So $A_1 = \frac{8}{3}$ (since area must be positive)

$A_2 = (12 - 4) \times 4 \div 2 = 16$ *[1 mark]*

So $A = A_1 + A_2 = \frac{8}{3} + 16 = \frac{56}{3}$ *[1 mark]*

Section 7 — Vectors

Page 63 — Vectors

Practice Questions

1 a) $\mathbf{b} - \mathbf{a}$ b) $\mathbf{a} - \mathbf{b}$ c) $\mathbf{b} - \mathbf{c}$ d) $\mathbf{c} - \mathbf{a}$

2 $2\mathbf{i} - 4\mathbf{j}$

3 $\begin{pmatrix} 13 \\ -10 \end{pmatrix}$

Exam Questions

1 $\overrightarrow{WX} = \overrightarrow{OX} - \overrightarrow{OW} = \begin{pmatrix} -2 \\ 1 \end{pmatrix} - \begin{pmatrix} 1 \\ 3 \end{pmatrix} = \begin{pmatrix} -3 \\ -2 \end{pmatrix}$ *[1 mark]*

$\overrightarrow{YZ} = \overrightarrow{OZ} - \overrightarrow{OY} = \begin{pmatrix} a \\ b \end{pmatrix} - \begin{pmatrix} 5 \\ 4 \end{pmatrix} = \begin{pmatrix} a - 5 \\ b - 4 \end{pmatrix}$ *[1 mark]*

$\overrightarrow{WX} = \overrightarrow{YZ} \Rightarrow \begin{pmatrix} a - 5 \\ b - 4 \end{pmatrix} = \begin{pmatrix} -3 \\ -2 \end{pmatrix} \Rightarrow a = 2,\ b = 2$

So $\overrightarrow{OZ} = \begin{pmatrix} 2 \\ 2 \end{pmatrix}$. *[1 mark]*

2 $\overrightarrow{AB} = (5\mathbf{i} + \mathbf{j}) - (-2\mathbf{i} + 4\mathbf{j}) = (5 - (-2))\mathbf{i} + (1 - 4)\mathbf{j} = 7\mathbf{i} - 3\mathbf{j}$ *[1 mark]*

P is $\frac{1}{4}$ of the way along $\overrightarrow{AB}$, so $\overrightarrow{AP} = \frac{1}{4}\overrightarrow{AB} = \frac{7}{4}\mathbf{i} - \frac{3}{4}\mathbf{j}$ *[1 mark]*

$\overrightarrow{OP} = \overrightarrow{OA} + \overrightarrow{AP} = \left((-2) + \frac{7}{4}\right)\mathbf{i} + \left(4 - \frac{3}{4}\right)\mathbf{j}$ *[1 mark]*

$= -\frac{1}{4}\mathbf{i} + \frac{13}{4}\mathbf{j}$ *[1 mark]*

Page 65 — More Vectors

Practice Questions

1 $-\frac{2}{\sqrt{29}}\mathbf{i} + \frac{5}{\sqrt{29}}\mathbf{j}$

2 a) $\sqrt{5}$ b) $\sqrt{10}$ c) $\sqrt{13}$

3 $7\cos 20°\mathbf{i} + 7\sin 20°\mathbf{j}$

4 108.4° (1 d.p.)

5 Distance = 5, angle = 41.8° (1 d.p.)

Exam Questions

1 $\overrightarrow{BC} = \overrightarrow{AC} - \overrightarrow{AB} = -2\mathbf{i} + 4\mathbf{j} - (-5\mathbf{i} + 2\mathbf{j}) = 3\mathbf{i} + 2\mathbf{j}$ *[1 mark]*

$\overrightarrow{BM} = \frac{1}{2}\overrightarrow{BC} = \frac{3}{2}\mathbf{i} + \mathbf{j}$

$\overrightarrow{AM} = \overrightarrow{AB} + \overrightarrow{BM} = -5\mathbf{i} + 2\mathbf{j} + \frac{3}{2}\mathbf{i} + \mathbf{j} = -\frac{7}{2}\mathbf{i} + 3\mathbf{j}$ *[1 mark]*

So, $|\overrightarrow{AM}| = \sqrt{\left(-\frac{7}{2}\right)^2 + 3^2} = \frac{\sqrt{85}}{2}$ *[1 mark]*

2 a) $\mathbf{p} = 7\cos 15°\ \mathbf{i} + 7\sin 15°\ \mathbf{j}$

[2 marks available — 1 for each correct component]

b) The speed is given by the magnitude of $\mathbf{q}$:

$|\mathbf{q}| = \sqrt{(2\sqrt{2})^2 + (2\sqrt{2})^2} = \sqrt{16} = 4$ m/s, *[1 mark]*

so the particle's speed has decreased by 3 m/s. *[1 mark]*

The direction of $\mathbf{q}$ is 45°. *[1 mark]*

3

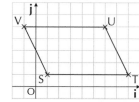

As STUV is a parallelogram, $\overrightarrow{TU}$ is parallel to $\overrightarrow{SV}$ and is the same length, so $\overrightarrow{TU} = \overrightarrow{SV}$. *[1 mark]*

$\overrightarrow{TU} = \overrightarrow{SV} = -\mathbf{i} + 5\mathbf{j} - (\mathbf{i} + \mathbf{j}) = -2\mathbf{i} + 4\mathbf{j}$ *[1 mark]*

$\overrightarrow{SU} = \overrightarrow{ST} + \overrightarrow{TU} = (8\mathbf{i} + \mathbf{j}) - (\mathbf{i} + \mathbf{j}) + (-2\mathbf{i} + 4\mathbf{j}) = 5\mathbf{i} + 4\mathbf{j}$ *[1 mark]*

$|\overrightarrow{SU}| = \sqrt{5^2 + 4^2} = \sqrt{41}$ *[1 mark]*

You could also find the position vector of U (6$\mathbf{i}$ + 5$\mathbf{j}$) — a diagram makes this pretty easy. Then $\overrightarrow{SU}$ = (6$\mathbf{i}$ + 5$\mathbf{j}$) − ($\mathbf{i}$ + $\mathbf{j}$) = 5$\mathbf{i}$ + 4$\mathbf{j}$ as before.

Answers

Section 8 – Data Presentation and Interpretation

Page 67 – Central Tendency and Variation

Practice Questions

1   mean = 1.375, median = 1, mode = 0
2   mean = 17.9 (3 s.f.), standard deviation = 5.57 (3 s.f.)
3   mean = 2.8, variance = 1
4 a) 513   b) 81.3

Exam Question

1 a) $\bar{a} = \dfrac{60.3}{20} = 3.015$ g *[1 mark]*

b) $s_A{}^2 = \dfrac{219}{20} - 3.015^2 = 1.860$ g^2 *[1 mark]*

    So $s_A = 1.36$ g (3 s.f.) *[1 mark]*

c) E.g. Brand A chocolate drops are heavier on average than brand B. Brand B chocolate drops are generally much closer to their mean weight than brand A.
[1 mark for each of 2 sensible statements]
"Mmm, chocolate drops" does not count as a sensible statement...

d) Mean of A and B $= \dfrac{\Sigma a + \Sigma b}{50} = \dfrac{60.3 + (30 \times 2.95)}{50}$
                       $= 2.976$ g *[1 mark]*

    $\dfrac{\Sigma b^2}{30} - 2.95^2 = 1$, so $\Sigma b^2 = 291.075$ *[1 mark]*

    Variance of A and B $= \dfrac{\Sigma a^2 + \Sigma b^2}{50} - 2.976^2$

                         $= \dfrac{219 + 291.075}{50} - 2.976^2 = 1.3449$ *[1 mark]*

    So s.d. $= \sqrt{1.3449} = 1.16$ g (3 s.f.) *[1 mark]*

Work through each step carefully so you don't make silly mistakes and lose any lovely marks.

Page 69 – Displaying Data

Practice Questions

1 a)
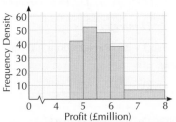

b) mode = 3
c) E.g. The distribution is fairly symmetrical about the mode.

2
```
7 | 7
8 | 5 7 9          Key: 8 | 7 means 87% attendance
9 | 0 2 5  5  8
10| 0
```

3 a) frequency density = 2.5   b) frequency density = 2.2

Exam Questions

1 a)
```
      A        B
    3 0 | 0 |
  7 5 2 | 1 | 7          Key: 2 | 1 | 7 means 12 for A
      6 | 2 | 0 2 7                   and 17 for B
      2 | 3 | 1 3 4 8
      5 | 4 | 1 4
    0 0 | 5 |
```
[2 marks – 1 for each side correct]

b) There are 10 data values for both cricketers, so the median is halfway between the 5th and 6th values.
A: median = (17 + 26) ÷ 2 = 21.5 *[1 mark]*
B: median = (31 + 33) ÷ 2 = 32 *[1 mark]*

2 a) There are 30 data values for the men, so the median is halfway between the 15th and 16th values.
Median = (62 + 65) ÷ 2 = 63.5 years *[1 mark]*

b) E.g. The women's median is 64.5 years, which is higher than the men's median. This suggests that, in general, the women were older when they became grandparents.
[2 marks for a sensible comment and interpretation]
You could've also commented on the women's mean being higher, or the women's range being smaller, meaning the ages at which the women became grandparents were more consistent.

Page 71 – Grouped Data

Practice Questions

1
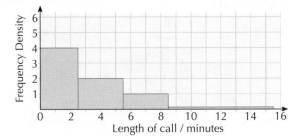

2   mean = 37.1 mph, median = 36.9 mph (3 s.f.),
     modal class = 35-39 mph

Exam Questions

1   Find the total area under the histogram: *[1 mark]*
2 + 1.5 + 2 + 2 + 1.5 + 4 + 5 + 3 + 4 = 25
So each grid square represents 2 lions. *[1 mark]*
The number of squares for lengths above 220 cm is 7, which represents 7 × 2 = 14 lions. *[1 mark]*
There are other ways you could reach this answer — any of them are fine, as long as you end up with the right number of lions in the end.

2 a)

Profit ($£p$ million)	Class width	No. of businesses	Frequency density
$4.5 \le p < 5.0$	0.5	21	42
$5.0 \le p < 5.5$	0.5	26	52
$5.5 \le p < 6.0$	0.5	24	48
$6.0 \le p < 6.5$	0.5	19	38
$6.5 \le p < 8.0$	1.5	10	6.67

[Histogram: Frequency Density against Profit (£million)]

[1 mark for correct axes, plus 2 marks if all bars drawn correctly, or 1 mark for at least 3 bars correct]

b)

Profit ($£p$ million)	Class midpoint (x)	No. of businesses (f)	fx	x^2	fx^2
$4.5 \le p < 5.0$	4.75	21	99.75	22.5625	473.8125
$5.0 \le p < 5.5$	5.25	26	136.5	27.5625	716.625
$5.5 \le p < 6.0$	5.75	24	138	33.0625	793.5
$6.0 \le p < 6.5$	6.25	19	118.75	39.0625	742.1875
$6.5 \le p < 8.0$	7.25	10	72.5	52.5625	525.625
Totals		100	565.5		3251.75

[1 mark for correct x and fx, 1 mark for correct x^2 and fx^2]

Estimated mean $= \dfrac{\Sigma fx}{\Sigma f} = \dfrac{565.5}{100} = £5.655$ million *[1 mark]*

Estimated variance $= \dfrac{\Sigma fx^2}{\Sigma f} - \bar{x}^2 = \dfrac{3251.75}{100} - 5.655^2$

                     $= 0.538475$ *[1 mark]*

So estimated s.d. $= \sqrt{0.538475} = £0.734$ million (3 s.f.) *[1 mark]*

Answers

c) $n \div 2 = 50$, $21 + 26 = 47$, so the median
is in the 5.5–6.0 class *[1 mark]*.
Estimated median = $5.5 + 0.5 \times \frac{50-47}{24}$ *[1 mark]*
$= £5.5625$ million *[1 mark]*

Page 73 — Interquartile Range and Outliers
Practice Question
1 a) 85 is not an outlier   b) 95 is an outlier   c) 0 is an outlier

Exam Question
1 a) Total number of people = 38, and $38 \div 2 = 19.2$
So the median is the average of the 19th and 20th values. *[1 mark]*
19th value = 15, 20th value = 16, so median = 15.5 hits *[1 mark]*
mode = 15 hits *[1 mark]*
b) Lower quartile = 10th value = 14,
Upper quartile = 29th value = 17 *[1 mark for both]*
So IQR = $17 - 14 = 3$, and upper fence = $17 + (1.5 \times 3) = 21.5$
This means that 25 is outlier. *[1 mark]*
c) E.g. The value of the mean is likely to be affected more than the
median by the presence of an outlier. *[1 mark]*

Page 75 — Cumulative Frequency Graphs and Boxplots
Practice Questions
1

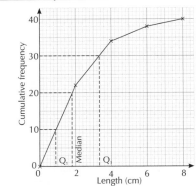

median ≈ 1.8 cm,
IQR ≈ 2.4 cm

These are estimates, so answers close to these are also correct.

2   median = £7, lower quartile = £5, upper quartile = £13.50

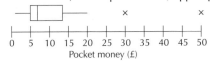

Exam Question
1 a) Times = 2, 3, 4, 4, 5, 5, 5, 7, 10, 12
$\frac{n}{2} = 5$ is a whole number, so the median is the average of the 5th
and 6th terms: $Q_2 = (5 + 5) \div 2 = 5$ minutes
$\frac{n}{4} = 2.5$ is not a whole number, so the lower quartile
is the 3rd term: $Q_1 = 4$ minutes
$\frac{n}{4} = 7.5$ is not a whole number, so the lower quartile
is the 8th term: $Q_3 = 7$ minutes
[2 marks available — lose 1 for each incorrect answer]
b) Worker A

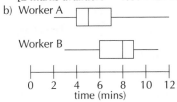

Worker B

*[4 marks available —
2 for correct values of Q_1,
Q_2 and Q_3 for Worker B,
1 for correctly drawn box
plots and 1 for putting both
on a common, labelled scale]*

If you used fences at 1.5 × IQR above Q_3 and below Q_1,
the data value 12 for Worker A would be an outlier.

c) E.g. The data supports Worker A's claim — the median for
Worker B is higher, so the times for Worker B are generally longer.
*[1 mark for a correct statement comparing A and B's times,
1 mark for a sensible conclusion about A's claim]*

Page 77 — Correlation
Practice Questions
1 a) No correlation
b) Weak negative correlation
c) Strong positive correlation
2   Explanatory variable = amount of sunshine
Response variable = barbecue sales

Exam Question
1 a)

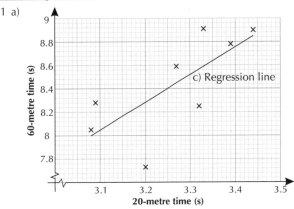

*[2 marks for all points plotted correctly, otherwise
1 mark for 4-7 points plotted correctly]*
b) Weak positive correlation *[1 mark]*
c) See graph *[1 mark for regression line plotted correctly]*
d) (i) When $x = 3.15$, $y = (2.367 \times 3.15) + 0.709 = 8.17$ s (3 s.f.)
3.15 m is within the range you have data for (this is interpolation),
so the estimate should be accurate.
[1 mark for correct y-value and sensible comment]
(ii) When $x = 3.88$, $y = (2.367 \times 3.88) + 0.709 = 9.89$ s (3 s.f.)
3.88 m is outside the range you have data for (this is
extrapolation), so the estimate might not be accurate.
[1 mark for correct y-value and sensible comment]

Section 9 — Probability
Page 79 — Random Events and Venn Diagrams
Practice Questions
1 a) $\frac{5}{12}$ b) $\frac{7}{36}$ c) $\frac{11}{18}$

2

	S	S'	Total
C	2%	18%	20%
C'	48%	32%	80%
Total	50%	50%	100%

a) 2%   b) 18%   c) 66%

Exam Question
1 a) The Venn diagram would look something like this:

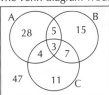

*[5 marks available — 1 for the central figure correct, 2 for '5', '7'
and '4' correct (or 1 mark for any 2 correct), 1 for '28', '15' and
'11' correct, and 1 for a box with '47' outside the circles.]*

Answers

b) (i) Add up the numbers in all the circles: 73 people out of 120 buy at least 1 type of soap. *[1 mark]*

So probability = $\frac{73}{120}$ *[1 mark]*

(ii) Add up the numbers in the intersections: 5 + 3 + 4 + 7 = 19, so 19 people buy at least two soaps, *[1 mark]* so the probability a person buys at least two types = $\frac{19}{120}$. *[1 mark]*

Page 81 — Mutually Exclusive and Independent Events

Practice Questions

1 a) The events are not mutually exclusive — e.g. if she picks 2 and 3, both events happen at the same time.

b) The events are not independent — the cards are not replaced, so the probability that the second number is odd will be different depending on whether or not the first number is even.

2 a)

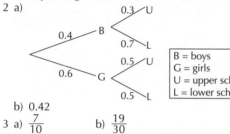

B = boys
G = girls
U = upper school
L = lower school

b) 0.42

3 a) $\frac{7}{10}$ b) $\frac{19}{30}$

You weren't asked to draw a tree diagram for this question, but you might find it makes it a lot easier if you do.

Exam Questions

1 a) (i) J and K are independent, so
P(J and K) = P(J) × P(K) = 0.7 × 0.1 = 0.07 *[1 mark]*

(ii) P(J or K) = P(J) + P(K) − P(J and K) *[1 mark]*
= 0.7 + 0.1 − 0.07 = 0.73 *[1 mark]*

b) Drawing a quick Venn Diagram often helps:

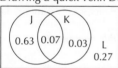

So you can see that (L and K′) = L (= J′ and K′) *[1 mark]*
All of L is contained in K′, so the bits in (L and K′) are just the bits in L.
So P(L and K′) = P(L) = 1 − P(K or J) = 1 − 0.73 = 0.27 *[1 mark]*

2 a)

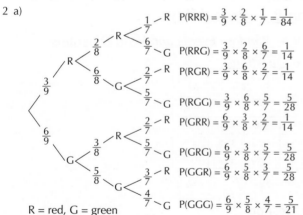

R   P(RRR) = $\frac{3}{9} \times \frac{2}{8} \times \frac{1}{7} = \frac{1}{84}$

G   P(RRG) = $\frac{3}{9} \times \frac{2}{8} \times \frac{6}{7} = \frac{1}{14}$

R   P(RGR) = $\frac{3}{9} \times \frac{6}{8} \times \frac{2}{7} = \frac{1}{14}$

G   P(RGG) = $\frac{3}{9} \times \frac{6}{8} \times \frac{5}{7} = \frac{5}{28}$

R   P(GRR) = $\frac{6}{9} \times \frac{3}{8} \times \frac{2}{7} = \frac{1}{14}$

G   P(GRG) = $\frac{6}{9} \times \frac{3}{8} \times \frac{5}{7} = \frac{5}{28}$

R   P(GGR) = $\frac{6}{9} \times \frac{5}{8} \times \frac{3}{7} = \frac{5}{28}$

G   P(GGG) = $\frac{6}{9} \times \frac{5}{8} \times \frac{4}{7} = \frac{5}{21}$

R = red, G = green

[3 marks available — 1 mark for a correctly-drawn tree diagram, 1 mark for multiplying along the branches to find combined probabilities, 1 mark for all probabilities correct.]

b) 'Third counter is green' means one of four outcomes: 'RRG', 'RGG', 'GRG' or 'GGG'. *[1 mark]*
So P(3rd is green) = $\frac{1}{14} + \frac{5}{28} + \frac{5}{28} + \frac{5}{21} = \frac{2}{3}$ *[1 mark]*

c) There are only two outcomes where all of the counters are the same colour: 'RRR' or 'GGG'. *[1 mark]*
So P(all same colour) = $\frac{1}{84} + \frac{5}{21} = \frac{1}{4}$ *[1 mark]*

d) 'At least one counter is red' is the complementary event of 'none of the counters are red', so:
P(at least one red) = 1 − P(no reds)
= 1 − P(GGG) *[1 mark]*
= 1 − $\frac{5}{21} = \frac{16}{21}$ *[1 mark]*

[Alternatively, 1 mark for giving P(at least one red) as the sum of all of the outcome probabilities other than P(GGG), and 1 mark for the correct answer]

Section 10 — Statistical Distributions

Page 84 — Probability Distributions

Practice Question

1 a) $k = \frac{1}{10}$ b) $P(X > 2) = \frac{7}{10}$ c) $P(1 \le X \le 3) = \frac{3}{5}$

d) i)

x	1	2	3	4
$P(X = x)$	$\frac{1}{10}$	$\frac{1}{5}$	$\frac{3}{10}$	$\frac{2}{5}$

ii)

x	1	2	3	4
$F(x) = P(X \le x)$	$\frac{1}{10}$	$\frac{3}{10}$	$\frac{3}{5}$	1

Exam Question

1   Use the fact that the probabilities add up to 1 to find k:
$\frac{1}{k}(1^2) + \frac{1}{k}(2^2) + \frac{1}{k}(3^2) + \frac{1}{k}(4^2) = 1$ *[1 mark]*
$\Rightarrow \frac{1}{k}(1 + 4 + 9 + 16) = 1 \Rightarrow \frac{30}{k} = 1 \Rightarrow k = 30$ *[1 mark]*
$P(X \le 2) = P(X = 1) + P(X = 2)$ *[1 mark]*
$= \frac{1}{30}(1^2) + \frac{1}{30}(2^2) = \frac{5}{30} = \frac{1}{6}$ *[1 mark]*

Page 87 — The Binomial Distribution

Practice Questions

1 a) 0.00977 (3 s.f.)   b) 0.0107 (3 s.f.)
2 a) P(X = 4) = 0.2286 (4 d.p.)   b) P(Y ≤ 15) = 0.9997 (4 d.p.)

Exam Questions

1 a) Using the binomial cdf:
P(X < 8) = P(X ≤ 7) *[1 mark]* = 0.562 (3 s.f.) *[1 mark]*
b) Using the binomial pdf: P(X = 5) = 0.101 (3 s.f.) *[1 mark]*
c) P(3 < X ≤ 7) = P(X ≤ 7) − P(X ≤ 3) *[1 mark]*
= 0.56182... − 0.01526... = 0.547 (3 s.f.) *[1 mark]*

2 a) Let X represent the number of apples that contain a maggot. Then X ~ B(40, 0.15). So P(X < 6) = P(X ≤ 5) *[1 mark]*
= 0.433 (3 s.f.) *[1 mark]*

b) P(X > 2) = 1 − P(X ≤ 2) *[1 mark]*
= 1 − 0.04859... = 0.9514... = 0.951 (3 s.f.) *[1 mark]*

c) The probability that a crate contains more than 2 apples with maggots is 0.9514... from b). So define a random variable Y, where Y is the number of crates that contain more than 2 apples with maggots. Then Y ~ B(3, 0.9514...). *[1 mark]*
Using your calculator:
P(Y > 1) = 1 − P(Y ≤ 1) *[1 mark]*
= 1 − 0.00685... = 0.993 (3 s.f.) *[1 mark]*
You could also do: P(Y > 1) = P(Y = 2) + P(Y = 3) = 3p²(1 − p) + p³.

d) E.g. maggots could spread to other nearby apples in a crate, some trees might have more apples with maggots than others, etc.
[1 mark for a suitable criticism]

Section 11 — Statistical Hypothesis Testing

Page 91 — Statistical Sampling

Practice Questions

1 a) Sample — a census is impossible as the number of coin tosses is infinite, so he can only examine a sample of them.

b) Sample — testing all 200 pies would take too long, and more importantly, the test will destroy the pies.

Answers

c) Census — the population is fairly small, and the result will be more accurate if all the marks are considered.
2   Opportunity (convenience) sampling
3   First, find out how many people are at the cinema that afternoon and decide on your sample size. Divide the total population by the sample size to find your value of n. Then, generate a random starting point and ask every n^{th} person after this starting point as they leave the cinema.

Exam Questions

1 a) i) All the Year 7 pupils in the school. *[1 mark]*
     ii) A list of all Year 7 pupils, e.g. the school registers. *[1 mark]*
  b) i) E.g. Biased — as all of the students in the sample have the same history teacher, their opinions are likely to be similar, while students with a different teacher would have different opinions on history lessons. *[1 mark]*
     ii) E.g. Not biased — the distance between a pupil's home and the school is unlikely to be affected by which history class they are in, so only using pupils from one class should not introduce bias. *[1 mark]*
2   Retired people = $98 \div 250 \times 25 = 9.8 \approx 10$ people *[1 mark]*
    Unemployed people = $34 \div 250 \times 25 = 3.4 \approx 3$ people *[1 mark]*
    People who work full- or part-time = $83 \div 250 \times 25 = 8.3$
    ≈ 8 people *[1 mark]*
    Students = $(250 - 98 - 34 - 83) \div 250 \times 25 = 3.5 \approx 4$ people
    [1 mark]
    Check your answer by adding up the number of people sampled:
    10 + 3 + 8 + 4 = 25 as required.

Page 93 — Hypothesis Tests

Practice Question

1   No — the result of the hypothesis test supports the claim that the percentage of library users has decreased, but doesn't support the claim that it has decreased by a specific amount.

Exam Question

1   Let p be the proportion of customers that rated the restaurant as 'Excellent'. Then $H_0: p = 0.43$ and $H_1: p > 0.43$.
    [1 mark for both hypotheses correct]

Page 95 — Hypothesis Tests and Binomial Distributions

Practice Questions

1 a) $H_0: p = 0.2$, $H_1: p \neq 0.2$, $\alpha = 0.05$ (so $\frac{\alpha}{2} = 0.025$) and $x = 1$:
     Under H_0, $X \sim B(20, 0.2)$. $P(X \leq 1) = 0.06917...$
     $0.06917... > 0.025$, so there is insufficient evidence at the 5% level of significance to reject H_0.
  b) $H_0: p = 0.4$, $H_1: p > 0.4$, $\alpha = 0.01$ and $x = 15$:
     Under H_0, $X \sim B(20, 0.4)$
     $P(X \geq 15) = 1 - P(X \leq 14) = 1 - 0.9983... = 0.00161...$
     $0.00161.. < 0.01$, so there is evidence at the 1% level of significance to reject H_0.
2   $H_0: p = 0.3$, $H_1: p < 0.3$, $\alpha = 0.05$
    Under H_0, $X \sim B(10, 0.3)$
    Critical region = biggest possible set of 'low' values of X with a total probability of ≤ 0.05.
    $P(X \leq 0) = 0.02824...$, $P(X \leq 1) = 0.14930...$,
    so critical region is $X = 0$.

Exam Question

1 a) Binomial *[1 mark]*   *'Proportion' should set the binomial bell ringing.*
  b) i) Start by stating the hypotheses:
         $H_0: p = 0.2$ and $H_1: p > 0.2$ *[1 mark for both correct]*
         X = number of tiramisu orders in sample
         Under H_0, $X \sim B(20, 0.2)$ *[1 mark]*
         $\alpha = 0.05$
         Either:
         Use the binomial cdf to find the p-value (the probability of getting a value greater than or equal to 7, under H_0):
         $P(X \geq 7) = 1 - P(X \leq 6)$ *[1 mark]*
         $= 1 - 0.9133... = 0.0866...$ *[1 mark]*
         $0.0866... > 0.05$, so the result isn't significant. *[1 mark]*
         Or:
         Use the binomial cdf to find the critical region:
         $P(X \geq 7) = 1 - P(X \leq 6) = 1 - 0.9133... = 0.0866...$
         $P(X \geq 8) = 1 - P(X \leq 7) = 1 - 0.9678... = 0.0321...$
         [1 mark for attempting to find the smallest value of x such that P(X ≥ x) ≤ 0.05]
         $0.0321... < 0.05$, so the CR is $X \geq 8$. *[1 mark]*
         7 isn't in the CR, so the result isn't significant. *[1 mark]*
         So there is insufficient evidence at the 5% level of significance to support the chef's theory that the proportion of dessert eaters ordering tiramisu on a Saturday is greater than on weekdays.
         [1 mark for a suitable conclusion]
     ii) You're looking for the smallest value of x such that $P(X \geq x) \leq 0.05$.
         You know $X = 7$ isn't significant from part (i).
         Try 8: $P(X \geq 8) = 0.0321... < 0.05$,
         so the answer is 8 tiramisu orders. *[1 mark]*
         Part (ii) here is really just asking for the lower boundary of the critical region (the critical value). So if you answered part (i) by finding the critical region, you've already worked out the answer. Bonus.

Section 12 — Kinematics

Page 97 — Constant Acceleration Equations

Practice Questions

1   12 m
2   0.714 s (3 s.f.)
3   6.20 ms^{-1} (3 s.f.)

Exam Questions

1 a) Using $v = u + at$ *[1 mark]*
     $17 = u + (9.8 \times 1.2)$ *[1 mark]*
     So $u = 5.24$ *[1 mark]*
  b) Using $s = ut + \frac{1}{2}at^2$ *[1 mark]*
     $s = (17 \times 2.1) + \frac{1}{2}(9.8 \times 2.1^2)$ *[1 mark]*
     So, $s = 57.309$ *[1 mark]*
     $h = \frac{s}{14} = 4.09$ m (3 s.f.) *[1 mark]*
2 a) Using $v^2 = u^2 + 2as$ *[1 mark]*
     $20^2 = u^2 + (2 \times 9.8 \times 8)$ *[1 mark]*
     $u = \sqrt{400 - 156.8} = \sqrt{243.2}$
     Ignore the negative solution as speed must be positive.
     So $u = 15.59487... = 15.6$ (3 s.f.) *[1 mark]*
  b) Using $v = u + at$ *[1 mark]*
     $20 = -15.59487... + 9.8t$ *[1 mark]*
     So, $9.8t = 35.59487...$
     hence $t = 3.63212... = 3.63$ s (3 s.f.) *[1 mark]*
     It's best to avoid using $s = ut + \frac{1}{2}at^2$ in this question, as it gives you a second, incorrect solution. If this ever happens in a question, try using another suvat equation to figure out which is the correct solution.

Answers

Page 99 — Motion Graphs

Practice Questions

1 a) From rest, the athlete travels 5 m in 3 seconds; then rests for
   2 seconds; then returns to the start, travelling 5 m in 1 second.
   b) 0 ms^{-1}
   c) 10 m
2 Distance = 68.75 m
3 a) $v = u + at \Rightarrow u = v - at$
   Substituting this into $s = \frac{1}{2}(u + v)t$ gives:
   $s = \frac{1}{2}(v - at + v)t = \frac{1}{2}(2v - at)t = vt - \frac{1}{2}at^2$
   b) Rearranging $v = u + at$ gives: $t = \frac{v - u}{a}$
   Substitute this into $s = \frac{1}{2}(u + v)t$:
   $s = \frac{1}{2a}(u + v)(v - u)$
   $\Rightarrow 2as = uv - u^2 + v^2 - vu \Rightarrow v^2 = u^2 + 2as$

Exam Questions

1 a) Area under graph (area of trapezium) = distance *[1 mark]*
   $\frac{120 + 180}{2} \times V = 2100$ *[1 mark]*
   $V = \frac{2100}{150} = 14$ ms^{-1} *[1 mark]*
   b) Distance = area under graph *[1 mark]*
   $= \frac{1}{2} \times 40 \times 14 = 280$ m *[1 mark]*
2 a) Acceleration is the gradient of the graph. *[1 mark]*
   acceleration $= \frac{\text{change in } y}{\text{change in } x} = \frac{50 - 10}{15 - 10} = 8$ ms^{-2} *[1 mark]*

b)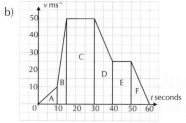

Distance is area so: area of A $= (10 \times 10) \div 2 = 50$
   area of B $= \frac{10 + 50}{2} \times 5 = 150$
   area of C $= 15 \times 50 = 750$
   area of D $= \frac{50 + 25}{2} \times 10 = 375$
   area of E $= 10 \times 25 = 250$
   area of F $= 10 \times 25 \div 2 = 125$
[1 mark for attempting to find the area under the graph]
First 30 s: $50 + 150 + 750 = 950$ m *[1 mark]*
Second 30 s: $375 + 250 + 125 = 750$ m *[1 mark]*
So Sean is correct. *[1 mark]*
c) Using the calculations from b), $15 < T < 30$ *[1 mark]*
   (i.e. T is within C).
   Find 'how far T is through C' (as a fraction):
   $700 - \text{area of A} - \text{area of B} = 700 - 50 - 150 = 500$ m
   $\frac{500}{750} = \frac{2}{3}$, so T is $\frac{2}{3}$ through C. *[1 mark]*
   So $T = 15 + \left(\frac{2}{3} \times 15\right) = 25$. *[1 mark]*

Page 101 — Using Calculus for Kinematics

Practice Questions

1 a) $a = 16t - 2$
   b) $s = \frac{8t^3}{3} - t^2 + C$
2 $a = -\frac{2}{3}\sin\left(\frac{1}{3}t\right)$ ms^{-2}
3 70.2 m (3 s.f.)

Exam Questions

1 a) $s = -\frac{1}{100}t(t^2 - 9t - 10) = -\frac{1}{100}t(t + 1)(t - 10)$ *[1 mark]*
   Draw a quick sketch:

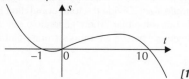

[1 mark]
Distance and time can't be negative so $0 \le t \le 10$ *[1 mark]*

b) s is at a maximum when $\frac{ds}{dt} = 0$, i.e. when $v = 0$ *[1 mark]*
   $v = \frac{ds}{dt} = \frac{1}{100}(-3t^2 + 18t + 10)$ *[1 mark]*
   When $v = 0$, $-3t^2 + 18t + 10 = 0$.
   Using the quadratic formula $t = 6.51188...$
   or $t = -0.511884...$ (ignore as $0 \le t \le 10$). *[1 mark]*
   When $t = 6.51188...$, $s = \frac{1}{100}[-(6.51188...)^3 + 9(6.51188...)^2$
   $+ 10(6.51188...)]$ *[1 mark]*
   $= 1.71$ m (3 s.f.) *[1 mark]*

2 a) v is at a maximum when $\frac{dv}{dt} = 0$, i.e. when $a = 0$
   So, in the interval $0 \le t \le 2$, $a = \frac{dv}{dt} = 9 - 6t$ *[1 mark]*
   When $a = 0$: $0 = 9 - 6t \Rightarrow t = 1.5$ s *[1 mark]*
   So: $v = (9 \times 1.5) - 3(1.5^2)$ *[1 mark]*
   $= 6.75$ ms^{-1} *[1 mark]*

b) (i) $s = \int v\, dt = \frac{9t^2}{2} - t^3 + C$ for $0 \le t \le 2$. *[1 mark]*
   When $t = 0$, the particle is at the origin, i.e. $s = 0$
   $\Rightarrow C = 0$ *[1 mark]*
   When $t = 2$, $s = \frac{9}{2}(2^2) - 2^3 = 10$ m *[1 mark]*

   (ii) $s = \int v\, dt = \int \frac{24}{t^2}\, dt = \frac{-24}{t} + C$ for $t > 2$ *[1 mark]*
   Use the answer to part i) as initial conditions:
   when $t = 2$, $s = 10$, so $10 = \frac{-24}{2} + C$ *[1 mark]*
   $\Rightarrow C = 22$ *[1 mark]*
   When $t = 6$, $s = \frac{-24}{6} + 22 = 18$ m *[1 mark]*

Section 13 — Forces and Newton's Laws

Page 103 — Forces and Modelling

Practice Questions

1 Mass: kg, volume: m^3, density: kg m^{-3} or kg/m^3
2 a) ⃝ Assumptions: The ball is a particle.
        There is no air resistance (*unless air resistance*
        is included on diagram).
        No other external forces act on the ball.
     $\downarrow W$
   b) ↑R Assumptions: The ball is a particle.
        The ball does not bounce or roll
        when it hits the cushion.
        The cushion is a horizontal plane.
     $\downarrow W$ No other external forces act on the ball.

Exam Question

1 Possible answers include:
   – It is unrealistic to model a car as a particle — the driver, the
     engine and the tyres may all have varying effects on its motion.
     Adjusting the model to account for these effects would make it
     more accurate.
   – The road is unlikely to be smooth — the model could include
     friction between the car and the road.
   – The car would realistically experience air resistance.
     Including this in the model would make it more accurate.
   – A constant speed is unrealistic — the model could account
     for how the speed varies with time.
   [2 marks available — 1 for each suggested improvement]

Answers

Page 105 — Newton's Laws
Practice Questions

1 $v = 4$ ms^{-1}

2 Magnitude = 0.283 N (3 s.f.), direction = 32.0° (1 d.p.)
Make sure you convert the mass into kg before using the formula.

3 Magnitude = 6.25 ms^{-2}, direction = 53.1° (1 d.p.),
$s = 28.1$ m (3 s.f.)

Exam Questions

1 a) $(8\mathbf{i} - 3\mathbf{j}) = (x\mathbf{i} + y\mathbf{j}) + (5\mathbf{i} + \mathbf{j})$
So, $x\mathbf{i} + y\mathbf{j} = (8\mathbf{i} - 3\mathbf{j}) - (5\mathbf{i} + \mathbf{j})$, so $x = 3$ and $y = -4$
[2 marks available — 1 for each correct value]

b) Using $F_{net} = ma$: $8\mathbf{i} - 3\mathbf{j} = 2.5a$ *[1 mark]*
$\Rightarrow a = 3.2\mathbf{i} - 1.2\mathbf{j}$ ms^{-2} *[1 mark]*
Magnitude of $a = \sqrt{3.2^2 + (-1.2)^2} = \sqrt{11.68}$
$= 3.42$ ms^{-2} (3 s.f.) *[1 mark]*
$\tan\theta = \frac{-1.2}{3.2} \Rightarrow \theta = -20.556...°$ *[1 mark]*
F_{net} acts down-right, so direction = 360° − 20.556...°
$= 339.4°$ (1 d.p.) *[1 mark]*

c) List variables: $u = 0\mathbf{i} + 0\mathbf{j}$, $v = v$, $a = 3.2\mathbf{i} - 1.2\mathbf{j}$, $t = 5$
$v = u + at \Rightarrow v = 0\mathbf{i} + 0\mathbf{j} + 5(3.2\mathbf{i} - 1.2\mathbf{j})$ *[1 mark]*
$= 16\mathbf{i} - 6\mathbf{j}$ ms^{-1} *[1 mark]*

2 a) List variables: $s = 200$, $u = 0$, $a = a$, $t = 7$
$s = ut + \frac{1}{2}at^2 \Rightarrow 200 = (0 \times 7) + \frac{1}{2} \times a \times 49$ *[1 mark]*
$\Rightarrow a = 200 \times 2 \div 49 = 8.163...$ ms^{-2} *[1 mark]*
$F_{net} = ma \Rightarrow F_{net} = 60 \times 8.163...$ *[1 mark]*
$= 489.79...$ N *[1 mark]*
Resolving forces, $F_{net} = W - R = mg - R$
$489.79... = (60 \times 9.8) - R$ *[1 mark]*
$\Rightarrow R = 588 - 489.79...$
$= 98.2$ N (3 s.f.) *[1 mark]*

b) Assumptions: The skydiver is a particle, the air resistance
force is not affected by the skydiver's speed,
acceleration due to gravity is a constant 9.8 ms^{-2},
no other external forces act on the skydiver.
[2 marks available — 1 each for any valid assumption]

Page 107 — Connected Particles
Practice Questions

1 $a = 0.867$ ms^{-2} (3 s.f.), $T = 7040$ N

2 $W = 30.6$ N (3 s.f.)

Exam Questions

1 a) Considering the car and the caravan together:
Resolving horizontally:
$F_{net} = ma$
$2500 - (1000 + 200) = 2000a$ *[1 mark]*
$a = 0.65$ ms^{-2} *[1 mark]*

b) Either:
Resolving horizontally for the caravan:
$F_{net} = ma$
$T - 200 = 500 \times 0.65$
$T = 525$ N
Or:
Resolving horizontally for the car:
$F_{net} = ma$
$2500 - (1000 + T) = 1500 \times 0.65$
$2500 - 1000 - T = 975$
$1500 - 975 = T$
$T = 525$ N
*[2 marks available — 1 for resolving horizontally,
1 for correct final answer]*
Two different methods, one correct answer. At the end of the day,
it doesn't matter which you use, although it's certainly a bonus if you
manage to pick the simpler way and save a bit of time in the exam.

2 a) Resolving forces acting on A:
$7g - T = 7a$ ① *[1 mark]*
Resolving forces acting on B:
$T - 3g = 3a \Rightarrow T = 3a + 3g$ ② *[1 mark]*
Substituting ② into ①:
$7g - 3a - 3g = 7a \Rightarrow 4g = 10a \Rightarrow a = 3.92$ ms^{-2} *[1 mark]*
List variables: $u = 0$, $v = 5.9$, $a = 3.92$, $t = t$
$v = u + at \Rightarrow 5.9 = 0 + 3.92t \Rightarrow t = 1.51$ s (3 s.f.) *[1 mark]*

b) $v^2 = u^2 + 2as \Rightarrow 5.9^2 = 0^2 + (2 \times 3.92 \times s)$ *[1 mark]*
$7.84s = 34.81 \Rightarrow s = 4.44$ m (3 s.f.) *[1 mark]*
You could have used one of the other *suvat* equations here,
but using $v^2 = u^2 + 2as$ means you don't have to rely on
your answer to part a) being right (I'm sure it was, of course).

c) When A hits the ground, speed of B = speed of A = 5.9 ms^{-1}.
B will then continue to rise, momentarily stop and then
fall freely under gravity. The string will be taut again when
the displacement of B = 0.
So, listing variables: $s = 0$, $u = 5.9$, $a = -9.8$, $t = t$ *[1 mark]*
$s = ut + \frac{1}{2}at^2 \Rightarrow 0 = 5.9t + \frac{1}{2}(-9.8)t^2 = 5.9t - 4.9t^2$ *[1 mark]*
Solve for t: $5.9t - 4.9t^2 = 0 \Rightarrow t(5.9 - 4.9t) = 0$ *[1 mark]*
$\Rightarrow t = 0$ or $t = 5.9 \div 4.9 = 1.204...$
So the string becomes taut again at $t = 1.20$ s (3 s.f.) *[1 mark]*

Index

Index

Formula Sheet

These are the formulas from the formula booklet that are needed for AS-Level Maths.

Binomial Series

$$(a + b)^n = a^n + \binom{n}{1}a^{n-1}b + \binom{n}{2}a^{n-2}b^2 + \ldots + \binom{n}{r}a^{n-r}b^r + \ldots + b^n \quad (n \in \mathbb{N})$$

$$\text{where } \binom{n}{r} = {}^nC_r = \frac{n!}{r!(n-r)!}$$

Differentiation From First Principles

$$f'(x) = \lim_{h \to 0} \frac{f(x+h) - f(x)}{h}$$

Standard Deviation

$$\sqrt{\frac{\sum(x - \overline{x})^2}{n}} = \sqrt{\frac{\sum x^2}{n} - \overline{x}^2}$$

The Binomial Distribution

If $X \sim B(n, p)$, then $P(X = x) = \binom{n}{x}p^x(1-p)^{n-x}$

Mean of $X = np$ Variance of $X = np(1 - p)$

Kinematics

$$v = u + at$$
$$s = ut + \frac{1}{2}at^2$$
$$s = \frac{1}{2}(u + v)t$$
$$v^2 = u^2 + 2as$$
$$s = vt - \frac{1}{2}at^2$$

MAHR52